Globalization in Question

Globalization in Question

THE INTERNATIONAL ECONOMY AND THE POSSIBILITIES OF GOVERNANCE

Paul Hirst and Grahame Thompson

Polity Press

First published in 1996 by Polity Press
in association with Blackwell Publishers Ltd.
Reprinted 1996, 1997, 1998

Editorial office:
Polity Press
65 Bridge Street
Cambridge CB2 1UR, UK

Marketing and production:
Blackwell Publishers Ltd
108 Cowley Road
Oxford OX4 1JF, UK

Published in the USA by
Blackwell Publishers Inc.
350 Main Street
Malden MA 02148, USA

ISBN 0–7456–1244–X
ISBN 0–7456–1245–8 (pbk)

A CIP catalogue record for this book is available from the British Library
and the Library of Congress.

Typeset in 10 on 11½pt Times
by Best-set Typesetter Ltd., Hong Kong
Printed in Great Britain by MPG Books Ltd, Bodmin, Cornwall

This book is printed on acid-free paper.

Contents

Acknowledgements

The author and publishers wish to thank the following who have kindly given permission for the use of copyright material.

American Economic Association/Journal of Economic Literature to reproduce Maddison 1987 table A/21, page 694.

The Bank for International Settlements, Basle, Switzerland for data from annual reports.

The Greenwood Publishing Group, Inc, Westport CT for Fig 19.1, page 347, in Nam, ed. *Handbook of International Migration*. Copyright © 1990 Greenwood.

Macmillan Press Ltd for a table from Appendix IV, page 67 from A Lewis, 'The Rate of Growth of World Trade, 1830–1973' in Grassman, S. and Lundberg, E (eds) *The World Economic Order*. Copyright © 1981 Macmillan Press Ltd.

OECD Publications and Information Centre for data.

United Nations for figure 3.1 from International Trade, GATT; figure 3.2 from UNCTC estimates based on *World Investment Directory*, UNCTC, 1991; International Monetary Fund balance of payments tape, retrieved 10 January 1991; *Monthly Bulletin of Statistics*, United Nations, 1984 and 1990; and figure 3.8 from J Kline, Transnational Corporations, Vol 2, 1993.

1

Introduction: Globalization – A Necessary Myth?

Globalization has become a fashionable concept in the social sciences, a core dictum in the prescriptions of management gurus, and a catch-phrase for journalists and politicians of every stripe. It is widely asserted that we live in an era in which the greater part of social life is determined by global processes, in which national cultures, national economies and national borders are dissolving. Central to this perception is the notion of a rapid and recent process of economic globalization. A truly global economy is claimed to have emerged or to be in the process of emerging, in which distinct national economies and, therefore, domestic strategies of national economic management are increasingly irrelevant. The world economy has internationalized in its basic dynamics, it is dominated by uncontrollable market forces, and it has as its principal economic actors and major agents of change truly transnational corporations, that owe allegiance to no nation state and locate wherever in the globe market advantage dictates.

This image is so powerful that it has mesmerized analysts and captured political imaginations. But is it the case? This book is written with a mixture of scepticism about global economic processes and optimism about the possibilities of control of the international economy and of the viability of national political strategies. One key effect of the concept of globalization has been to paralyse radical reforming national strategies, to see them as unviable in the face of the judgement and sanction of international markets. If, however, we face economic changes that are more complex and more equivocal than the extreme globalists argue, then the possibility remains of political strategy and action for national and international control of market economies in order to promote social goals.

We began this investigation with an attitude of moderate scepticism. It was clear that much had changed since the 1960s, but we were cautious about the more extreme claims of the most enthusiastic globalization theorists. In particular it was obvious that radical expansionary and redistributive strategies of national economic management were no longer possible in the face of a variety of domestic and international constraints. However, the closer we looked the shallower and more unfounded became the claims of the more radical globalists. In particular we began to be disturbed by three facts: first, the absence of a commonly accepted model of the new global economy and how it differs from previous states of the international economy; second, in the absence of a clear model against which to measure trends, the tendency casually to cite examples of internationalization of sectors and processes as if they were evidence of the growth of an economy dominated by autonomous global market forces; and third, the lack of historical depth, the tendency to portray current changes as both unique and without precedent and firmly set to persist long into the future.

To anticipate, as we proceeded our scepticism deepened until we became convinced that globalization, as conceived by the more extreme globalizers, is largely a myth. Thus we argue that:

1   The present highly internationalized economy is not unprecedented: it is one of a number of distinct conjunctures or states of the international economy that have existed since an economy based on modern industrial technology began to be generalized from the 1860s. In some respects, the current international economy is *less* open and integrated than the regime that prevailed from 1870 to 1914.

2   Genuinely transnational companies (TNCs) appear to be relatively rare. Most companies are nationally based and trade multinationally on the strength of a major national location of production and sales, and there seems to be no major tendency towards the growth of truly international companies.

3   Capital mobility is not producing a massive shift of investment and employment from the advanced to the developing countries. Rather, foreign direct investment (FDI) is highly concentrated among the advanced industrial economies and the Third World remains marginal in both investment and trade, a small minority of newly industrializing countries apart.

4   As some of the extreme advocates of globalization recognize, the world economy is far from being genuinely 'global'. Rather, trade, investment and financial flows are concentrated in the Triad of Europe, Japan and North America and this dominance seems set to continue.

5 These major economic powers, the G3, thus have the capacity, especially if they coordinate policy, to exert powerful governance pressures over financial markets and other economic tendencies. Global markets are thus by no means beyond regulation and control, even though the current scope and objectives of economic governance are limited by the divergent interests of the great powers and the economic doctrines prevalent among their elites.

These and other more detailed points challenging of the globalization thesis will be developed in later chapters. We should emphasize that this book challenges the strong version of the thesis of *economic* globalization, because we believe that without the notion of a truly globalized economy many of the other consequences adduced in the domains of culture and politics would either cease to be sustainable or become less threatening. Hence most of the discussion here is centred on the international economy and the evidence for and against the process of globalization. However, the book is written to emphasize the possibilities of national and international governance and, as it proceeds, issues of the future of the nation state and the role of international agencies, regimes and structures of governance are given increasing prominence.

It is one thing to be sceptical about the concept of globalization, it is another to explain the widespread development and reception of the concept since the 1970s. It will not do to wheel out the concept of 'ideology' here, for this view is so widespread that it covers the most diverse outlooks and social interests. It covers the political spectrum from left to right, it is endorsed in diverse disciplines – economics, sociology, cultural studies and international politics – and it is advanced by both theoretical innovators and traditionalists. The literature on globalization is vast and diverse. We deliberately chose not to write this book by summarizing and criticizing this literature, in part because that would be a never-ending enterprise given the scale and rate of publication on the topic, but mainly because we concluded that the great bulk of the literature was based on untenable assumptions. Hence we decided to examine the evidence against concepts that could specify what a distinctive global economy would look like but which did not presuppose its existence.

We are well aware that there are a wide variety of views that use the term 'globalization'. Even among those analysts that confine themselves to strictly economic processes, some make far more radical claims about changes in the international economy than others. It might therefore be argued that we are focusing too narrowly in concentrating on delineating and challenging the most extreme version of the thesis of economic globalization. Indeed, in criticizing such positions we might be held to be demolishing a straw man. On the contrary, we see these extreme views as strong, relatively coherent and capable of being developed into a clear ideal typical conception of a globalized economic system. Such views are also important in that they have become politically highly consequential. The most eloquent proponents of the extreme view are very influential and tend to set the tone for discussion in business and political circles. Views that shape the perception of key decision-makers are important, and thus are a primary target rather than a marginal one.

Some less extreme and more nuanced analyses that employ the term 'globalization' are well established in the academic community and concentrate on the relative internationalization of major financial markets, of technology, and of certain important sectors of manufacturing and services, particularly since the 1970s. Emphasis is given in many of these analyses to the increasing constraints on national-level governance that prevent ambitious macroeconomic policies that diverge significantly from the norms acceptable to international financial markets. Indeed, both authors have over some time drawn attention to such phenomena in their own work.

Obviously, it is no part of our aim here to deny that such trends to increased internationalization have occurred or to ignore the constraints on certain types of national economic strategy. Our point in assessing the significance of such internationalization as has occurred is to argue that it is well short of dissolving distinct national economies in the major advanced industrial countries or of preventing the development of new forms of economic governance at the national and international levels. There are, however, very real dangers in not distinguishing clearly between certain trends toward internationalization and the strong version of the globalization thesis. It is particularly unfortunate if the two become confused by using the same word, 'globalization', to describe both. Often we feel that evidence from cautious arguments is then used carelessly to bolster more extreme ones, to build a community of usage when there needs to be strict differentiation of meanings. It also confuses public discussion and policy-making, reinforcing the view that political actors can accomplish less than is actually possible in a global system.

The strong version of the globalization thesis requires a new view of the international economy, as we shall shortly see, one that subsumes and subordinates national-level processes. Whereas tendencies toward internationalization can be accommodated within a modified view of the world economic system, that still gives a major role to national-level policies and actors. Undoubtedly, this implies some greater or lesser degree of change: firms, governments and international agencies are being forced to behave differently, but in the main they can use existing institutions and practices to do so. In this way we feel it makes more sense to consider the international economic system in a longer historical perspective, to recognize that current changes while significant and distinctive are not unprecedented and do not necessarily involve a move toward a new type of economic system. The strong versions of the globalization thesis have the advantage that they clearly and sharply pose the possibility of such a change. If they are wrong they are still of some value in enabling us to think out what *is* happening and why. In this sense, challenging the strong versions of the thesis is not merely negative but helps us to develop our own ideas.

However, the question remains to be considered of how the myth of the globalization of economic activity became established as and when it did. In answering one must begin with the end of the post-1945 era in the turbulence of 1972–3. A number of significant changes ended a period of prolonged economic growth and full employment in the advanced countries, sustained by strategies of active national state intervention and a managed multilateral regime for trade and monetary policy under US hegemony. Thus we can point to:

1 The effects of the collapse of the Bretton Woods system and the OPEC oil crisis in producing turbulence and volatility in all the major economies through the 1970s into the early 1980s. Significant in generating such turbulence and undermining previous policy regimes was the rapid rise in inflation in the advanced countries brought about by domestic policy failures, the international impact of US involvement in the Vietnam War, and the oil price hikes of 1973 and 1979.

2 The efforts by financial institutions and manufacturers, in this period of turbulence and inflationary pressure, to compensate for domestic uncertainty by seeking wider outlets for investments and additional markets. The results were widespread bank lending to the Third World during the inflationary 1970s, the growth of the Eurodollar market, and the increasing foreign trade to GDP ratios in the advanced countries.

3 The public policy acceleration of the internationalization of financial markets by the widespread abandonment of exchange controls and other market deregulation in the late 1970s and early 1980s, even as the more extreme forms of volatility in currency markets were being brought under control by, for example, the development of the European monetary system (EMS) in 1979 and the Louvre and Plaza accords in the 1980s.

4 The tendency towards 'de-industrialization' in Britain and the United States and the growth of long-term unemployment in Europe, promoting fears of foreign competition especially from Japan.

5 The relatively rapid development of a number of newly industrializing countries (NICs) in the Third World and their penetration of First World markets.

6   The shift from standardized mass production to more flexible pro-
    duction methods, and the change from the perception of the large
    nationally rooted oligopolistic corporation as the unchallengeably
    dominant economic agent towards a more complex world of multi-
    national enterprises (MNCs), less rigidly structured major firms, and
    the increased salience of smaller firms – summed up in the wide-
    spread and popular concept of 'post-Fordism'.

These changes are undoubted and they were highly disturbing to those
conditioned by the unprecedented success and security of the post-1945
period in the advanced industrial states. The perceived loss of national
control, the increased uncertainty and unpredictability of economic relations, and rapid institutional change were a shock to minds conditioned
to believe that poverty, unemployment and economic cycles could all be
controlled or eliminated in a market economy based on the profit mo-
tive. If the widespread consensus of the 1950s and 1960s was that the
future belonged to a capitalism without losers, securely managed by
national governments acting in concert, then the later 1980s and 1990s
are dominated by a consensus based on contrary assumptions, that global
markets are uncontrollable and that the only way to avoid becoming a
loser – whether as nation, firm or individual – is to be as competitive as
possible. The notion of an ungovernable world economy is a response to
the collapse of expectations schooled by Keynesianism and sobered by
the failure of monetarism to provide an alternative route to broad-based
prosperity and stable growth. 'Globalization' is a myth suitable for a
world without illusions, but it is also one that robs us of hope. Global
markets are dominant, and they face no threat from any viable contrary
political project, for it is held that Western social democracy and socialism of the Soviet bloc are both finished.
  One can only call the political impact of 'globalization' the pathology
of over-diminished expectations. Many over-enthusiastic analysts and
politicians have gone beyond the evidence in over-stating both the extent
of the dominance of world markets and their ungovernability. If this is
so, then we should seek to break the spell of this uncomforting myth. The
old rationalist explanation for primitive myths was that they were a way
of masking and compensating for humanity's helplessness in the face of
the power of nature. In this case we have a myth that exaggerates the
degree of our helplessness in the face of contemporary economic forces.
If economic relations are more governable (at both the national and
international levels) than many contemporary analysts suppose, then we
should explore the possible scale and scope of that governance. It is not
the case currently that radical goals are attainable: full employment in
the advanced countries, a fairer deal for the poorer developing countries,
and more widespread democratic control over economic affairs for the

world's people. But this should not lead us to dismiss or ignore the forms of control and social improvement that could be achieved relatively rapidly with a modest change in attitudes on the part of key elites. It is thus essential to persuade reformers of the left and conservatives who care for the fabric of their societies that we are not helpless before uncontrollable global processes. If this happens, then changing attitudes and expectations might make these more radical goals acceptable.

Models of the international economy

We can only begin to assess the issue of globalization if we have some relatively clear and rigorous model of what a global economy would be like and how it represents both a new phase in the international economy and an entirely changed environment for national economic actors. Globalization in its radical sense should be taken to mean the development of a new economic structure, and not just conjunctural change toward greater international trade and investment within an existing set of economic relations. An extreme and one-sided ideal type of this kind enables us to differentiate *degrees* of internationalization, to eliminate some possibilities and to avoid confusion between claims. Given such a model it becomes possible to assess it against evidence of international trends and thus enables us more or less plausibly to determine whether or not this former phenomenon of the development of a new supranational economic system is occurring. In order to do this we have developed two basic contrasting ideal types of international economy: a fully globalized economy, and an open international economy that is still fundamentally characterized by exchange between relatively distinct national economies and in which many outcomes, such as the competitive performance of firms and sectors, are substantially determined by processes occurring at the national level. These ideal types are valuable in so far as they are useful in enabling us conceptually to clarify the issues, that is, in specifying the difference between a new global economy and merely extensive and intensifying international economic relations. Too often evidence compatible with the latter is used as if it substantiated the former. With a few honourable exceptions, the more enthusiastic advocates of globalization have failed to specify that difference, or to specify what evidence would be decisive in pointing to a structural change towards a global economy. Increasing salience of foreign trade and considerable and growing international flows of capital are not *per se* evidence of a new and distinct phenomenon called 'globalization': as we shall see in chapter 2, they were features of the international economy before 1914.

Type 1: An inter-national economy

We shall first develop a simple and extreme version of this type.

An *inter-national economy* is one in which the principal entities are national economies. Trade and investment produce growing interconnection between these still national economies. Such a process involves the increasing integration of more and more nations and economic actors into world market relationships. Trade relations, as a result, tend to take on the form of national specializations and the international division of labour. The importance of trade is however progressively replaced by the centrality of investment relations between nations, which increasingly act as the organizing principle of the system. The form of interdependence between nations remains, however, of the 'strategic' kind. That is, it implies the continued relative separation of the domestic and the international frameworks for policy-making and the management of economic affairs, and also a relative separation in terms of economic effects. Interactions are of the 'billiard-ball' type: international events do not directly or necessarily penetrate or permeate the domestic economy but are refracted through national policies and processes. The international and the domestic policy fields either remain relatively separate as distinct levels of governance or work 'automatically'. In the latter case adjustments are thought to be not the subject of policy by public bodies or authorities, but a consequence of 'unorganized' or 'spontaneous' market forces.

Perhaps the classic case of such an 'automatic' adjustment mechanism remains the Gold Standard, which operated at the height of the *pax Britannica* system from mid-century to 1914. Here 'automatic' is put in inverted commas to signal the fact that this is a popular caricature. The actual system of adjustment took place very much in terms of overt domestic policy interventions (see chapter 2). The flexibility in wages and prices that the Gold Standard system demanded (the international value of currencies could not be adjusted since these were fixed in terms of gold) had to be engendered by governments through domestic expenditure reducing policies to influence the current account and through interest rate policy to influence the capital account.

Great Britain acted as the political and economic hegemon and the guarantor of this system. But it is important to recognize that the system of the Gold Standard and the *pax Britannica* was merely one of the several structures of the international economy in this century. Such structures were highly conditional upon major socio-political conjunctures. Thus the First World War wrecked British hegemony, accelerating a process that would have occurred far more slowly merely as a consequence of British industrial decline. It resulted in a period of protectionism and national autarchic competition in the 1930s, followed by the establishment of American hegemony after World War II and the re-opened international economy of the Bretton Woods system. This indicates the danger of assuming that current major changes in the international economy are unprecedented and that they are inevitable or irreversible. The lifetime of a prevailing system of international economic relations in this century has been no more than thirty to forty years. Indeed, given that most European currencies did not become fully convertible until the late 1950s, the full Bretton Woods system after World War II only lasted upwards of thirteen to fourteen years. Such systems have been transformed by major changes in the politico-economic balance of power and the conjunctures that have effected these shifts have been large-scale conflicts between the major powers. In that sense, the international economy has been determined in its structure and the distribution of power within it by the major nation states.

The period of this world-wide inter-national economic system is also typified by the rise and maturity of the multinational corporation (MNC), as a transformation of the large merchant trading companies of a past era. From our point of view, however, the important aspect of these MNCs is that they retain a clear national home base; they are subject to the national regulation of the mother country, and by and large they are effectively policed by that home country.

The point of this ideal type drawing on the institutions of the *belle époque* is not, however, a historical analogy: for a simple and automatically governed international economic system *like* that before 1914 is unlikely to reproduce itself now. The current international economy is relatively open, but it has real differences from that prevailing before World War I: it has more generalized and institutionalized free trade through GATT; foreign investment is different in its modalities and destinations, although a high degree of capital mobility is once again a possibility; the international monetary system is quite different; and freedom of labour migration is drastically curtailed. The pre-1914 system was, nevertheless, genuinely international, tied by efficient long-distance communications and industrialized means of transport.

The late twentieth century communications and information technology revolution has further developed, rather than created, a trading system that could make day-to-day *world* prices. In the second half of the nineteenth century the submarine inter-continental telegraph cables enabled the integration of world markets. Modern systems dramatically increase the possible volume and complexity of transactions, but we have had information media capable of sustaining a genuine international trading system for over a century. The difference between a trading system in which goods and information moved by sailing ship and one in which they moved by steam ships and electricity is qualitative. If the theorists of globalization mean that we have an economy in which each part of the world is linked by markets sharing close to real-time information, then that began not in the 1970s but in the 1870s.

Type 2: a globalized economy

A *globalized economy* is an ideal type distinct from that of the international economy and can be developed by contrast with it. In such a global system distinct national economies are subsumed and rearticulated into the system by international processes and transactions. The inter-national economy, on the contrary, is one in which processes that are determined at the level of national economies still dominate and international phenomena are outcomes that emerge from the distinct and differential performance of the national economies. The international economy is an aggregate of nationally located functions. Thus while there are in such an economy a wide and increasing range of international economic interactions (financial markets and trade in manufactured goods, for example) these tend to function as opportunities or constraints for nationally located economic actors and their public regulators.

The global economy raises these nationally based interactions to a new power. The international economic system becomes autonomized and socially disembedded, as markets and production become truly global. Domestic policies, whether of private corporations or public regulators, now have routinely to take account of the predominantly international determinants of their sphere of operations. As systemic interdependence grows, the national level is permeated by and transformed by the international. In such a globalized economy the problem this poses for public authorities is how to construct policies that coordinate and integrate their regulatory efforts in order to cope with the systematic interdependence between their economic actors.

The first major consequence of a globalized economy would thus be the fundamental problematicity of its governance. Global socially decontextualized markets would be difficult to regulate, even supposing effective cooperation by the regulators and a coincidence of their interests. The principal difficulty is to construct both effective and integrated patterns of national and international public policy to cope with global market forces. The systematic economic interdependence of countries and markets would by no means necessarily result in a harmonious integration in which world consumers benefit from truly independent allocatively efficient market mechanisms. On the contrary, it is more than plausible that the populations of even successful and advanced states and regions would be at the mercy of autonomized and uncontrollable, because global, market forces. Interdependence would then readily promote *dis-integration* – i.e. competition and conflict – between regulatory agencies at different levels. Such conflict would further weaken effective public governance at the global level. Enthusiasts for the efficiency of free markets and the superiority of corporate control over that of public agencies would see this as a rational world order freed from the shackles of obsolete and ineffective national public interventions. Others, less sanguine but convinced globalization *is* occurring, may see it as a world system in which there can be no generalized or sustained public reinsurance against the costs imposed on particular localities by unfavourable competitive outcomes or market failures.

Even if one does not accept that the full process of globalization is taking place, this ideal type can help to highlight some aspects of the importance of greater economic integration within the major regional trade blocs. Both the European Union (EU) and the North American Free Trade Area (NAFTA) will soon be highly integrated markets of continental scale. Already in the case of the EU it is clear that there are fundamental problems of the integration and coordination of regulatory policies between the different public authorities at Union, national and regional level.

It is also clear that this ideal type highlights the problem of weak public governance for the major corporations. Even if such companies were truly global, they will not be able to operate in all markets equally effectively and, like governments, will lack the capacity for reinsurance against unexpected shocks from their own resources alone. Governments would no longer be available to assist as they have been for 'national champions'. Firms would, therefore, seek to share risks and opportunities through inter-corporate investments, partnerships, joint ventures, etc. Even in the current internationalized economy we can recognize such processes emerging.

A second major consequence of the notion of a globalizing international economy would be the transformation of MNCs into transnational corporations (TNCs) as the major players in the world economy.[1] The TNC would be genuine footloose capital, without specific national identification and with an internationalized management, and at least potentially willing to locate and relocate anywhere in the globe to obtain either the most secure or the highest returns. In the financial sector this could be achieved at the touch of a button and in a truly globalized economy would be wholly dictated by market forces, without reference to national monetary policies. In the case of primarily manufacturing companies the TNC would source, produce and market at the global level as strategy and opportunities dictated. The company would no longer be based on one predominant national location (as with the MNC) but would service global markets through global operations. Thus the TNC, unlike the MNC, could no longer be controlled or even constrained by the policies of particular national states. Rather it could escape all but the commonly agreed and enforced international regulatory standards. National governments could not thus effectively adopt particular regulatory policies that diverged from these standards to the detriment of TNCs operating within their borders. The TNC would be the main manifestation of a truly globalized economy.

Julius (1990) and Ohmae (1990; 1993; 1995), for example, both consider this trend toward true TNCs to be well established. Ohmae argues that such 'stateless' corporations are now the prime movers in an Interlinked Economy (ILE) centred on North America, Europe and Japan. He contends that macroeconomic and industrial policy intervention by national governments can only distort and impede the rational process of resource allocation by corporate decisions and consumer choices on a global scale. Like Akio Morita of Sony, Ohmae argues that such corporations will pursue strategies of 'global localization' in responding on a world-wide scale to specific regionalized markets and locating effectively to meet the varying demands of distinct localized groups of consumers. The assumption here is that TNCs will rely primarily on foreign direct investment and the full domestication of production to meet such specific market demands. This is in contrast to the strategy of flexibly specialized core production in the company's main location and the building of branch assembly plants where needed or dictated by national public policies, a strategy compatible with nationally based companies. But the evidence from Japanese corporations that are the most effective operators in world markets favours the view that the latter strategy is predominant (Williams et al. 1992). Japanese companies appear to have been reluctant to locate core functions like R&D or high-value-added parts of the production process abroad. Thus national companies with an international scope of operations currently and for the foreseeable future seem more likely than the true TNCs. Of course, such multinational companies, although they are nationally based, are internationally oriented. Foreign markets influence their domestic strategies and foreign competitors their production processes. Although MNCs continue to trade substantially *within* their national economies, significant percentages of foreign sales influence their actions. The point, however, is that this is not new: companies in the era of the post-1945 long boom were influenced in this way too, and were successful only if they met the standards of international competition.

A third consequence of globalization would be the further decline in the political influence and economic bargaining power of organized labour. Globalized markets and TNCs would tend to be mirrored by an open world labour market. This market would operate not primarily by *actual* labour mobility from country to country but by mobile capital selecting locations with the best deal in terms of labour costs and supply. Thus while companies requiring highly skilled and productive labour might well continue to locate in the advanced countries, with all their advantages, rather than merely seek low wages, the trend of the global mobility of capital and the relative national fixity of labour would favour those advanced countries with the most tractable labour forces and the lowest social overheads relative to the benefits of labour competence and motivation. 'Social democratic' strategies of enhancement of working conditions would thus only be viable if they assured the competitive advantage of the labour force, without constraining management prerogatives, and at no more overall cost in taxation than the average for the advanced world. Such strategies would clearly be a tall order and the tendency of globalization would be to favour management at the expense of even moderately organized labour, and, therefore, public policies sympathetic to the former rather than the latter. This would be the 'disorganized capitalism' of Lash and Urry (1987) with a vengeance, or it could be seen as placing a premium on moderate and defensive strategies where organized labour remains locally strong (Scharpf 1991).

A final and inevitable consequence of globalization is the growth in fundamental multipolarity in the international political system. The hitherto hegemonic national power could no longer impose its own distinct regulatory objectives in either its own territories or elsewhere, and lesser agencies (whether public or private) would thus enjoy enhanced powers of denial and evasion *vis-à-vis* any aspirant 'hegemon'. A variety of bodies from international voluntary agencies to TNCs would thus gain in relative power at the expense of national governments and, using global markets and media, could appeal to and obtain legitimacy from consumers/citizens across national boundaries. Thus the distinct disciplinary powers of national states would decline, even though the bulk of their citizens, especially in the advanced countries, remained nationally bound. In such a world, national military power would become less effective as the rationality of the objectives of 'national' state control in respect of the economy evaporated. The use of military force would be increasingly tied to non-economic issues, such as nationality and religion. A variety of more specific powers of sanction and veto in the economic sphere by different kinds of bodies (both public and private) would thus begin to compete with national states and begin to change the nature of international politics. As economics and nationhood pulled apart the international economy would become even more 'industrial' and less 'militant' than it is today. War would be increasingly localized, and wherever it threatened powerful global economic interests it would be subject to devastating economic sanction.

The argument in outline

We have spent some time elaborating this idea of a globalized international economy and contrasting it with that of an inter-national one.

This is to try to clarify exactly what would be involved in making the strong claim either that we are firmly within a globalizing economy, or that the present era is one in which there are strong globalizing tendencies. To consider these claims conclusively is a difficult task. This task is made harder because of a number of specific and politically driven changes in the international economy since the First World War. Chief amongst these have been the collapse in hegemonic leadership during the inter-war period and then the decline of the *pax Americana* in the post-1970s period.

The world trading system has never just been an 'economy', a distinct system governed by its own laws. In this sense the term 'international economy' has always been a shorthand for what is actually the product of the complex interaction of economic relations and politics, shaped and reshaped by the struggles of the Great Powers. The international economy has been most open, it appears, when the trading system has been sustained by a hegemonic power which for reasons of its own perceived interests was willing to accept the costs of underwriting the system. If the globalizers are correct, then all this is about to come to an end. British hegemony was followed by a period of turbulence and competition between the Great Powers after 1918. Are we currently witnessing a slightly different period of turbulence after the weakening of American hegemony in the early 1970s or the formation of an entirely new global system in which economic laws finally prevail over political power and thus can eschew a guarantor?

US economic and military power made possible the *pax Americana* after 1945, a deliberate political attempt to reopen the international economy that was remarkably successful. The liberal multilateral market system created by the US permitted the massive growth in world trade that helped to fuel the long boom. But US hegemony was multi-dimensional and it is by no means clear that it is entirely over. Militarily the US is still hegemonic in the sense that its strength ensures that no other state can use political power to restructure the international economy. In this sense the *pax* continues: the US remains the only possible guarantor of the world free-trading system against politically inspired disruption and thus the openness of global markets depends on American policy. The US also remains the largest single national economy and the power-house of world demand. Even though US monetary policy is unable to operate hegemonically and unilaterally, the dollar remains the medium of world trade. Thus the US has more than residual elements of hegemony and no obvious political competitors, neither the EU nor Japan being capable of taking over its world role or wishing to do so.

The immediate conjuncture of the weakening of US hegemony led to conditions in which it might appear that a globalized economy could emerge. The crisis of the early 1970s led to a totally floating rate monetary regime. These developments combined with fashionable theories led to the policies of the abandonment of exchange controls and the liberalization of international financial markets. The floating exchange rate regime quickly began to exhibit perverse 'over-shooting'. At the same time the OPEC oil hikes (a coordinated national policy action of the oil exporters) increased the volatility of the international economy by producing inflationary crises in the advanced nations, massive increases in the liquidity of the OPEC countries, and a massive growth of borrowing by the Third World (leading subsequently to the debt crisis and recessions, particularly in Latin America). These changes also produced a generalized recession in the advanced world and the widespread increase in government indebtedness. The US changed from being a major creditor nation and became a massive capital importer, principally to fund its trade deficit with Japan.

The point is that these changes were conjunctural, although important in their effects and large scale, and that they were at least in part policy driven. The period of extreme volatility and turbulence did not last for long. The totally floating rate monetary regime was replaced by partial regularization through the creation of the EMS in 1979, and the Louvre and Plaza accords between the G7 advanced industrial countries in the 1980s. The old post-1945 multilateral order was not restored, but a drift into uncontrolled market forces on the one hand, or negative competition between the major emerging trading blocs on the other, was prevented. The recent Uruguay Round of the GATT Treaty has helped, despite conflicts and divergent interests over agricultural products, financial services and intellectual property rights, to keep the world trading system both open and at least potentially subject to calculable rules. Thus the maximum point of change in the post-1945 international regime does not seem to have produced an acephalous system based on unregulated supra-national markets.

The history of the international economy will be considered in the next chapter: we rehearse these issues here to register the purely contingent nature of a lot of these events which have often been used to argue for a structural transformation in the international economy. Many of these trends have been reversed or interrupted as the international economy has evolved. This goes to make the point, then, that we should be cautious in a wider sense of ascribing structural significance to what may be conjunctural and temporary changes, dramatic though some of them have been.[2]

The strong concept of a globalized economy outlined above acts as an ideal type which we can measure against the actual trends within the international economy. This globalized economy has been contrasted with the notion of an inter-national economy in the above analysis in order to distinguish its particular and novel features. The opposition of these two types for conceptual clarity conceals the possibly messy combination of the two in fact. This would make it difficult to determine major trends on the basis of the available evidence. These two types of economy are not inherently mutually exclusive: rather, in certain conditions the globalized economy would *encompass and subsume* the inter-national economy. The globalized economy would rearticulate many of the features of the inter-national economy, transforming them as it reinforced them. If this phenomenon occurred there would thus be a complex combination of features of both types of economy present within the present conjuncture. The problem in determining what is happening is to identify the dominant trends: either the growth of globalization or the continuation of the existing inter-national patterns.

It is our view that such a process of hybridization is not taking place, but it would be cavalier not to consider and raise the possibility. Central in this respect is the evidence we present later for the weak development of TNCs and the continued salience of MNCs (chapter 4) and also the ongoing dominance of the advanced countries in both trade and FDI (chapter 3). Such evidence is consistent with a continuing inter-national economy, but much less so with a rapidly globalizing hybrid system. Moreover, we should remember that an inter-national economy is one in which the major nationally based manufacturers and the major financial trading and service centres are strongly externally oriented, emphasizing international trading performance. The opposite of a globalized economy is thus not a nationally inward-looking one, but an open world market based on trading nations and regulated to a greater or lesser degree both by the public policies of nation states and by supra-national agencies (chapter 6). Such an economy has existed in some form or another since the 1870s, and has continued to re-emerge despite major setbacks, the most serious being the crisis of the 1930s. The point is that it should not be confused with a global economy.

Structure of the book

The rest of this book is organized as follows.

In chapter 2 the history of the international economy and its regimes of regulation is considered in some detail. In particular we contrast the economic integration of the Gold Standard period before 1914 with the international economy developing during the 1980s and early 1990s. The analysis looks at a wide range of measures of integration and finds that there is nothing unprecedented about the levels of integration experienced at present, in either the real or the monetary economy. The governed nature of the international system is stressed, and the relationships between domestic and international activity during different periods are explored.

Chapter 3 moves on to examine the specific issues of trade and foreign direct investment. FDI is key to the proposition that capital mobility is restructuring the world economy, and the chapter considers its distribution and the question of its regulation, relative to or distinct from that of international trade. The dominance of the Triad blocs – North America, Europe and Japan – in trade and FDI flows is stressed, and the relationships between these and the Third World are explored.

Chapter 4 presents the evidence about the economic role of MNCs and explores the best readily available data sets to show that companies are not becoming footloose global capital. Chapters 3 and 4 represent a closely related couple, dealing with the nature of the international real economy through a thorough examination of the strategies of international companies and real resource flows. Their overall conclusion is that the globalization of production has been exaggerated: companies remain tethered to their home economies and are likely to remain so.

Chapter 5 considers the issue of whether present patterns of trade and investment centred on the advanced countries will be transformed by rapid growth in the developing world, and concludes that on balance such predictions are highly optimistic and that First World dominance is likely to continue well into the next century. This chapter thus addresses whether our analysis is backward looking by assessing the possible future shape of the international economy.

Chapter 6 examines the present structure of governance of the world economy, particularly the financial system, and goes on to consider the possibilities for economic regulation at international, national and regional levels. We conclude that there are real potentialities for developing regulatory and management systems, that the international economy is by no means out of control, but that the political will is lacking at present to gain extra leverage over undesirable and unjust aspects of international and domestic economic activity. Chapter 7 considers the European Union as the most developed trade bloc and examines the issue of the future evolution of its institutions. The outcomes here, we argue, will be crucial to whether the international economy develops with a minimalist or more extended regulatory regime.

Chapter 8 examines the political dimensions of governance. It explores the changing role and capacities of the nation state and the possible roles that such entities may perform in promoting and legitimating extended governance in the international system. Our argument here is that, far from the nation state being undermined by the processes of internationalization, these processes strengthen the importance of the nation state in many ways. Chapter 9 concludes the book by re-examining the notion of 'globalization' in the light of the foregoing analyses.

2

Globalization and the History of the International Economy

The 'globalization' of economic activity and the governance issues it raises are often thought to have appeared only since the Second World War, and particularly during the 1960s. The post-1960s era was one of the emergence of MNC activity on the one hand and the rapid growth of international trade on the other. Subsequently, with the collapse of the Bretton Woods semi-fixed exchange rate regime in the 1971–3 period, the expansion of international securities investment and bank lending began in earnest as capital markets rapidly internationalized, adding to the complexity of international economic relations and heralding the genuine globalization of an integrated and interdependent world economy. In this chapter we scrutinize this popular history and trace the main periods of the internationalization of economic activity, which it will be shown have developed in a cyclical and uneven fashion. The key issue at stake in our assessment is the changing autonomy of national economies in the conduct of their economic activity.[1]

MNCs, TNCs and international business

The history of the internationalization of business enterprises is a long one and not something confined just to the period since 1960. Trading activities, for instance, date from the earliest civilizations, but it was the Middle Ages in Europe that initiated systematic cross-border trading operations carried out by institutions of a private corporate nature (though often with strong state backing and support). During the fourteenth century, for instance, the Hanseatic League organized German merchants in the conduct of their Western European and Levantine commerce – which involved them in agricultural production, iron smelting and general manufacturing. Around the same time the merchant adventurers organized the sale of UK produced wool and cloth to the Low Countries and elsewhere. In addition, Italian trading and banking houses occupied a key position in the general internationalization of business activity during the early Renaissance period. By the end of the fourteenth century it is estimated that there were as many as 150 Italian banking companies already operating multinationally (Dunning 1993, pp. 97–8).

During the seventeenth and eighteenth centuries state patronage extended as the great colonial trading companies were established. Thus came into existence the Dutch and British East India Companies, the Muscovy Company, the Royal Africa Company and the Hudson Bay Company. These pioneered wholesale trading operations in what were to become the leading colonial areas.

However, it is the development of international manufacturing as the industrial revolution took hold that presents the closest precursor to the modern-day MNC. Here the early pre-eminence of British firms as multinational producers becomes apparent. Initially North and South America presented the most favourable investment opportunities, but these were soon followed by Africa and Australasia. There is some dispute as to whether 'colonial investments' should be considered a true precursor of FDI, but production for the local market began in this way. Technical and organizational developments after the 1870s allowed a wider variety of similar products to be produced domestically and abroad within the boundaries of the same firm, while the exploration and development of minerals and other raw material products also attracted large amounts of FDI (Dunning 1993, ch. 5).

One of the problems with such a retrospective classification, however, is that the modern concepts of 'direct' investment on the one hand (involving some notion of managerial control from abroad) and 'portfolio' investment on the other (involving the acquisition of securities issued by foreign institutions so as to claim returns without any associated control or management participation) were only developed in the early 1960s, at the same time as the term MNC was itself introduced. The US Department of Commerce had reported outward FDI from 1929, but this was the exception.

Despite this lack of consistently classified data it is generally agreed that manufacturing multinationals appeared in the world economy after the mid nineteenth century and that they were well established by the First World War. International business activity grew vigorously in the 1920s as the truly diversified and integrated MNC matured, but it slowed

Table 2.1   Estimated stocks of FDI by country of origin, 1914 (current US$ million)

UK	8,172
US	2,652
Germany	2,600
France	1,750
Netherlands	925

Sources: UK, Corley 1994; Germany, Schröter 1984; US and France, Dunning 1993; Netherlands, Gales and Sluyterman 1993: all drawn from Jones 1994

down during the depressed 1930s and war-torn 1940s, and began a fluctuating expansion again after 1950.

There have been two approaches to quantifying the growth of international business over time. The first involves looking at whatever statistics on international investment are available, generating additional data, and then reclassifying these on the basis of modern distinctions. The second approach focuses on the businesses themselves. It traces the history of firms and the internationalization of their activity, which involves counting multinationals and their business affiliations over time (Jones 1994).

Recent estimates of FDI held by the leading countries in 1914 are shown in table 2.1. The analysis of companies and their history also shows the developed nature of international production before the First World War. The pioneer country here was the UK, but there was also a surprising extent of multinational production organized by the smaller advanced economies. Company-based analysis reveals that a good deal of this early FDI was modest in scale, though extensive in scope, and often made by quite small foreign companies (Jones 1994).

Trade and international integration

A better statistical base is available for exploring the trends in international trade. Again the history of this part of international economic activity goes back a long way. But good statistical evidence exists from 1830 onwards (Maddison 1962; 1987; Lewis 1981). The important period from our point of view concerns developments this century, and particularly from the First World War. A similar pattern emerges here as in the case of FDI, though perhaps more pronounced in its features. The volume of world foreign trade expanded at about 3.4 per cent per annum between 1870 and 1913. After 1913 trade was adversely affected by the growth of tariffs, quantitative restrictions, exchange controls and then war, and it expanded by less than 1 per cent per annum on average between 1913 and 1950. After 1950, however, trade really took off to grow at over 9 per cent per annum until 1973. Between 1973 and the mid 1980s the growth rate fell back to nearer the late nineteenth century levels, expanding at a rate of only 3.6 per cent (see also figure 3.1).

The experience of the development of export volumes for six main economies between 1913 and 1984 is shown in table 2.2, indicating the different rates of volume growth and their fluctuation. This table demonstrates that there was a definite fall in the volume of world trade during the 1930s. Clearly, the brunt of the fall in trade volume in this inter-war period was borne by Germany, France, the UK and to a lesser extent the US and the Netherlands. Japan only suffered as a consequence of the Second World War (as also did Germany).

The estimated value of manufacturing exports for a number of countries in 1913 is shown in table 2.3. The UK and Germany were thus the leading exporters of manufactures at the outbreak of the First World War, and were over twice as important as the US and France. Yearly export values were already less than accumulated FDI stocks by this time (compare table 2.3 with table 2.1).

The relationship between growth in output and growth in trade is a central one for international economics analysis. It is not our intention to explore the theoretical links between these here (see Kitson and Michie 1995). However, table 2.4 gives empirical data on the relationship between the two over various cyclical periods. Trade growth from 1853 to 1872 was already faster than the growth in world production, while from 1872 to 1911 it grew at about the same rate. The devastating effects of the inter-war period and the Second World War are shown for both series. Only since 1950 has there been a consistent expansion of trade relative to production, even during the cyclical downturn after 1973 (see also chapter 3).

Table 2.2   Volume of exports, 1913–1984 (1913 = 100)

	France	Germany	Japan	Netherlands	UK	US
1913	100.0	100.0	100.0	100.0	100.0	100.0
1929	147.0	91.8	257.9	171.2	81.3	158.2
1938	91.0	57.0	588.3	140.0	57.3	125.7
1950	149.2	34.8	210.1	171.2	100.0	224.6
1960	298.4	154.7	924.4	445.1	120.0	387.9
1973	922.4	514.3	5,672.7	1,632.1	241.9	912.0
1984	1,459.5	774.0	14,425.2	2,383.7	349.1	1,161.5

Source: Maddison 1987, table A-21, p. 694

Table 2.3 Estimated value of manufacturing exports, 1913 (current US$ million)

UK	1,928
Germany	1,824
US	896
France	813
World Total	7,227

Source: Lewis 1981, appendix IV, p. 67

Table 2.4 Relationship between growth of output and growth of foreign trade, 1853–1984 (per cent per annum)

	1853–72	1872–99	1899–1911	1913–50	1950–73	1973–84
Average growth of trade volume[a]	4.3	3.1	3.9	0.5	9.4	3.6
Average growth of output[b]	3.7	3.3	3.6	1.9	5.3	2.1

[a] 1853–1911: UK, US, France and Germany.
  1913–1984: UK, US, France, Germany, Netherlands and Japan.
[b] 1853–1911: industrial production only.
  1913–1984: GDP.
Sources: 1853–1911, Lewis 1981, table 5, p. 70; 1913–1984, Maddison 1987, table 14, p. 670

Migration and the international labour market

A third broad area of analysis in the context of the history of the international economy concerns migration and the consequences of this for the integration of the global labour market. It is generally agreed that migration is becoming (or has become) a 'global phenomenon' (e.g. Serow et al., 1990, p. 159; Segal 1993, ch. 7; Castles and Miller 1993, ch. 4). However, by 'global' these authors mean that, since the mid 1970s in particular, many more countries have been affected by migration, there has been a growing diversity of areas of origin for migrants, and migrants are of a wider range of socio-economic statuses than ever before. Thus for these authors globalization registers a quantitative change in the extent and scope of migration rather than a feature of a potentially different socio-economic order.

There are a number of different kinds of migrants. Clearly the early slave trade was a form of 'involuntary' migration (it is estimated that 15 million slaves were moved from Africa to the Americas before 1850: Castles and Miller 1993, p. 48). Refugees and asylum seekers can also be considered as migrants. But for the purposes of our analysis we focus on 'voluntary' migration. The period considered extends from the 'mass migration' after 1815 (mainly from Europe) to the emergence and extension of labour migration of the 'guest worker' variety after the Second World War.

It is difficult to judge exactly how many migrants there have been since 1815, so all the following numbers should be treated with some caution. Castles and Miller (1993) report that there could have been as many as 100 million migrants of all kinds in 1992 (including some 20 million refugees and asylum seekers, and 30 million overseas workers). They point out, however, that this represented only about 1.7 per cent of the world population. Thus the vast majority of the world's population remain in their country of origin.

The greatest era for recorded voluntary mass migration was the century after 1815 (figure 2.1). Around 60 million persons left Europe for the Americas, Oceania, and South and East Africa. An estimated 10 million voluntarily migrated from Russia to Central Asia and Siberia. A million went from Southern Europe to North Africa. About 12 million Chinese and 6 million Japanese left their homelands and emigrated to Eastern and Southern Asia. One and a half million left India for South Eastern Asia and South and West Africa (Segal 1993, p. 16: the statistics for Indian migration are probably severely underestimated here).

Between the two world wars international migration decreased sharply. To a large extent this was in response to the depressed economic conditions during much of the inter-war period, but it was also due to restrictive immigration policies instigated in many of the traditional recipient countries, particularly the United States.

An upsurge in international migration began in the post-1945 period, particularly involving Europe and the United States once again (Livi-Bacci 1993). This was the period, however, of the relative growth of migration from the developing countries to the developed ones, and the introduction of the 'guest worker' phenomenon (figure 2.2). During the 1970s and 1980s global trends favoured the controlled movements of temporary workers and entry for immigrants was restricted to the highly skilled or those with family already in the country of destination.

It is generally agreed that the United States has been, and remains, the great immigrant country. Figure 2.3 neatly summarizes the history of immigration into the US, which mirrors the trends in the history of migration for the world as a whole sketched above. The steady growth of migration to the US since the Second World War is evident from this graph. For the 1980s estimates of global flows of migrants run at approximately 25–30 million a year (Segal 1993, p. 115). Up to 4 million of these

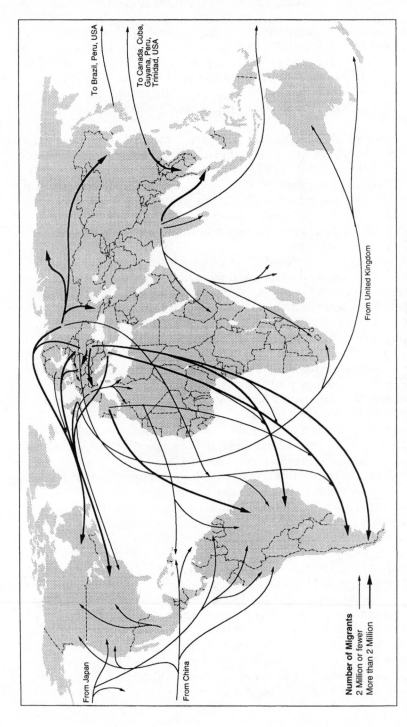

Figure 2.1 Global voluntary migrations, 1815–1914

Source: Based upon Segal 1993, p. 17

To Brazil, Peru, USA

To Canada, Cuba, Guyana, Peru, Trinidad, USA

From United Kingdom

From Japan

From China

Number of Migrants
2 Million or fewer
More than 2 Million

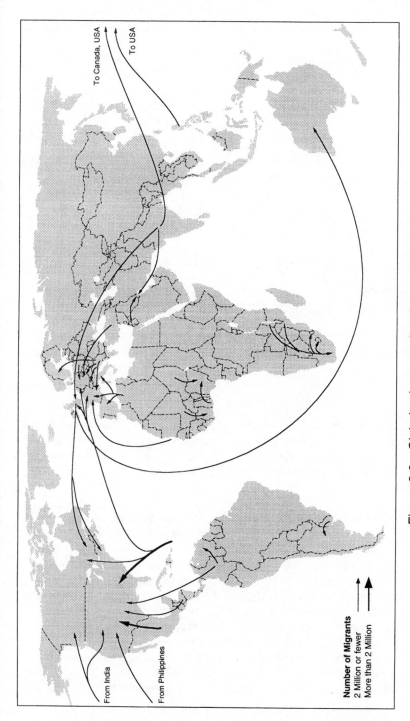

Figure 2.2 Global voluntary migrations, 1945–1980
Source: Based upon Segal 1993, p. 21

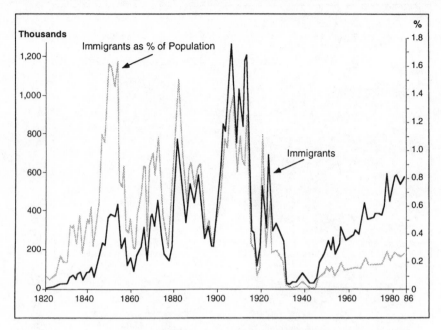

Figure 2.3   Legal immigration to the United States, 1820–1986 (numbers and as percentage of population)
Source: Serow et al. 1990, figure 19.1

were refugees and a good proportion of the others consisted of new temporary migrant labour (labour with the intent of returning home). The era of mass family migration has yet to repeat itself in the way that it operated in the period up to the First World War.

The relative openness and interdependence of the international system

A key question posed by the preceding analysis is whether the integration of the international system has dramatically changed since the Second World War. Clearly, there has been considerable international economic activity ever since the 1850s, but can we compare different periods in terms of their openness and integration?

One way of doing this is to compare trade and GDP ratios. Table 2.5 provides information on these for a range of countries. Apart from the dramatic differences in the openness to trade of different economies demonstrated by these figures (e.g., compare the US and the

Table 2.5   Ratio of merchandise trade to GDP at current prices (exports and imports combined), 1913, 1950 and 1973

	1913	*1950*	*1973*
France	35.4	21.2	29.0
Germany	35.1	20.1	35.2
Japan	31.4	16.9	18.3
Netherlands	103.6	70.2	80.1
UK	44.7	36.0	39.3
US	11.2	7.0	10.5

Source: Maddison 1987, derived from table A-23, p. 695

Netherlands), the startling feature is that trade to GDP ratios were consistently higher in 1913 than they were in 1973 (with the slight exception of Germany where they were near enough equal), indicating a greater international openness in the earlier year. It might be objected that the years shown here are rather unusual and non-representative, particularly that for 1950. But there is further evidence to show that the UK at least was consistently more open in these terms over the entire period between 1905 and 1914 compared with 1965 to 1986 (Tomlinson 1988, table 1, p. 3).

If we look at just the post-war period, however, and define trade openness slightly differently than so far (i.e. using purchasing power parity weights instead of market weights), then a steady increase in openness across most of the developed and the developing worlds becomes apparent, as shown in table 2.6. The position of the East Asian economies is particularly revealing (here defined as Hong Kong, Indonesia, Korea, Malaysia, Singapore, Taiwan and Thailand).

What is more, getting back to the longer-term trends, the evidence suggests greater openness to capital flows in the period before the First World War compared with more recent years. Grassman (1980), measuring 'financial openness' in terms of current account balance to GNP ratios, finds no increase in openness between 1875 and 1975: indeed, there is a decline in capital movements for his leading six countries (Great Britain, Italy, Sweden, Norway, Denmark and the USA). This is even the case for the period after the Second World War, though from the mid 1970s there is some sign of an increasing trend in financial openness. Measuring things slightly differently, the figures shown in table 2.7 confirm the general finding of a decrease in openness, but not an increase for all the countries after 1975.

In addition, Lewis (1981, p. 21) reports that capital exports rose steadily over the thirty years before the First World War, though subject to

Table 2.6   Trade openness since the Second World War (percentage of GDP)[a]

	1950–59	1960–69	1970–79	1980–89
Industrial countries	23.3	24.6	32.0	36.8
North America	11.2	11.7	17.8	21.9
Western Europe	37.2	38.9	48.7	56.9
Japan	21.8	19.5	22.9	23.9
Developing countries	–	28.0	34.4	38.4[b]
Africa	–	48.2	55.1	54.4
Asia				
East	–	47.0	69.5	87.2
Other[c]	–	17.2	19.6	24.0
Middle East	–	41.5	60.4	46.9
Western Hemisphere	26.3	23.9	24.9	27.9

[a] Openness is defined as nominal merchandise exports plus imports as a percentage of nominal output. Aggregates are calculated on the basis of purchasing power parity (PPP) weights.
[b] 1980–87.
[c] Excluding China.
Source: *World Economic Outlook,* October 1994, IMF, table 21, p. 89

Table 2.7   Ratio of total capital flows to GDP

	Britain	France	Sweden
1905–14	6.61	–	2.01
1965–75	1.17	1.59	1.02
1982–86	1.10	0.99	1.48

Source: Tomlinson 1988, table 2, p. 4

wide fluctuations. But when compared with the period 1953–73 the order of magnitude of capital exports was much lower in the latter period (Lewis 1981, p. 21). Finally, in a comprehensive comparison of the pre-1914 Gold Standard period with the 1980s, Turner (1991) also concludes that current account imbalances and capital flows, measured in relation to GNP, were larger before 1914 than they were in the 1980s.

Thus using gross figures for ratios of trade and capital flows relative to output confirms unequivocally that 'openness' was greater during the Gold Standard period than even in the 1980s. But these gross figures can disguise important differences between the periods. For instance, the composition of output might be important in judging the real extent of interdependence. The fact is that the proportion of 'non-tradable' output has increased in overall GDP since the First World War, particularly as the importance of the public sector has grown, so that we might expect the trade to GDP ratio to fall just as a result of this. In the case of financial flows we should also recognize the change in the character of these and the significance of the financial regimes under which they took place. This issue is discussed at greater length below but at this stage it is worth pointing to the nature of the Gold Standard as a quintessential fixed exchange rate system compared with the 1980s floating position. In a fixed exchange rate regime, short-term capital flows are highly interest rate elastic, with only small changes in interest rates causing significant capital movements (though this also means that the capital flow to interest rate sensitivity can limit the variability of short-term interest rates). Some of the capital flow could thus be accounted for by the interest rate variation as between the two periods, which was significantly different, though again the post-war Bretton Woods system did not show any greater interest rate variability than the Gold Standard period (Turner 1991, table 2, p. 16).

Moving away from trade and capital flows for the moment, we can now look at the implications of the trends in international migration. First, it must be emphasized that these are set within the twin considerations of the labour market and governmental policy. A world market for labour just does not exist in the same way as it does for goods and services. Most labour markets continue to be nationally regulated and accessible only marginally to outsiders, whether legal or illegal migrants or professional manpower. Moving goods and services is infinitely easier than moving labour. Even a rapid and sustained expansion of the world economy is unlikely to significantly reduce the multiple barriers to the movement of labour. Other than in the context of regionally developing free-trade agreements of the EU type, freedom of labour movement still remains heavily circumscribed. Even the NAFTA explicitly excludes freedom of movement of persons, though there is *de facto* freedom between Canada and the US, and enormous illegal flows between Mexico and the US. Extra-regional migration of all kinds is a small percentage of global labour movements, however. Most migration is of the country next door variety. During the nineteenth century the mass movement of workers to the sources of capital was accepted and encouraged; now it is rejected except as a temporary expedient.

In as much as there is global international migration for employment it is concentrated on the Gulf States, North America and Western Europe. A crude estimate of this category gives about 20 million in 1990 (prior to the Gulf War, which saw a massive return home of particularly Third World migrant workers). This form of international labour force reached its peak in the early 1970s. The world-wide recession and subsequent developments like the Gulf War interrupted the growth of temporary migrant employment. A large proportion of these workers are illegally residing and working abroad. Legal expatriate workers tend to be in the managerial, skilled and technical employment categories.

One consequence of these levels of international migration and employment is that remittances now constitute an important component of international financial flows and of the national incomes of some small states. It is estimated that remittances rose from $3,133 billion in 1970 to $30,401 billion in 1988 (Segal 1993, p. 150). But this still represents less than 5 per cent of the total value of world trade, though it has been increasing at a faster pace than has the value of that trade. This suggests either that the incentives to move this kind of labour have grown relative to the movements of goods and services or that the rewards to this kind of labour have grown relatively. The latter explanation could in turn be because more of the migrants are now to be found in the higher-income categories of employment. The days of the unskilled, low-income migrant seem to be numbered, though there may remain considerable scope for continued temporary female migration to undertake domestic tasks in the richer countries.

Indeed, this is where government policy enters the picture explicitly. Policy is tightening on the growth of migrant workers, and even more so on the rights to permanent family immigration. There are differences here, particularly between Europe and the USA where the latter country still maintains a much more open and liberal regime (Livi-Bacci 1993, p. 41). But as Castles and Miller suggest:

> Prospects are slim for significant increased legal migration flows to Western democracies over the short to medium term…Political constraints will not permit this…[There is] some room for highly skilled labour, family reunification and refugees, but not for the resumption of massive recruitment of foreign labour for low level jobs. (1993, pp. 265–6)

The adverse labour market conditions in the advanced countries and the difficulty of providing work for existing citizens and resident alien workers will also mean the curtailment of unwanted and illegal immigration.

Two sets of more general points are worth making in the light of these remarks. The first is that there have been phases of massive international migration over many centuries and there seems nothing unprecedented about that since the Second World War or that of more recent decades. The second related point is that in many ways the situation between 1815 and 1914 was much more open than it is today. The supposed era of 'globalization' has not seen the rise of a new unregulated and internationalized market in labour migration. In many ways, for the world's underprivileged and poor there are fewer international migratory options nowadays than there were in the past. At least in the period of mass migration there was the option to uproot the whole family and move in the quest for better conditions, something that now seems to be rapidly closing off for present-day equivalent sections of the world's population. They have little option but to remain in poverty and stick it out. The equivalent of the 'empty lands' available to European and other settlers in the USA and Canada, South America, Southern Africa, and Australia and New Zealand just do not exist today, with a concomitant loss of 'freedom' for the world's poor.

Things look different for the well-off and privileged however. Those with professional qualifications and technical skills still have greater room for manoeuvre and retain the option to move if they wish. The 'club class' with managerial expertise, though relatively few in number in global population terms, are the most obvious manifestation of this inequity in migratory opportunities.

As a preliminary conclusion, then, we can say that the international economy was in many ways more open in the pre-1914 period than it has been at any time since, including that from the late 1970s onwards. International trade and capital flows, both between the rapidly industrializing economies themselves and between these and their various colonial territories, were more important relative to GDP levels before the First World War than they probably are today. Adding to this the issue of international migration just explored, we have an extraordinarily developed, open and integrated international economy at the beginning of this century. Thus the present period is by no means unprecedented.

International monetary and exchange rate regimes

An issue thrown up by the previous analysis is the existence of the general monetary and exchange rate regimes in which economic activity takes place and by which the international economy is ordered and governed. Broadly speaking we can divide the twentieth century into a number of fairly discrete periods as far as these regimes are concerned, as indicated by table 2.8.

There are two important preliminary points to note about this table. The first is the diversity of regimes it displays. It is often thought that there have been just two regimes in the twentieth century, the Gold Standard and the Bretton Woods system – the former breaking down in the inter-war period and the latter in the post-1973 period. Clearly, these are two of the main systems characterizing the twentieth century, but they are not the exclusive ones. In addition, there are important subperiods within some of the regimes depicted. All in all a rather more complex picture of international economic orders and systems needs to be painted if we are to have an adequate analysis.

Table 2.8   History of monetary and exchange rate regimes

Regime	Period
1 International Gold Standard	1879–1914
2 Inter-war instability	1918–1939
(a) Floating	1918–1925
(b) Return to Gold	1925–1931
(c) Return to floating	1931–1939
3 Semi-fixed rate dollar standard	1945–1971
(a) Establishing convertibility	1945–1958
(b) Bretton Woods system proper	1958–1971
4 Floating rate dollar standard	1971–1984
(a) Failure to agree	1971–1974
(b) Return to floating	1974–1984
5 EMS and greater Deutschmark zone	1979–1993
6 Plaza-Louvre intervention accords	1985–1993
7 Drift towards renewed global floating	1993–

Sources: compiled from Eichengreen 1990; 1994; McKinnon 1993; and authors' own assessments

Secondly, other than the number of regimes, what is striking about the table is the short period over which they have operated. Only the Gold Standard existed for more than thirty years, and most of the others operated for considerably less. Clearly, what is designated here as 'inter-war instability' does not conform to any obvious regime since the 'rules of the game' during this period defy a consistent characterization. Thus we have split this period into three sub-periods, none of which can be said to display exclusive (or inclusive) system-like features since arrangements were very fluid and overlapping, being either in decay or in embryonic reconstruction (sometimes both at the same time).

The regime emerging immediately after the Second World War is characterized as a 'semi-fixed rate dollar standard', which has two subperiods. This is really a period of significant stability in exchange rates since few and only slight adjustments were made, but they were possible and sanctioned within this regime.[2] The period in its entirety is often classified as the Bretton Woods system (BWS), after the agreement signed in 1944, but we prefer to divide it into two sub-periods, since full current account convertibility of the major currencies was not established until the end of 1958 (though this was a condition of the 1944 Treaty). Thus the Bretton Woods system proper only operated for some thirteen years between 1958 and 1971,[3] perhaps a surprisingly short period.

The following period is designated the 'floating rate dollar standard'. The tumultuous events of 1971–4 are termed here 'the failure to agree' sub-period. This was one during which the international community successively gave up any attempt to collectively manage its exchange rates after the Nixon administration unilaterally suspended convertibility of the US dollar against gold in August 1971 and subsequently devalued. Despite various plans and schemes designed to shore up the previous system during this period, the writing for it was already on the wall. But the advent of 'flexible' rates did little to dislodge the dollar as the *de facto* standard for the conduct of official and most private international monetary transactions. Also, this sub-period, despite its designation as one of a 'return to floating', displayed a definite set of 'rules of the game' in the conduct of international monetary transactions, which were closely adhered to by the industrialized countries involved (McKinnon 1993, pp. 26–9: also see below).

Although the period of floating rates lasted for ten years, an important sub-regime interrupts this after the EMS was established in 1979. This is termed a 'greater Deutschmark zone' to indicate the central importance of the German currency in acting as the standard for the other European currencies that were or remain in the EMS. The EMS began to unscramble after the autumn of 1992 with first the departure of a number of its key currencies and then the widening of the bands in which the remaining currencies were allowed to fluctuate. Further devaluations of the Spanish peseta and Portuguese escudo followed in early 1995. The remains of the EMS, in this modified form, still functions however.

The sixth regime characterized in table 2.8 follows the Plaza and Louvre accords struck in 1985 and 1987, which had as their objective the stabilization (and, indeed, initially the reduction) of the value of the US dollar against the two other main currency blocs: the EMS-DM zone and the Japanese yen. Formally these accords inaugurated broad 'target zones' between the three currency blocs, allowing 'interventions' to stabilize around these rates (with concomitant sterilization of monetary impacts), and sanctioned adjustment of the central rates according to 'economic fundamentals' when necessary. Whilst monitoring by the G3 continues, it is arguable whether there was ever a real commitment to managing the rates (and thereby also to managing the G3 economies more generally: see also chapter 6). This is why, when considered alongside the partial demise of the EMS after 1992, we suggest a final possible regime, emerging during 1993–4, that hints at a drift toward the more obvious floating rate regime of 1974–84. This is despite the still informal or formal existence of the Plaza-Louvre accord regime.

The main purposes of this brief history of international monetary arrangements are as follows. First, it demonstrates the governed nature of the system throughout this century (with the possible exception of the twenty inter-war years). Secondly, it suggests that there is nothing radically unusual about the present situation. In these terms at least, there remains a definite system or order of governance. Thirdly, given the volatile nature of the international regimes and their short-lived character, it provides no reason to believe that things cannot change significantly in the future, even the near future. The length of regimes may be getting shorter. But even if they are not, thirty years looks like an absolute maximum before strains begin to pull things apart (or perhaps push things together again). With this in mind we should remember that what is often thought to have been the key regime 'watershed' year of 1973 was already twenty-two years behind us by 1995.

Openness and integration: what is at stake?

Returning to the broad issue of integration preliminarily discussed above, the actual measurement of the degree of integration in financial markets is difficult both theoretically and empirically. Economic analysis in this area tends to be driven by the idea of 'efficient (international) capital market' theory: that is, that capital markets operate competitively to allocate (international) savings and capital so as to equalize returns on investment. Thus key indicators of the degree of integration would be measures such as the interest rates between countries or the value of the same shares on domestic and international stock markets; the nearer these are to equality between different national financial markets, the more integrated the international economy has become. With a fully integrated capital market there would be single international rates of interest on short-term and long-term loans, and a single share or bond price, other things remaining equal.

Of course, the key constraint here is 'other things remaining equal'. In reality they just do not, so the task of empirical analysis from within this dominant perspective is to account for, and then adjust for, these 'imperfections' so as to arrive at a proxy measure of the degree of 'true' integration.[4] As might be expected this all requires some formidable assumptions to be made, which few other than the true *cognoscenti* might either appreciate or accept. However, despite some scepticism about this underlying approach it is worth considering its main results.[5]

There are a number of forms and levels at which the degree of international financial integration could be analysed (Frankel 1992; Herring and Litan 1995; Harris 1995). These can be grouped under three overlapping headings: those associated with interest rate differentials, those associated with differential prices of securities, and those associated with real resource flows and capital mobility. We deal with these each in turn, beginning with a discussion of the relationships between interest rates and exchange rates.

One of the most straightforward indicators of financial integration concerns offshore markets like that for Eurocurrencies. Formally, measures of offshore financial market integration can be established in terms of covered interest rate parities. This implies that depositors can receive the same return on whatever Eurocurrency they hold, taking into account the cost involved in protecting against possible exchange rate changes. Such interest rate parity seems to hold in the Eurocurrency markets. A more developed form of integration would be when offshore and onshore markets are closely linked, but it is here that difficulties begin to arise. Banking regulations and capital controls establish a separation between these two spheres, and these have often been introduced and maintained for public policy reasons. But with the progressive harmonization of banking regulations and the abandonment of capital controls this form of integration was effectively established between the advanced countries by 1993: thus covered interest rate parity between national rates has now also been more or less achieved.

Deeper forms of integration would be signalled by first uncovered interest rate parity and then real interest rate parity between deposits in different currencies. If the first condition holds, expected returns on investments in different currencies are the same when measured in terms of a single currency, so that capital flows equalize expected rates of return regardless of exposure to exchange rate risk. This introduces an unobservable variable into the calculation, the 'speculative premium' associated with expectational changes. In the case of real interest rate parity, differential inflation rates are already anticipated in the nominal rates, so that real exchange rates are maintained and capital flows serve to equalize real interest rates across countries. Whilst tests to measure the presence of these latter two forms of integration are complex and controversial, real interest rate parity seemed far from established by the early 1990s, so that the current level of international financial integration fell short of what would prevail in a truly integrated system. By contrast the Gold Standard period was one where short-term interest rates were closely correlated, and there was a strong tendency for real rates of return to be equalized internationally (Turner 1991, pp. 16–17).

The second broad approach is to focus on asset prices in different national financial systems. Here one problem is to distinguish domestic influences on prices from international ones, but there is a *prima facie* case that stock markets are closely linked, with disruption in one being quickly transmitted to others. In this context it is changes in the 'volatility' of price movements that would represent an indicator of increased globalization, not the existence of links as such, and the evidence on this score remains at best ambiguous (Harris 1995, pp. 204–6). In fact, historically based studies have reinforced the impression of greater financial integration, measured in these terms, before the First World War. From within the broad perspective of the efficient capital market approach, Neal (1985) focused on asset-price movements during the main financial crises occurring between 1745 and 1907. He measured the rapidity with which financial panics were spread between one financial centre and another. This analysis found that there was already a surprisingly high degree of capital market integration between European financial centres as early as the mid eighteenth century, but suggested that the degree of financial integration did not develop much further between then and 1900. Zevin (1992), in his survey of a wide range of the financial integration literature, reports on a number of measures supporting the highly integrated nature of the international economy before the First World War. He sums up thus:

> All these measures of transnational-securities trading and ownership are substantially greater in the years before the First World War than they are at present. More generally, every available descriptor of financial markets in the late nineteenth and early twentieth centuries suggests that they were more fully integrated than they were before or have been since. (pp. 51–2)

The Gold Standard period was thus also the one displaying the most interdependent and integrated international economy in terms of security markets, the extent of which seems yet to have been repeated.

A third important related approach in trying to identify the extent of financial integration involves measuring real resource flows. Can increased financial integration be implied from increased capital mobility? In this case it is the relationship between international savings and investment that becomes the object of analysis. This approach has generated the most extensive literature, but its results remain controversial.

The more integrated the capital markets the more mobile capital will become internationally and the more likely it is that domestic savings and investment will diverge. Thus national economies will lose their ability to 'regulate' or 'determine' domestic investment. In fact, this is just another way of pointing to the key role of interest rate differentials as a measure of integration and as the determinant of investment. As openness increases domestic savings become irrelevant to domestic investment since interest rates converge and savings and investment adjust accordingly.

The evidence for the separation of savings and investment has not been forthcoming, however. Feldstein and Horioka (1980) and Feldstein (1983) found that the relationship remained strong between 1960 and 1979. More recently, Bosworth (1993, pp. 98–102) confirmed the Feldstein and Horioka findings. His analysis covered a period (1965–90) in which the floating rate regime discussed above emerged, in which most capital controls were removed, and in which major deregulations of the capital markets took place. Despite these changes there was no obvious unloosening of the close correlation between national investment and savings. This is confirmed by the way that international portfolio diversification has yet to develop very far. In terms of the distribution of equity and fixed income assets managed by leading fund managers in 1991, foreign assets as a percentage of total assets were: US, 5 per cent; Germany, 27 per cent; France, 3.7 per cent; UK, 34.2 per cent, total US and Europe, 11.4 per cent (Padoa-Schioppa and Saccomanni 1994, table 4, p. 250). The position for Japan was approximately 23 per cent (OECD 1993, table 7, p. 38). What is more, the analysis of Frankel et al. (1986) found that the positive relationship between national savings and investment was higher for the industrialized countries than it was for less developed ones, and that it became *stronger* for both sets of countries after 1973 than it was before.

However, the basic Feldstein-Horioka findings, while proving very robust and reproducible, have attracted heavy criticism, mainly because they are so counter-intuitive. Against the conclusion that the high correlation between national savings and investment is the result of a lack of financial integration are arguments that: if the data are disaggregated into private and public sector flows, lower correlations are produced for just private sector behaviour, so that it is government policy that accounts for the strong overall relationship (Bayoumi 1990); floating exchange rates and associated uncertainties have lowered capital mobility (Bayoumi and Rose 1993); the close correlations may be because of exogenously determined productivity shocks and the way they are domestically handled (Ghosh 1995); and finally, although the original findings are robust, they have been fatally undermined by the emergence of the large US balance of payments deficits since the mid 1980s, and this has yet to be properly picked up by econometric analyses (Frankel 1992).

Clearly, there are a number of possible reasons for the high correlation between aggregate savings and investment. Most of the points just made do not so much undermine this relationship as serve to explain it in the context of a range of contemporary conditions. One problem is to distinguish those points that pertain to the determinants of real capital investment flows as opposed to overall financial ones. With the exception of the final point, they do not undermine the result of a continued separation of capital markets. They provide reasons for the results which are compatible with a relatively un-integrated international financial system – one that continues to allow for more national autonomy than might be generally appreciated. Indeed, there is no robust evidence to suggest that even after 1973 and during the 1980s the degree of integration, on these measures alone, increased. In a longer-term perspective

Zevin compares the post-1960 findings with a similar type of analysis for the 1890s onwards. This only went to confirm his other results that the Gold Standard period was an era of more effective capital mobility and financial openness than that from the 1960s onwards. Investment/savings autarky was much less between 1870 and 1910 (Zevin 1992, table 3.2, p. 57). We return to the fourth point made above – concerning the significant change in the post-1985 period *vis-à-vis* the USA – below and in chapter 6, but this pertains to general financial flows between the US and Japan and not just real resource flows.

One further possible explanation for these results, particularly over the recent period, has to do with the rate of return on financial investments in different economies. If there is no significant difference in the return on financial investment then we would not expect a large redistribution of capital relative to savings compared with a situation where there was extreme variation in returns. Thus the current situation of low financial asset mobility could be accounted for by a general convergence of returns between different economies. As figure 2.4 shows there was considerable convergence of underlying productivity between the main industrial economies from 1962 to 1991, and a striking general decline in productivity levels (which has yet to be reversed). Of course this does not preclude an intense short-term movement of funds between financial centres in search of small arbitrage gains on currency transactions, which is something that has characterized the contemporary currency markets (indeed, underlying convergence may encourage this very activity). We discuss this further below and in chapters 6 and 8.

However, on the general issue of convergence and non-convergence – which itself could constitute a measure of integration between economies – whatever indications there were of this, as the real economic business cycles of the major economies synchronized in the mid 1970s and early 1980s, came undone with the upturn of the late 1980s and early 1990s when a general desynchronization set in (OECD 1994, pp. 37–43). Thus it is inappropriate to read too much into any measure of 'convergence' as an indicator of integration which does not have a long-term empirical provenance or carry robust explanatory significance.

Of particular importance in this context was the growing asymmetric relationship between the G3 countries over the 1970s and 1980s in terms of financial flows, even though the close relationships between their domestic savings and investment levels did not alter much (Bosworth 1993, ch. 3). While there was a decline in the savings ratios in most advanced countries, so that investment ratios also fell, there was a stronger fall of both of these for the US than in other countries. The US in effect imported capital to make up for a decline in its domestic savings, and not to sustain higher levels of investment. This happened along with the emergence there of a persistent current account deficit. This led to

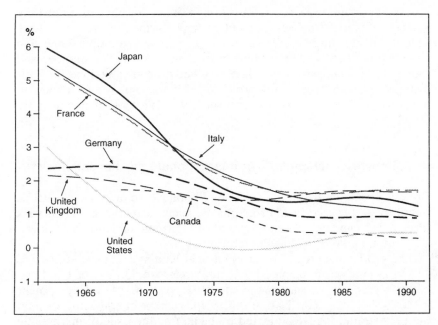

Figure 2.4 Trend total factor productivity, 1962–1991 (percentage change). Total factor productivity growth is calculated as the growth of output less a weighted average of growth of inputs, with weights equal to period averages of the factor income shares. A Hodrick-Prescott filter, corresponding roughly to two-sided moving averages, is used to calculate the trend.

Source: *OECD Economic Outlook*, no. 50, December 1991, chart A, p. 6

financing problems in the context of the so-called 'twin deficits' which have undoubtedly affected the entire international economy. How far these international financing problems were the result of the twin deficits, rather than the abandonment of fixed exchange rates and of capital controls and financial market deregulation, remains a point of dispute. In chapter 6 we discuss this issue further.

The importance of this assessment of openness and integration is obvious. It has to do with the ability of distinct national economies to devise and regulate their own economic policies. The fact that the degree of constraint on national economies in the Gold Standard period seems to have been consistently greater than at any time since should not blind us to the problems and issues facing economies because of the level of integration at the present time. It is certainly the case that, on the basis of some of the measures discussed above, the level of economic integration has increased since 1960 – though this is not obvious on just the savings/investment measure, except perhaps for the most recent period. In addition, it would be difficult to accept that the qualitative dimension has been constant over the entire period since 1870. The number and range of financial instruments have changed dramatically since 1960, for instance, and with them new problems of management and regulation have arisen (Turner 1991; Cosh et al. 1992). We look at this in more detail now.

Recent developments in international financial activity

Broadly speaking the period since the liberalization moves of the 1970s has seen an upsurge in international financial activity associated with three developments: increased extent of international lending, financial innovation and financial agglomeration.

The prodigious growth of international lending is indicated in table 2.9. In 1994 it was anticipated that total loans would be over US$1,000 billion – a tenfold increase on the late 1970s position. A key development is the growth of 'securitization': the displacement of conventional loan business (traditionally conducted by banks) by the issue of marketable bonds and other securities. The other significant feature is the growth of 'uncommitted facilities', particularly in the Eurobond market.

As part of these processes, financial innovation has become rife, which itself involves several features. The range of new instruments is shown in table 2.10. Since most of these are derivative of the move towards security lending – they provide borrowers and lenders with the possibility of hedging against the risk of interest rate and exchange rate

Table 2.9 Borrowing on international capital markets, 1976–1993 (US$ billion, annual averages)

	1976–80	1981–85	1986–90	1991	1992	1993
Securities[a]	36.2	96.4	234.7	332.1	357.2	521.7
Loans	59.4	72.0	103.1	116.0	117.9	136.7
Committed backup facilities		35.2	18.7	7.7	6.7	8.2
Uncommitted facilities[b]			70.9	80.2	127.7	152.0
Total	95.6	203.6	427.4	536.0	609.5	818.6
% change on previous year				+23.2	+13.8	+34.3

[a] International and foreign bonds and, as from 1986, issues of international equities.
[b] Mainly Eurocommercial paper and medium-term note programmes.
Sources: *OECD Financial Markets Trends*, no. 55, June 1993; no. 58, June 1994

Table 2.10 Markets for selected derivative instruments: national principal amounts outstanding at year end, 1986–1992 (US$ billion equivalent)

	1986	1990	1991	1992
Exchange-traded instruments[a]	*588*	*2,291*	*3,520*	*4,783*
Interest rate futures	370	1,454	2,157	3,048
Interest rate options[b]	146	600	1,073	1,385
Currency futures	10	16	18	25
Currency options[b]	39	56	59	80
Stock market index futures	15	70	77	81
Options on stock market indices[b]	8	95	136	164
Over-the-counter instruments[c]	*500*(E)	*3,451*	*4,449*	–
Interest rate swaps[d]	400(E)	2,312	3,065	–
Currency and cross-currency interest rate swaps[d,e]	100(E)	578	807	–
Other derivative instruments[d,f]	–	561	577	–
Memorandum item				
Cross-border plus local foreign currency claims of BIS reporting banks	4,031	7,578	7,497	7,352

E = estimate.

[a] Excludes options on individual shares and derivatives involving commodity contracts.

[b] Calls plus puts.

[c] Only data collected by ISDA. Excludes information on contracts such as forward rate agreements, over-the-counter currency options, forward foreign exchange positions, equity swaps and warrants on equity.

[d] Contracts between ISDA members reported only once.

[e] Adjusted for reporting of both currencies.

[f] Caps, collars, floors and swap options.

Source: *OECD Financial Markets Trends,* no. 55, June 1993, table 3, p. 26

movements – they are collectively termed 'derivatives'. A lot of these are very esoteric instruments, which are quite difficult to understand, monitor or control. In part this is because new ways of trading have emerged, in particular over-the-counter (OTC) markets in which intermediaries deal amongst themselves in large monetary volumes, by-passing the established exchanges which use traditional trading floors. The importance of these OTC instruments can be seen in table 2.10. By 1991 they were larger than exchange-traded instruments and were over 50 per cent as big as total foreign currency claims of all Bank for International Settlements (BIS) reporting banks. Such instruments are often traded 'off balance sheet': they earn a fee income rather than constituting part of a financial institution's asset or liability structures. These developments provide opportunities for the intermediaries to engage in risk arbitrage in a lower-cost and less regulated environment, but they thereby raise important new problems of systemic risk exposure. We discuss these problems again in chapter 6.

Financial innovation continues apace. The latest developments represent a resurgence of bond instruments with so-called 'dragon bonds' and 'global bonds'. 'Dragon bonds' are issued and traded simultaneously on just East Asian markets, while their 'global' counterparts are issued and traded in all major international financial centres on a 24 hour basis. Since the first global bond was marketed by the World Bank in 1989, this market had expanded to over US$100 billion by mid 1994, capturing 8 per cent of the total external bond issue in that year (OECD 1993, table 1, p. 57).

This latest development in bond markets testifies to the strength of the trend toward internationalization in the world financial systems. But as mentioned above, the penetration of foreign assets into domestic institutional investment markets is still relatively light. The US in particular remains highly undiversified and autonomous on this score. In as much as global trading of securities and derivatives exists, it still remains within a single region (North America, Europe or Asia-Pacific). But again, as table 2.11 indicates, the trend in the government bond market certainly seems towards further openness.

The final issue to discuss in this sub-section is the development of financial conglomerates. The international financial services industry is

Table 2.11   Foreign penetration of national central government bond markets, 1983–1989: non-resident holdings as a percentage of outstanding domesticbonds and Eurobonds

	1983	1985	1988	1989
Australia[a]	20	33	55	54
Belgium	4	10	13	14
Canada	16	21	31	37
France	4	2	6	15
Germany[a]	9	17	31	34
Italy	3	4	4	6
Japan	6	6	4	4
Netherlands	33	28	35	37
Spain[b]	0	0	2	5
United Kingdom	9	11	15	15
United States	13	14	17	19
Average	10	13	13	15

[a] Central and local government.
[b] Excluding Eurobonds.
Source: Turner 1991

increasingly characterized by a small number of highly capitalized securities and banking houses, which are global players with diversified activities. In part this is the result of the continuing trend towards predominantly institutional investment. 'Collective saving' is a strengthening feature of all OECD countries, as shown in table 2.12, so the institutions managing these funds could become key international players.

Broadly speaking, there is world-wide excess capacity in this industry, leading to intense competitive pressures to which cost-cutting and diversification are the strategic commercial responses. As a result, the financial conglomerates operate through very complex and often opaque corporate structures. Attempts at risk transfer between a shrinking number of players, and even between the different components of the companies themselves, are legion. Thus contagion risk, market risk and systemic risk have all increased, presenting new and important regulatory problems for governments and international bodies (see chapter 6).

An important point to note about the present era as compared with the Gold Standard period is that the recent growth of international lending has not just dramatically increased the range of financial instruments, but changed the whole character of capital flows. Late nineteenth century lending was mainly long term in nature, going to finance investment in real assets. Even that part of total flows comprising investment in financial assets was mainly used to finance real investment. This is no longer so. The explosion of aggregate lending had until very recently been made up almost exclusively of financial assets. Only since the mid

Table 2.12 The growth of institutional investment, 1980–1990: financial assets as a percentage of total household assets

	1980	1985	1990
United States	20.0	26.0	31.2
Japan	15.6	20.2	26.4
Germany	22.6	29.0	35.1
France	10.6	23.6	36.3
Italy[a,b]	–	2.9	6.1[c]
United Kingdom[a]	41.5	53.1	58.6[c]
Canada	20.4	24.9	29.7

[a] Total assets.
[b] At book value.
[c] Figures for 1989.
Source: *OECD Financial Markets Trends*, no. 55, June 1993, derived from table 3, p. 22

1980s has substantial real investment reappeared with the growth of FDI (see chapters 3 and 4).

The overall picture: history and current situation

In the final section of this chapter we review the changing nature of national economic management and its interaction with international mechanisms of integration so as to chart the broad contours of the present situation facing the international economy. This has as its objective an analysis of the economic autonomy implications of the main regimes indicated in table 2.8.

To a large extent the Gold Standard (GS) must act as a bench-mark in this discussion because of its pivotal position as the first integrated economic mechanism and the key features it displayed. It is the system which carries great ideological and theoretical significances since it was not only 'voluntarily' entered into by the parties involved (there was no 'founding treaty'), but it is also supposed to have embodied the principle of 'automaticity' in its operation and adjustments. In most orthodox accounts other, subsequent, systems are measured against the Gold Standard – and often found wanting, it must be added.

The basics of the system involved the fixing of an official gold price for each currency, and then allowing the free export and import of gold with no current or capital account restrictions. The persistent movement of gold in or out of a country is then permitted to influence the domestic money supply in each country. Thus the issue of bank notes and coinage is directly linked to the level of gold reserves. Any short-run liquidity crisis (e.g. a gold drain) is first met by lending by the central bank at premium rates ('lender of last resort' facility). If the gold price ('mint parity') has to be suspended, this should only be temporary, and convertibility is restored as soon as possible – if necessary with the aid of domestic deflationary policies. Here arises the crucial link between domestic and international conditions: there must be domestic wage and price/cost flexibility to allow the nominal price level to be determined endogenously by the world-wide demand and supply of gold. Thus the GS, in as much as it actually functioned along these lines, represented the quintessential integrated economy, where 'national autonomy' was minimal.

As might be expected the GS never worked quite in this automatic manner. There was great difficulty experienced at times in generating the deflationary domestic measures that the system implied as a condition of its operation. This led to various 'gold devices' that cushioned the domestic economy from the full rigours of gold movements, most important amongst these being disguised changes in the exchange rates of the domestic currency against gold to protect reserves or to maintain the level of domestic economic activity (so-called 'massaging of the gold points'). Despite this, however, the exchange rates stayed within remarkably narrow bands between 1870 and 1914.[6] It also required a remarkable degree of cooperation between central bankers because all manner of discretionary judgements and actions were necessary if the system was to function: there were a good many asymmetrical adjustments that needed to be made which in effect circumvented the formal rules.

Within the terms of the GS there was no single currency that provided the nominal anchor for the money supply or price level, since that was done by the system as a whole and by the supply and demand for gold. No single country took responsibility for monitoring 'the money supply' which was the supposed key to the success of the system, not even the British authorities. It was the UK's commitment to free trade (along with its ability to police this) and the depth of its financial markets in London that supported the system, however, and that provided the key political anchor for its effective functioning. The economic weakness of the Gold Standard arose from the way supply and demand shocks were designed in this way to be outside any national jurisdiction, so that volatile economic activity was magnified, a constant feature of the system. In addition, any excessive accumulation of gold stocks by a single country could also trigger off a generalized deflation of the system, whether this were involuntary or not.

It is the instability of the inter-war years that still haunts the international economic system, and provides the main reason for the concern and uncertainty associated with current trends in the international economy. The constant worry of the international community is to avoid a repeat of this period, when, as we have seen, international (and domestic) economic activity fell dramatically (foreign trade fell by two-thirds between 1929 and 1933, comprehensive capital controls were introduced, devaluations and deflations took place). In the wake of all this, belligerent protectionist power blocs emerged which eventually fought to challenge one another's existence.

The Bretton Woods system was designed to avoid the external constraint imposed on national economies by the GS, which had operated so disastrously in the inter-war period. What was needed was flexibility to support nationally decided policies on the one hand but enough stability to avoid competitive devaluations on the other. The solution negotiated at Bretton Woods was for a fixed but adjustable system, linked to the dollar standard as *numéraire*. Currencies were fixed in terms of the US dollar, which itself was to be convertible into gold; 'fundamental disequilibriums' were adjustable with International Monetary Fund (IMF) consent; national economies were given autonomy to pursue their own price level and employment objectives unconstrained by a common nominal price anchor. National capital markets were kept relatively separate by sanctioning capital controls on transactions other than current ones, and the domestic impacts of exchange rate interventions were 'sterilized' by drawing on official exchange reserves and IMF credits, which thereby acted as the buffers between the domestic and international monetary conditions, adding to domestic autonomy.

The well-known and tortuous story of how the BWS fared and its shortcomings in the post-war period will not be repeated here. Its key feature was a reliance on American 'passivity', and when this was no longer viable (because of fears of the loss of American international competitiveness) neither was the system itself. The above remarks are designed to demonstrate (a) how this was a definite regime, and (b) how the issue of (relative) national economic autonomy was built into that regime. What the BWS demonstrated, however, was that there was no economic autonomy, in the terms laid out so far, for the US economy if the system was to function as described. This may sound odd given the leading role that the US played in the international economy over the period and the way that it is perceived as dictating the 'rules of the game' to its own advantage. But one of the paradoxes here is that, strictly speaking, once those rules were in place the behaviour of the US economy was just as much circumscribed by them as was the conduct of the other economies in the system, if in different ways. The US could not 'choose' its own price and employment levels independently of others. It had to remain passive in terms of its exchange rate, hold minimal reserves of foreign exchange, provide liquidity to the system by acting as its creditor, and anchor the world price of internationally tradable goods in terms of dollars by its own domestic monetary policy. If there was to be no international inflation, then that domestic monetary policy was constrained by the dictates of a system in which partner choices were paramount: *formal* American monetary independence was just that.[7] Clearly, up to a point this also benefited the US since while it remained the strongest export economy in such a system it required a stable exchange rate and inflation proof regime. However, as this position changed, and as the US manoeuvred for some domestic economic autonomy, the system collapsed.

The floating rate regime, which followed the unsuccessful attempts to shore up the BWS in the period of the 'failure to agree', was again designed to increase national economic autonomy. But the rules of this game changed surprisingly little from the period before. As mentioned above, the US dollar remained the 'currency of choice' for the conduct of international monetary transactions – largely because of its path dependent embeddedness. The US also continued to remain relatively 'passive' in the face of changes in the dollar's value, though other countries conducted systematic interventions to try to stabilize their own currency dollar-equivalent rates. In the short run, other countries' national money supply policies were set so as to adjust to the relative weaknesses of their exchange rates *vis-à-vis* the dollar (reduce domestic money supply as the currency value against the dollar weakened, increase it as that value strengthened, i.e. the non-sterilization of exchange rate movements); while in the long run, secular adjustments in the par values were sanctioned so as to set national price level and money supply targets independently of US policy (this being the major change on the previous system). The US on the other hand no longer tried to anchor a common world price level, but conducted its own monetary and exchange rate policy independently of what other countries were doing.

One (unintended) consequence of this relative autonomy in the conduct of monetary policies was an increase in the world's money supply. As the dollar weakened between 1971 and 1980 (implying a strengthening of other currencies against the dollar) other countries' money supplies increased. The passivity of the US on the other hand meant it did not offset this with a reduction of its own money supply. Inflation resulted. Then when the dollar unexpectedly strengthened after 1980, the adjustment took the form of severe deflations and world output contracted sharply. Thus perhaps somewhat bizarrely, this period saw the closer and deeper integration of the international economy as the business cycles of all the main participants synchronized and became more pronounced. That regime, designed to increase autonomy (by allowing floating exchange rates and independent monetary policies), had actually led in the opposite direction. There is an important lesson to be learned here about the need to design particular rules for whatever governance mechanism is adopted.

Of course that lesson was partly learned in the case of the attempt to stabilize exchange rates associated with the Plaza-Louvre accord period. The US abandoned its 'hands-off' policy and initiated an attempt at more concerted action to manage exchange rates with 'discrete but clustered' interventions. The rules of this game were mentioned above. There were seventeen such concerted interventions between 1985 and 1992, most of which worked successfully in moving the exchange rates at least in the direction anticipated – and often against the prevailing trend. Thus at the level of exchange rates this cooperation between the G3 powers implied a heavy integration between them. But they were exercising their 'autonomy' independently of those outside the G3 framework, these other countries having to support or not oppose any G3 intervention (by buying or selling dollars with their national currency when the dollar was either weak or strong).

Quite whether the G3 regime remains robust is a moot point, however. The key issues are the existence or otherwise of 'target zones' and how seriously they are taken; whether the implied sterilization works (itself leading to differences in short-term interest rates between financial centres); and the macroeconomic effects of all of these. Without direct and more continuous coordination of policies (as opposed to indirect and discrete cooperation), exchange rate volatility is likely to remain large and international inflation and output fluctuations serious. We take some of these issues up again in chapter 6.

A good many of the points made above in connection with the various international regimes could be repeated for the case of the EMS. This system in many ways parallels the rules of the fixed rate dollar standard of the Bretton Woods system, though it has had different objectives. The EMS, for instance, has as one of its objectives the successive convergence of national macroeconomic policies at an unchanging par value of the exchange rates, which some have interpreted as an eventual commitment to complete (economic and political) integration of the European Union economies. This strong convergence/union theme was something missing from the BWS. The EMS also fixed the par value of exchange rates of the participants in terms of a basket of EMS currencies, weighted according to the relative country size, though the DM became the *de facto* anchor of the system, much like the dollar under the BWS. Its formal rules include a commitment to keeping currency values stable within bilateral bands, though adjustments in par values were allowed to reposition price levels with the agreement of the EMS (all this before eventual convergence or full monetary union). Central bank intervention is also sanctioned if breaching of the bilateral rate bands are threatened.

The *de facto* operation of the system has been to stabilize national exchange rates *vis-à-vis* the DM (partly because of the DM's importance in the currency basket), increasingly using the DM as the intervention currency; to adjust short-term monetary targets and interest rates so as to support exchange rate interventions; to organize long-term money growth so that domestic inflation in tradable goods converges to, or remains the same as, price inflation in Germany; and to progressively liberalize capital controls. Germany, much like the US in the case of the BWS and the floating rate regime, was thus to remain 'passive' in respect of foreign exchange rates of other members, but to anchor the DM (and therefore the EMS) price level for tradables by adopting an independently chosen German monetary policy.

The history of this system is well known. What it provided – indeed was explicitly designed to provide – was a reduction of autonomy in connection with monetary policy, at least for the participants (see Thompson 1992, ch. 4, and chapters 6 and 7 in this book for a discussion of its implications in connection with other aspects of macroeconomic management, particularly that of fiscal policy). The country gaining the most formal autonomy was Germany, but, rather like the case of the US discussed above, if the system was to operate properly German policy would also have to be heavily constrained by the 'burden' of managing the system overall, and would have to circumscribe its own objectives at times in the interest of the other members. However, this has proved the crunch point in terms of the success or otherwise of the EMS. Partly as a consequence of constitutional issues – summed up in the so-called 'Emminger letter' (see Kenen 1995, pp. 183–4) – and partly for domestic political reasons, the Bundesbank has not been required to fully support partner currencies in times of EMS crisis. The result has been to undermine its credibility as a regime of financial governance.

Conclusion

We have striven to argue a number of things in this chapter.

First, we have asserted that the level of integration, interdependence, openness, or however one wishes to describe it, of national economies in the present era is not unprecedented. Indeed, the level of autonomy under the Gold Standard up to the First World War was much less for the advanced economies than it is today. This is not to minimize the level of that integration now, or to ignore the problems of regulation and management it throws up, but merely to register a certain scepticism over whether we have entered a radically new phase in the internationalization of economic activity.

Secondly, we have maintained that governance mechanisms for the international economy have been in place over almost the entire twentieth century, in one form or another. This is just as much the case today as it was at the turn of the century. We may not like the particular mechanisms that are in place now and how they work, but they are there all the same. The issue then becomes how to devise better or more appropriate ones.

Thirdly, we have argued that there are some new and different issues of economic interdependence in the present era which are particular to it. Our argument is not that things have remained unchanged: quite fundamental reorganizations are going on in the international economy to which an imaginative response is desperately needed. This issue we take up later in the book.

Finally, we have traced the trajectory of 'national economic autonomy' through the various regimes of governance operating over the twentieth century. This has shown such autonomy to have oscillated between periods of strong and then weak forces, and operated with various degrees of effectiveness. Perhaps the overall trajectory of this assessment is to point to the impossibility of complete national economic autonomy as the twentieth century has progressed. The debacle of the floating rate regime of 1974–84, if nothing else, seems to have confirmed the demise of this form of governance as a viable long-term objective in the present era. The consequences of this are perused in the concluding chapter.

3

Trade, Foreign Direct Investment and International Inequality

In this chapter we move away from the history of the international trading and financial system. Here we concentrate on the major changes in the structure of the international economy since the early 1980s and consider how policy on the part of various micro-agencies of economic governance might respond to these structural changes. The dominant change we identify and explore here is the increased salience of, and rapid growth in, foreign direct investment (FDI). In the period 1945–73 the dominant factor driving the world economy was growth in international trade; from the early 1980s onwards, we argue, it has been growth in FDI.

We are concerned with those international mechanisms that impact on the structure and growth in the real economy: trade and FDI. International short-term financial flows have expanded rapidly since the abandonment of fixed exchange rates and capital controls in the 1970s. Short-term capital flows have some indirect impact upon economic growth since they affect the exchange rate and the interest rate. But we contend that these short-term flows mainly redistribute success and failure around the system, and add little to the structural capacity of economies to generate aggregate growth.

It is multinational corporations (MNCs) that are the agents responsible for FDI. In this chapter we analyse the strategies of these organizations as they shape the roles and distribution of FDI. As we shall see, that distribution is socially and geographically uneven on a world scale. FDI is almost exclusively concentrated in the advanced industrial states and a small number of rapidly developing industrial economies. This analysis is complemented by a detailed empirical investigation into the geographical distribution of advanced country business activity – contrasting home and foreign concentration of this activity – in the next chapter.

In relation to the major change from a primarily trade driven to a primarily FDI driven system we examine the problems this poses for the governance of the international economy. This analysis acts as a preliminary discussion of these issues which are taken up in much greater detail in chapters 6, 7 and 8. In this chapter we argue that the regulatory regime proposed by the recent Uruguay Round of negotiations of the General Agreement on Tariffs and Trade (GATT) is backward looking because it has emphasized trade as the dominant issue. GATT, and its successor organization the World Trade Organization (WTO), is seeking to promote growth through liberalization, a regime perhaps appropriate to trade but one quite incapable of governing the flows and the consequences of FDI. These regulatory issues, trade and FDI, are in fact quite distinct, and we shall argue that the current ungoverned and skewed distribution of FDI threatens to limit the growth of the whole world economy and also sets limits on the growth of output and employment in the wealthiest countries by limiting effective demand in the poorer countries.

While FDI and trade can often function as alternatives, the regulatory problems underlying FDI are specific and the governance mechanisms appropriate to them are novel and complex. These need new forums and new strategies, creating forms of governance appropriate to the issues that are newly emergent. One problem is that there is a tendency to look backwards on the part of the opponents of 'globalization', to a world of largely self-sufficient and locally regulated national economies, and, on the part of enthusiasts for open global markets, to dismiss the possibility or desirability of any form of policy intervention other than deregulation. Thus opponents of the new GATT settlement tend to put forward two arguments: first, that it increases the dangers of footloose capital relocating to low-wage areas to the detriment of employment and, ultimately, demand in the advanced countries; and second, that it tilts the terms of trade even further to the advantage of the advanced countries and their TNCs and to the detriment of the poor countries. Our view is that a linkage of these issues is a misconception and that opponents of GATT are wrong to see the main danger as free trade and the remedy new forms of protectionism (Lang and Hines 1993). The major problem is, on the contrary, the composition and distribution of FDI. Free trade in combination with the management of investment offers the best prospect for promoting growth through fairer redistribution. By contrast, protectionism will do little in the long run to promote growth in either rich or poor countries and will, of course, fail to control the consequences of flows of FDI and would enhance the tendency to trade through investment.

Our concern and our arguments centre on FDI because this has become the key feature of the international economy and is less tractable to governance than short-term monetary and financial flows. The enthusiasts for 'globalization' may be mistaken about what is happening – the idea of an open global market-place with no institutional or locational constraints is an illusion, as will become clear in the next chapter – but it is true that the dominant problems of economic governance now lie in the international domain. Only if these are addressed can specific national routes to economic stability and prosperity be assessed, even in the most successful advanced countries. Economies may have internationalized to a considerable degree, but wealth and output remain local and extremely unevenly distributed. The danger of the rhetoric of globalization is that it tends to ignore these distributions: it treats the world as a single open competitive market and the location of economic activity as dictated by purely commercial considerations.

MNCs in the early 1990s

There were an estimated 37,000 MNCs in the early 1990s, controlling about 170,000 affiliated organizations (United Nations 1993a, from which much of the following information is drawn[1]). Of these, 24,000 (about 70 per cent) were 'home based' in the fourteen major developed OECD countries. Ninety per cent of MNC headquarters are in the developed world.

In 1992 the stock of FDI was US$2 trillion. The MNCs controlling this stock were responsible for (domestic and international) sales of US$5.5 trillion. This was much more than the total of world trade at US$4 trillion in 1992. Only 5 per cent of the stock of FDI had its origins with a developing country's MNC.

Some 80 per cent of US trade was conducted by MNCs, which is not untypical for the developed countries as a whole. For total US trade as much as a third was estimated to be *intra*-MNC trade (Bonturi and Fukasaku 1993). Intra-MNC trade – that conducted within the boundaries of the company, involving transfers across borders between different parts of the organization – is difficult both to ascertain and to assess. Clearly, MNCs' FDI and trade are very closely linked, but important changes are occurring here and differences in the patterns between the two are emerging about which we have more to say in a moment.

There is great concentration in FDI. The largest 100 MNCs accounted for a third of the total FDI stock and 14 per cent of the total flow in 1990. In as much as these distinctions can still be made, 60 per cent of MNC stock was associated with manufacturing, 37 per cent with services and only 3 per cent with the primary sector. It is the growth in service sector FDI that has been a particular feature of the latest surge in overall investment levels.

Character of FDI and trade

The 'long boom' after the Second World War was typified by a massive increase in world trade and domestic (and to a lesser extent foreign) investment. The prosperity of the international economy was in large part based on these trends: it was 'export driven'. The main characteristics of this period can be seen in figure 3.1, which shows the 'export gap' between the growth of world output and that of exports – that is, exports increasing at a much faster rate than production between 1960 and 1990 (see also table 2.4).

Since the early 1980s, however, a different trend has emerged, which can be seen in figure 3.2. Here what is striking is the sudden increase in FDI relative to exports. This is not to say that export growth itself had stopped relative to growth in output, but only that export growth was eclipsed by the expansion of FDI. For instance, between 1983 and

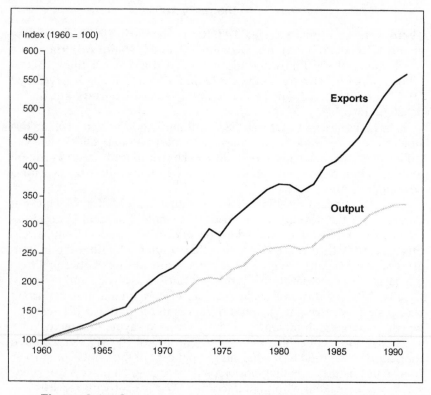

Figure 3.1   Gap between exports and output, 1960–1991
Source: *International Trade*, GATT, various years

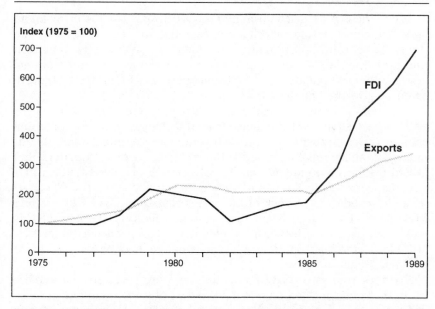

Figure 3.2   Current value of exports and FDI outflows, 1975–1989

Source: UNCTC estimates based on *World Investment Directory*, UNCTC, 1991; International Monetary Fund balance of payments tape, retrieved 10 January 1991; *Monthly Bulletin of Statistics*, United Nations, October 1984 and 1990

1990 FDI flows expanded at an average annual rate of 34 per cent compared with an annual rate of 9 per cent for global merchandise trade (OECD 1992, p. 12). The rest of this section is concerned with the consequences of this very basic change in the nature of the international economy.

One slight caveat is in order at this stage. Since the early 1990s there has been a slowdown in the growth of FDI, and indeed a slight fall in 1992 and 1993. The fall was mainly due to the slower growth rate in the major home economies. Thus it raises the issue of whether the growth in FDI since the early 1980s indicates a robust structural change as opposed simply to a cyclical upturn which came to an end a decade later. Our argument is that there will be no return to the pre-1980s position, but that the surge in FDI flows of the 1984–9 period in particular will not be repeated until there is another coincidental upturn in advanced country economic growth rates. The UN FDI forecasting model predicts a modest increase in FDI flows for the advanced countries between 1989 and 1995, with a more rapid increase going to Latin America, Africa and Asia (though from a much lower base, so that the *share* going to these areas does not change much: United Nations 1993c, pp. 34–6).

It was the GATT mechanism that governed the post-1945 long boom and the increase in trade which accompanied it. Indeed it may have been the trade liberalization promoted by the GATT that largely stimulated this growth. The question now is: what mechanism of international governance can regulate this new distinct period of FDI growth? Indeed, can it be governed at all?

Many of the problems besetting the Uruguay Round of GATT negotiations have stemmed from these structural changes in the international economy. Broadly speaking, the tactic of the international inter-governmental organizations committed to the preservation of a multilateral and liberal trading environment, particularly the OECD, was to attach FDI governance issues to the GATT negotiating framework. They have attempted to ride on the back of the past successes of GATT by grafting FDI negotiations directly on to it (the so-called TRIPs and TRIMs issues: see below). This strategy of linkage has been encouraged by attitudes stemming from the traditional close connection between trade and investment matters.

Previous rounds of GATT negotiations were successful largely because they concentrated on one main aspect of trade – the reduction of various forms of trade barriers to the international exchange of raw materials and manufactured goods. But the Uruguay Round has been different. It took on some very thorny issues that were not obviously intrinsically linked one to another.

The first of these is the issue of agricultural trade and subsidies. This is not such a straightforward issue as manufacturing because of the difficult 'cultural' connotations and interests involved with agricultural protection.

The second issue is trade in services. Here it is FDI that is progressively substituting for trade because it is not possible to internationally trade many services. They are locationally specific, so that MNCs must invest abroad in order to provide these services. In the context of the Uruguay Round the objective was to negotiate a comprehensive accord on trade and investment in services so as to facilitate their liberalization.

The third issue concerns trade-related investment measures proper (TRIMs). These refer to items like investment incentives (subsidies, tax and tariff concessions, grants); performance requirements (local content agreements, domestic sales requirements, technological transfer requirements, remittance restrictions, foreign exchange restrictions, export requirements, etc.); and finally, measures affecting general corporate activity (competition policy issues, pricing restrictions, collusive tendering, etc.). The reason these items were up for negotiation under GATT is that they are thought to be 'trade distorting'. The analytical framework behind this attempt to eliminate policy obstacles is the supposed 'gains from trade' generated from a modelling strategy in the context of perfectly competitive markets. Removing market imperfections is supposed to generate significant levels of international trade, and therefore provide greater stimulus to economic growth than specific national internationalist policy measures can do. The same logic underlay the creation of the single market in the EU and the Checcini Report on which the growth stimulus of liberalization was based.

Now, while this emphasis on perfect competition remains the established theoretical framework for analysing international trade, it is increasingly being challenged by an alternative approach that analyses international trade and growth in the context of *imperfectly* competitive market structures. This is the programme of the new trade theory (NTT) and new growth theory (NGT). These theories envisage a universe of oligopolistic firms, increasing returns to scale, barriers to trade, 'first mover advantage', 'lock-ins' and the like. The upshot of this new analytical framework is that a good many of the 'distortions' referred to above cease to be regarded as obstacles to growth and become quite legitimate objects of public intervention in the context of trade and industrial policies operated by governments in specific national territories. Such policies can achieve advantages in terms of rent and producer surplus appropriation, which do not necessarily result in an overall welfare loss (this remains controversial however: Krugman 1986; 1987; Moran 1992; Tyson 1993). Thus, to a large extent the way GATT has treated the TRIMs issue derives from an intellectual milieu that no longer conforms either to the features of the evolving international economy or to a robust theoretical orthodoxy. This has made it increasingly difficult to legitimize the TRIM negotiations.[2]

The fourth Uruguay Round negotiating issue concerned trade-related aspects of intellectual property rights (TRIPs). These involve items like genetic engineering and patent protection, trade marks, minimum standards on copyrights, industrial designs, computer integrated circuitry, layout designs, etc. Almost all of these areas centrally involve the protection of R&D investments. Again, an attempt was made to establish tighter international rules on property rights and common procedures in respect to these areas.

Thus this particular round of negotiations involved rather a rag-bag of only loosely related issues, though the attempt was made to solve them all together. Many of these issues intimately concerned FDI as well as trade measures in the strict sense. Indeed, with most of these issues it was the investment aspect in their constitution that was more important than trade (with respect to services and TRIMs, and some TRIP issues as well).

The general question raised by the preceding discussion is: can trade and investment issues be dealt with in this directly linked way? Would it be better to split them off: that is, to try to develop a whole new regime of FDI governance for example that was separate from, but running in parallel with, the existing GATT framework?[3] Should there be a new General Agreement on International Investment or International Business (GAII or GAIB)? It is to these questions that we return near the end of the analysis, and discuss again in chapter 6. First something needs to be said about the organizational strategies of the key players in the international economy, the MNCs or TNCs themselves.

Pattern of FDI flows and stocks, and the operation of MNCs

One of the most noticeable developments in recent years with regard to FDI activity has been the emergence of distinct regional patterns of its distribution. This regional clustering is associated with the formation of trading blocs such as the EU and NAFTA. While these are still called trading blocs, it might be better to describe them as investment blocs. A scrutiny of the recently negotiated NAFTA, for instance, demonstrates that it has as much if not more to do with investment relationships between the US and Mexico as with trade as such.

Important elements in this clustering have been regionally based production networks, a classic example of which was the Ford motor company's strategy in the rapidly integrating EU market. This was to develop a genuine network of integrated sourcing, production and marketing exclusively at the European level (Dicken 1992, p. 300). But it also interestingly demonstrates the still fluid situation for FDI in the international economy, since Ford announced in April 1994 that it was abandoning its purely regionalized approach to car manufacturing (producing a different range of models in each of its regionalized markets) and was adopting instead a genuinely 'global' strategy of producing a single different model in its various manufacturing environments and then selling these world-wide.

Many other examples of continuing regionalized strategies could be provided however. What they show is that a contributory factor in the stalling of the Uruguay Round was the emergence of these types of regionally based trading and investment blocs and the specific and mutually contradictory interests attaching to them. We will return to this theme in a moment.

Another typical example of the integration developing at the international level concerns strategic high-tech R&D-led production alliances in semiconductor manufactures (Hirst and Thompson 1994, figure 4). The products here are being developed and manufactured within quite different forms of collaborative arrangement between firms and national subsidiaries of the same firm. Diverse strategies are being followed by companies in these and other fields, which are not easy to comprehensively categorize or explain clearly (see Commission of the European Communities 1994; Dunning 1993; United Nations 1993a; Howells and Wood 1993; amongst others, for details of these diverse strategies).

Some have seen developments like this, involving new information technologies, as heralding the key to a new stage of TNC evolution, that is the uncoupling of companies and networks from distinct national bases, and the move towards a genuine global economy centred upon truly global companies. The best example of this argument is the work of Kenichi Ohmae (Ohmae 1990; 1993). The virtue of Ohmae's case is that he does at least say what he thinks the structure of a borderless truly global economy would look like: it is summed up in the idea of an 'inter-linked economy'. Ohmae argues that 'stateless' corporations are now the prime movers in an inter-linked economy (ILE) centred on North America, Europe and Japan. He contends that macroeconomic and industrial policy intervention by national governments can only distort and impede the rational process of resource allocation by corporate decisions and consumer choices on a global scale. The emergence of 'electronic highways' enables anyone, in principle, to 'plug into' the global market-place. All corporate players need to do is to shake off the burden of a nationally oriented bureaucracy, and the government intervention that goes along with this, and enter the new world of open global marketing and production. The vision is of one large inter-linked network of producers and consumers plugged into an efficiently operating 'level playing field' of the open international and globalized economy. International markets provide coordinative and governance mechanisms in and of themselves, which national strategies and policy interventions can merely distort. Like Robert Reich (1992) Ohmae believes that the era of effective national economies and state policies corresponding to them is over.

Pace Ohmae, the international economy looks nothing like the ILE and does not seem to be converging towards it. Current practice of international corporations is more complex, and much more akin to that of MNCs. Strategic alliances like those mentioned above are creating an extremely uneven international market-place, which is being duplicated in many other manufacturing and service sectors. To the extent that a globalized economy exists at all it is *oligopolistically* organized, not organized according to the dictates of the perfectly competitive model as Ohmae and others wish to believe. The major corporate players are involved in a deadly competitive game, one in which they deploy all manner of business strategies to exclude some competing players from their networks whilst locking others firmly into them. For oligopolists there are massive 'first mover' advantages. If a firm can secure the originating industry standard for instance it can reap enormous potential benefits by moving down the cost curve to achieve economies of scale and scope. The providers of the 'super electronic highways', for instance, compete with one another over standards and conditions of connection, which preclude any open plugging in at will (Mansell 1994). They seek to attract the right kind of customers and 'trap' them by locking them early into their own particular standards and connections so that sales can be guaranteed from then on. These companies seek to strongly protect by market resources and public policy any advantages gained in this way.

A clear illustration of this can be seen in figure 3.3. The airline groupings emerging here in the context of different computer reservation systems will help to dictate the particular nature of the international airline industry of the future. One specific collaboration is threatening to dominate all the others: that between the European Galileo system and the North American Covia/Apollo system. The airlines involved with these two systems – some of the major European 'national carriers' and

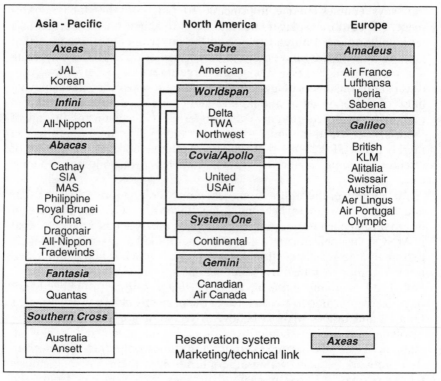

Figure 3.3   Alliances among airline computer reservation systems
Source: United Nations 1993a

two of the largest American carriers (along with Canadian and Air Canada) – stand to gain great marketing advantages if this liaison comes off.

In addition, we should not forget the still massive and important *national* differences in the attractiveness of locations for investment. Countries vary considerably in the effectiveness of their economies in delivering FDI advantages to MNC firms which cannot be ignored. Successful MNCs are those that can tap into these specific advantages. These advantages are not just those associated with the cost of labour. Companies also need national legal and commercial policy provisions to protect their investments – constraints that prevent them being entirely extra-territorial, as we emphasize in chapter 8.

The literature on 'national systems of innovation' (Ludval 1992; Nelson 1993; McKelvey 1991; Porter 1990), 'production regimes' (Wilkinson 1983; Rubery 1994) and 'national business systems' (Whitley 1992a; 1992b) is instructive here. These authors point to real differences in the way countries have traditionally gone about their innovative activity, established their typical business environment and conducted business therein, which continue even in a 'globalizing' world. Not all countries are the same in the way they perform quite basic economic functions and productive tasks. There are differences in the ingrained 'culture' of business, in the financial systems, and in the typicality and effectiveness of their R&D efforts, technical innovation, product development life-cycles and the like, which are deeply embedded both institutionally and nationally. These differences both inform the character of the firms that have their traditional home base in one major country or another, and affect the nature of the national environment into which FDI is inserted. The key to the success of MNC FDI is not whether it simply seeks a low-cost location to generate maximum profit advantage, but how it adapts its strategy to fit into the particular institutionalized national environments of business and innovation into which it settles.

MNCs are not monolithic entities, with a single strategic direction and intent. Increasingly they are networks of 'loosely coupled but highly aligned' semi-autonomous units. These units articulate themselves within specific national environments. The strategies of successful companies must precisely allow for this flexibility, which means the activities of their sub-units engage with the embedded national systems in which they function but also have an effect upon them. It is this double move that is crucial to an understanding of the nature of the 'transformations' being wrought by MNCs as they integrate their sourcing, production and marketing internationally.

One consequence of this emphasis on national specificities in production advantage is that there is increasing evidence of national sectoral trade specialization and diversity rather than a homogenization of inter-country trade (Archibugi and Pianta 1992; Archibugi and Michie 1995).

Perhaps an alternative related way of expressing this, from the MNCs' point of view this time, is via the three competences that Bartlett and Ghoshal (1989) suggest are the key to managing a network of cross-border value-adding activities: (a) taking advantage of the economies of scale and scope offered by international integration (the 'global' dimension); (b) appreciating consumer needs in different countries and tailoring local production and supply to meet these (the 'local' dimension); (c) using the experience so gained in global and local markets to strengthen the resource base of the firm as a whole (the 'learning' dimension). A careful balance between these three dimensions needs to be crafted for commercial success, they suggest, the precise nature of which will vary between different sectors and product ranges.

Thus what we have here is not only a set of commercial oligopolists operating in the international market-place but the possibility of a set of national governments that can act as strategic oligopolists as well (Dunning 1993, p. 612). Governments can *create* asset endowment advantages rather than simply rely on 'natural' ones (Porter 1990). Increasingly these are taking the form of infrastructure provision, the generation of a highly trained and skilled labour force, and the like. This is not to say, of course, that MNCs operating in some sectors are not looking for cheap labour: some are. But even in those sectors traditionally associated with this strategy, like auto assembly, circumstances are changing. In Mexico's auto assembly industry, for instance, it is estimated that up to a third of the workers are graduates.

Finally we should note the role of small and medium MNCs. There has been a growing interest in small and medium enterprises (SMEs) generally, and this has spilled over into their role as generators of FDI (United Nations 1993b). SM-MNCs are growing in significance as international investors and they are particularly important in the case of new innovative technologies, not all of which are necessarily of a 'high-tech' kind. Their technological transfer can be in a labour-intensive form and one more 'appropriate' to the circumstances of less developed economies, for instance. SMEs' investments also tend to be more 'trade intensive' than those of larger MNCs, so their impact on the trade balance of recipient countries is often favourable. But as yet SMEs' multinational investment activity represents a very small share of total FDI (though they are more important in terms of *numbers* of companies involved). In addition, the distribution of SMEs' FDI is heavily skewed towards the advanced countries. To the extent that their activity is directed towards non-advanced countries, it is concentrated in the rapidly growing South and East Asian countries.

Triad power and influence

This discussion of the diverse strategies and tactics of firms and governments in the context of FDI should not blind us to another overarching
feature of these relationships, illustrated in figure 3.4. Seventy-five per
cent of the total accumulated stock, and 60 per cent of the flow, of FDI
were located in just three players at the beginning of the 1990s. North
America, Europe and Japan dominate as both the originators and the
destination for international investment. In the case of investment the

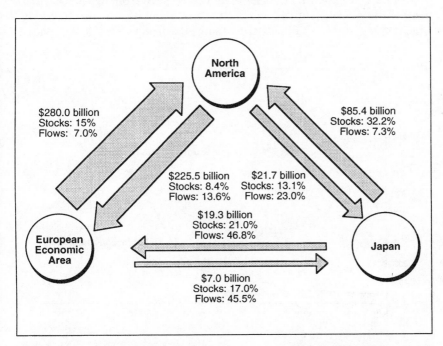

Figure 3.4   Intra-Triad foreign direct investment, 1990 (US$ billion)
Dollar figures show estimated values of stock of FDI based on data on
inward and outward investment from North America, Japan and the
European Economic Area (EEA): investment within North America and
the EEA has been netted out. Percentages show average annual
growth rates of stocks (1980–1990) and flows (1985–1991). North
America includes Canada and the US. The EEA includes the EU and
EFTA exceptIceland and Liechtenstein.
Source: UNCTAD Programme on Transnational Corporations, foreign direct investment
data base

flows were particularly intense between North America and Europe (the European Economic Area, EEA). Japan remained a net exporter of FDI in 1990 to both the other areas.

Particularly noticeable is that the US was a net importer of FDI in 1990. The background to this is shown in figure 3.5. The US became a net debtor nation in 1985 (for the first time since the First World War). Even the growth of foreign assets owned by US residents faltered in the early 1990s. The implication of all this is that domestic US assets are being bought up by foreigners at a faster rate than US residents are investing abroad.

A further noteworthy development can be seen from figure 3.6. Relatively isolated clusters of main actor and client states are emerging, which are geographically discrete and stabilizing. This figure shows

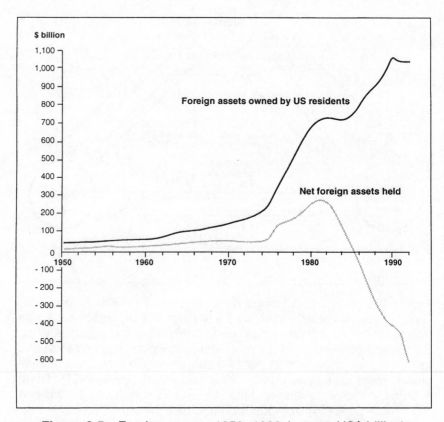

Figure 3.5   Foreign assets, 1950–1992 (current US$ billion)

Source: Balance Sheet for the US Economy, 1945–1992, Federal Reserve, Washington DC, 1993

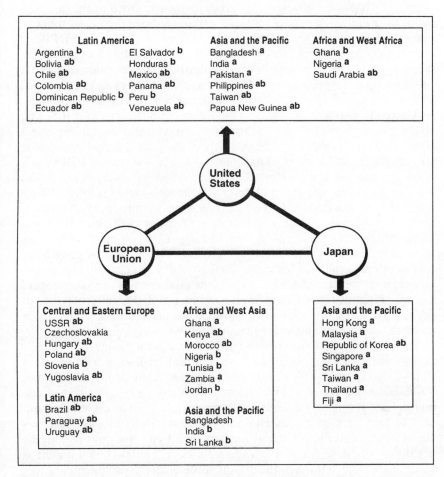

Figure 3.6 Foreign direct investment clusters of Triad members, 1990: economies in which a Triad member dominates inward foreign direct investment stocks and/or flows
a In terms of average inward FDI flow, 1988–1990.
b In terms of inward FDI stock, 1990.
Source: UNCTAD Programme on Transnational Corporations, foreign direct investment data base

which member of the Triad dominates the inward FDI in particular countries. Thus whilst *intra*-Triad investment relationships are particularly dense, a pattern of further discrete but robust *inter*-linkages between each of these and more marginalized country groupings is also evident. These country groupings tend to be regionally specific and 'adjacent' to one or other of the Triad members. Once again this goes against the idea of a 'neutral' or 'level playing field' in the global marketplace. Indeed it testifies to the relative *lack of integration* in FDI flows and stocks since the clusters indicate a geographical and regional discreteness in the relationships between countries. The direction of the FDI relationship is between one or other of the Triad powers and its clustered 'client' states, rather than between these client states themselves.[4]

There are two sets of points to be drawn from this analysis. The first concerns the *intensity* of the relationships involved and the consequences of these. Broadly speaking, the intensity of the relationship between the core members and their regional clients is *less* in the case of FDI than it is in the case of trade (United Nations 1993a, ch. VII). This is just another way of saying that multilateral trade integration is lower than is integration in the case of FDI, even though, as we have seen, it remains very geographically discrete in the case of investment. But there is a more multilateral set of integrative linkages between all the countries shown in figure 3.6 where investment is concerned, so that the geographical discreteness (and any associated 'clientism') is potentially less important than in the case of trade. Investment relationships are more 'open' to cross-integration between core countries and the different sets of clients than are trade relationships, which are more intensive and hence more closed to these cross-fertilizations between regionalized blocs.

This has two possible further implications. First it means that 'protectionist' sentiment on the part of the different trading blocs and major states is likely to be lower in the field of investment than in the field of trade. Secondly, it makes investment potentially more liable to genuine multilateral regulation than is trade (and trade has shown itself amenable to this form of management in the past). Both of these features might be responsible for undermining any intense and inward-looking development of regionalized trading blocs. Given that investment is tending to displace trade as the driving force of international integration, the likelihood of competitive and antagonistically poised trade blocs emerging is reduced if this analysis is correct.

Why are investment relationships less sticky and intense than those involving trade? The UN (1993a) report suggests there are two possible reasons: (a) geographical distance is less of an inhibitor to FDI than it is to trade because transactions costs are lower with respect to the former; (b) national endowment advantages in respect to FDI are less specific than they are with respect to trade. The factors important for successful FDI are more widely distributed geographically and not as concentrated as those concerning trade.

The second major point to draw from the analysis is to re-emphasize the still enormous *geographical concentration* of FDI in the big three and a few other states. And similarly it is to re-emphasize this even more so in respect to trade flows, as just pointed out above.

Table 3.1 Net FDI flows to developing countries, 1973–1993 (US$ billion, annual averages)

	1973–76	1977–82	1983–89	1990–93
Africa	1.1	0.8	1.1	1.4
Asia	1.3	2.7	5.2	19.8
Middle East and developing Europe	−1.0	2.5	2.6	1.6
Latin and South America	2.2	5.3	4.4	11.0
Total[a]	3.7	11.2	13.3	34.2

[a] Rounding may mean totals differ from additions of specific areas.
Source: derived from *World Economic Outlook*, October 1994, IMF, table 7

Before we proceed to the possible consequences of this concentration of FDI it is important to mention two provisos. The first is that concentration seems to have fallen a little in 1992 and 1993, as the major core areas continued to experience a recession, particularly that in Japan. This has meant a slight widening of the geographical spread of FDI, which may continue into the future. The net FDI flows to developing countries are shown in table 3.1, indicating a substantial increase since 1990 to Asia (overwhelmingly to China) and to Latin and South America.[5] However, the other areas have been seriously neglected.

The second proviso is to emphasize the growing importance of some developing countries as the *source* of FDI on the basis of their indigenous MNC activity. In particular this trend affects the rapidly growing East Asian countries, and a few in Latin America. Whilst these are important trends, as yet they do not threaten to undo the pattern outlined above of the continued dominance of the Triad in FDI.

FDI, trade and income inequalities

So what is the problem with the type and level of concentration of FDI elaborated above? The data presented in table 3.2 identify some of the issues. It is divided into three levels, A, B and C, showing the population and distribution of global FDI for different groups of countries and areas.

Level A concerns only the Triad countries, which, whilst making up only 14 per cent of world population in 1990, attracted 75 per cent of FDI flows over the 1980s. Level B adds the populations of the ten most important developing countries in terms of FDI flows over the period (which together received 66 per cent of all non-Triad flows and accounted for another 29 per cent of world population). Adding these together (A + B, shown near the bottom of the table) gives a total of 43 per cent of the world's population in receipt of 91.5 per cent of FDI flows.

Table 3.2   Investment flows and populations, 1981–91

	Population, 1990 (million)	(%)	Investment flows, 1980–91 (%)
Total world	5,292.195	100	
A			
USA and Canada	275.865 ⎫		
EC and EFTA	357.767 ⎬ 14		75
Japan	123.460 ⎭		
B			
Ten most important developing countries in terms of flows[a]	1,519.380	29	16.5 (66% of total flows to developing countries)
C			
Nine most important developing countries plus nine main Chinese coastal provinces[b]	758.820	14	
A + B		43 ⎫	91.5 (approx.)
A + C		28 ⎭	

[a] Singapore, Mexico, China, Brazil, Malaysia, Hong Kong, Argentina, Thailand, Egypt, Taiwan.
[b] Beijing, Tianjin, Hebei, Shanghai, Jiangsu, Zhejiang, Fujian, Shandong, Guangdong.
Sources: World Population Prospects, 1990, UN, 1991, various tables; *China Statistical Yearbook*, 1991, table T3.3; *Statistical Yearbook of the Republic of China*, 1991, p. 5, table 1; *TNCs and Integrated International Production*, UN, 1993, np. 255, annex table 4

But the group of countries included under level B is dominated by China with a population of nearly 1.2 billion in 1990. It is unlikely that all China's population is 'benefiting' from inward FDI. It is known that FDI and growth are highly concentrated in the coastal provinces, particularly in the south. Thus level C includes only the populations of the eight Chinese coastal provinces, along with Beijing province, to give a rough estimate of where the FDI is actually going within China. With this recalculation, A + C, only 28 per cent of the world's population receives 91.5 per cent of the FDI.

On the basis of these admittedly rough and ready calculations, between 57 and 72 per cent of the world population is in receipt of only 8.5 per cent of global FDI. In other words nearly two-thirds of the world is virtually written off the map as far as any benefits from this form of investment are concerned. The question is, for how long can this kind of severe inequality continue?

What is more, this inequality is paralleled by the case of trade. Table

Table 3.3   Global distribution of trade, 1992 (exports only)

	I *Including intra-EU trade (shares of US$3731b) (%)*	II *Excluding intra-EU trade (shares of US$2843b) (%)*
A		
USA and Canada	15.6	20.5
EU and EFTA[a]	45.2	27.9
Japan	9.1	12.0
Total	69.9	60.4
B		
Ten most important developing countries in terms of 1980s FDI flows (see table 3.2)	14.0	18.2
A + B	83.9	78.6

[a] Includes Switzerland.
Source: *1993 International Trade Statistics*, GATT, Geneva, based upon tables 1.4 and 1.5

3.3 shows the distribution of world trade (exports) in 1992. The table is divided into two main parts: part I includes intra-European trade, while part II excludes it. On the basis of this evidence the equivalent of A + B in table 3.2 accounted for between 84 and 79 per cent of trade in 1992, again demonstrating an incredible inequality in terms of the populations involved.

If we now look at the 'bottom line' of these developments, table 3.4 indicates the persistence of inequality in the world distribution of income for the dominant FDI investment group of countries (measured in terms of GDP). This distribution changed little from the 1970s to the 1980s. Looking at the global distribution of income more generally (figure 3.7), on the basis of the two measures indicated this has become more unequal rather than less since the 1970s.[6] All these measures go against the sentiment that benefits to the less well-off nations and regions will 'trickle down' as investment and trade are allowed to follow strictly market signals. Inequalities are dramatic, remain stubborn to change and indeed have grown since the 1970s.

There are good ethical arguments against this situation. Its consequences for living conditions, life expectancy and security on the part of the world's poor are obvious. It should not be *allowed* to go on and we should do something about it urgently as a matter of *conscience*. Ethics, however, have rarely moved economists, Western policy-makers and company executives. These need other rationales in terms of the economic and business opportunities. These non-ethical arguments are

Table 3.4   Global distribution of GDP, 1970–1989 (percentage share)

	Market exchange rate data[a]		Purchasing power currency data[b]	
	Average 1970–9	Average 1980–9	Average 1970–9	Average 1980–9
A				
USA and Canada	29.03	29.50	31.22	29.81
EC and EFTA	29.54	28.13	29.25	26.91
Japan	8.78	11.97	10.11	9.66
Total	67.35	69.60	70.58	66.38
B				
Ten most important developing countries in terms of 1980s FDI flows (see table 3.2)	7.34[c]	7.29[c]	8.68[d]	9.2[d]
A + B	74.69	76.89	79.26	75.58

[a] Based upon data for 178 countries.
[b] Based upon data for 117 countries.
[c] Excludes Taiwan.
[d] Excludes China, Hong Kong and Taiwan.
Source: derived from *Trends in International Distribution of Gross World Product*, UN, 1993, various tables

therefore emphasized here, that is, the practical economic and political objections to the continuation of these trends. These objections concern the self-interest of the successful in not neglecting the world's poor.

One of these implicates problems for world order. With an increasingly interconnected international system and the majority of the world's population excluded from prosperity, even greater political, social, environmental and therefore *economic* disruption of the world economy can be anticipated. This is not a new argument but it is one worth re-emphasizing in the contemporary conditions of the absence of superpower rivalry and an increasing plurality of antagonistically poised voices and social forces. Greater disruption in and by the 'periphery' now tends to have more immediate consequences within the 'core', and the 'core' itself is not immune from many of these trends: it 'imports' the consequences of poverty. The pressure on Europe and the USA of refugees and migrants fleeing conflict and poverty is obvious (chapter 2). Any new migration and its containment constitute a major new security risk, and this is likely to be exacerbated by the continuing reproduction of extreme inequality in the distribution of wealth on a global scale.

Secondly, there are good economic arguments in terms of direct benefits to the First World against the continuation of this unequal situation.

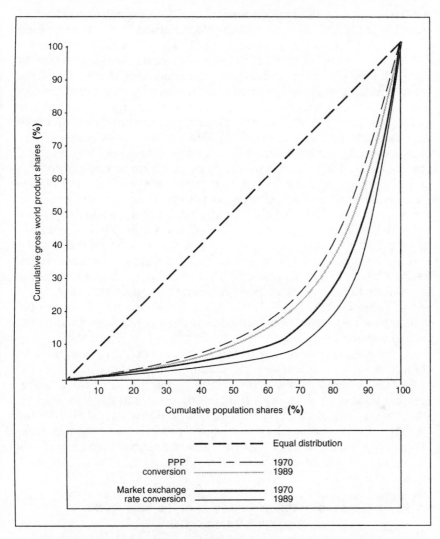

Figure 3.7   Lorenz curves of gross world product shares
PPP for 117 countries; market exchange for 178 countries.

Source: *Trends in International Distribution of Gross World Product, National Accounts Statistical Special Issue*, series X, no. 18, United Nations

Even while the high levels of concentration between the Triad members were developing in the 1980s, this did not prevent them from falling into recession. Indeed the post-1973 period more generally has been one of continued economic difficulties for many of the advanced countries of the Triad. One of the reasons for this could be the relative growth of cross-border merger and acquisition (M&A) expenditure at the expense of 'new establishment' investment in the 1980s. M&A activity expanded dramatically in the US (from 67 per cent of inward investment in the first half of the 1980s to 80 per cent in the second half: OECD 1992, p. 21), but it was a feature of the other Triad countries as well. The significance of this is that it may mean simply the transfer of ownership and speculative activity, rather than any net new productive investment. Be that as it may, stagnant aggregate demand, the under-utilization of resources and excess capacity, and an inability to launch a sustained recovery and upturn, have all typified this period. What this hints at is the need for a more balanced redistribution of world resources, a generation of new effective demand on a world scale, so as to promote a robust long-term recovery in the Triad as well as some hope for a sustainable upturn amongst the so far excluded countries of the 'South'. Spare capacity in the Triad is matched by excess but frustrated demand in the South. What is required is some mechanism (and the political will) to redistribute between them. It is to the credit of UNCTAD that it has been one of the few international voices to have consistently argued this case (for a recent effort see UNCTAD 1993).[7] Both rich and poor countries would benefit by such a move, and it would be in their joint long-term interests to engineer it.

As it stands, however, any of this looks unlikely. But there must be some question as to whether the existing situation analysed above is sustainable even in its own terms over the long run. How can a 'global system', however partial in its truly internationalized features, manage when two-thirds of its population is systematically excluded from the benefits of that system whilst the limited prosperity it generates is increasingly concentrated amongst the already employed and successful in the wealthy 14 per cent of the world and a few client states?

Issues in the governance of the new world investment order

What these issues bring to the fore are the possibilities of new institutional mechanisms of governance for the newly emerging international economic system. They throw up major issues for the kind of world investment order that could develop in the future.

Here we can return to the analysis of the GATT mechanism made earlier. There it was argued that GATT had been burdened with many of these new issues, but that it was ill equipped to deal with them. But the GATT is not the only international organization involved in initiatives in this area. Both the World Bank and the OECD have been in the forefront of attempts to generate new instruments to codify and regulate aspects of FDI and MNC activity. Perhaps the most comprehensive attempt to come to terms with some of these issues is represented by the UN Economic and Social Council's efforts to negotiate a *Draft Code of Conduct on TNCs* (Dunning 1993, appendix to ch. 21, provides the full text of this). The work on this code began in the early 1970s but by the 1990s it had come to nothing. It now seems to represent a stalled initiative that lacks any momentum. One of the reasons for this could be that it was begun in a different era as far as attitudes towards MNCs and FDI are concerned. It represents the final phase of a long post-war hostility towards MNC activity, embodied in a perception of an antagonistic relationship between such organizations and national states. The developing world saw multinationals as exploiters and a threat to national economic autonomy.

Rethinking these issues in a new political context less concerned with quasi-autarkic development has led to the revival of another old idea from the 1970s, presented as a new start: a comprehensive multilateral agreement on international investment or international corporations, a GAII or a GAIB as mentioned above (Bergsten and Graham 1993; Kline 1993; Scaperlanda 1993). The objectives of this agreement would be to codify and bring together the legitimate goals of both business and government in the conduct of FDI; to recognize in international law the continued 'dual personality' of MNCs, being part 'national' and part 'global'; and finally to design rules that would avoid 'beggar-my-neighbour' policies, first by governments in terms of their competitive attempts to attract FDI, and second by firms in their attempts to try to play one country off against another, both of these being recognized as leading to sub-optimal outcomes.

This kind of initiative can be viewed in the context of a matrix such as illustrated in figure 3.8. Along the horizontal axis is measured the extent or degree of economic convergence, while on the vertical axis is measured the degree of or approach to regulation. The way this developed in respect to FDI, as the degree of convergence moved from the national (unilateral) towards the global (multilateral), was for the approach to or degree of regulation to move from the 'harder' integrative realm of laws and regulation to the 'softer' standards and procedures approach associated with cooperation and coordination. The suggestion for a comprehensive package of measures (outlined further in a moment) is to push the international agencies involved with this activity in the opposite direction, towards the lower right hand corner of 'global integration'.

What might such a comprehensive agreement involve? First, it should define, codify and guarantee the property rights of MNCs in their FDI in various ways. Second, it would protect the rights of labour and conditions of work. Third, it would recognize the rights of governments to defend

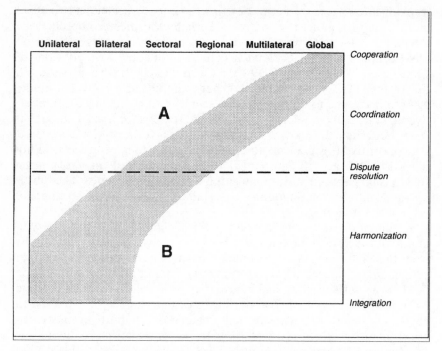

Figure 3.8 The regulatory environment
A, 'soft' standards and procedures; B, 'hard' laws and regulation.
Source: based on Kline 1993

certain of their legitimate national functions in respect to the economy –
support for R&D, defence considerations, balance of payments issues,
etc. Fourth, it would establish binding protocols on company taxation.
Fifth, it would establish a disputes mechanism that would be written into
international law. Finally, there should be some strengthened protocols
on environmental protection as well.

   This is a long list of very worthy and necessary provisions that begs to
be properly agreed and sanctioned by the international community.
However, one suspects that in the current international climate this kind
of a comprehensive agreement would be very difficult, if not impossible,
to achieve. It would be in danger of going down the road of the UN's
1970s initiative. It would certainly require a degree of political commitment and negotiating convergence not seen amongst the G5 or G7
countries in the 1980s and early 1990s.

   Thus perhaps a less comprehensive and totalizing approach is called
for, which might make progress along a number of different fronts in

parallel. This would go along with the sentiment emerging from some of the 'governance without government' literature (Ostrom 1990; Rosenau and Czempiel 1992), which has stressed the virtue of small-scale, highly focused organizational forms for the effectiveness of 'non-government' agreements in situations that lack an obvious hegemon.

One possibility, therefore, would be for the Triad to 'go it alone' – to try to reach some collaborative trilateral agreement on how FDI is treated within their own borders by companies over which they have influence in their investments in poorer countries. This may have the edge on a truly multilateral approach, if nothing else because it is just more feasible to reach agreement between three parties than between over 100 as presently in the GATT. In addition, of course, the three account for three-quarters of FDI and 70 per cent of trade anyway.

A second possibility is to think in terms of negotiations amongst a greater number of countries but along discrete 'functional' lines. Thus it might be possible to have separate negotiations and agreements on taxation, environmental standards, TNC property rights, etc., all running in parallel. The danger here is that inconsistencies will arise between all of these and a mess will result, much along existing lines. Further analysis of these issues is left to chapter 6.

Whatever the outcome, however, whether in terms of a comprehensive multilateral approach or along the more speculative lines sketched here (which, in fact, largely build on existing practice), this will not solve the extreme inequality and distributional problem discussed in connection with tables 3.2–3.4 and figure 3.7. Quite how that could be tackled remains another matter altogether. Nor do the prospects for tougher environmental regulation in connection with investment and trade look promising as the GATT is transformed into a bureaucratic WTO where decisions are increasingly likely to be made administratively behind closed doors (Chase 1993; Northrope 1993). Whatever the shortcomings of the GATT mechanism at least it represented a relatively open forum for negotiation and one subject to legitimate political pressure.

4

Multinational Corporations and the Globalization Thesis*

This chapter explores where the multinational corporations from the advanced industrial countries conduct their business activity. Such an investigation is important because until we know where and why MNCs operate in particular locations, we will not be in a position to adequately assess whether there are the strong tendencies towards 'globalization' as suggested by both the enthusiasts for this process and those for whom it represents an unwelcome threat. Thus in part here we are testing whether there is any strong tendency towards the conversion of MNCs into TNCs.

This chapter follows from the preceding chapter's investigation into the extent and nature of international business. Here we consider three main questions. The first is the issue of where MNCs conduct their business activity. The second is whether there are any systematic differences in the spread of activity between MNCs based in different countries. The third is to what extent there are differences between MNC activity in the manufacturing and the service sectors.

The analysis relies upon company-based data: it is derived from two large data sets that are discussed in the appendix to this book. Clearly there is already information available on where MNCs operate from balance of payments flow data between countries, which have been extensively analysed, and this formed the basis of the discussion in the

* This chapter is partly based upon a joint paper written by Grahame Thompson and John Allen, 'Transnational Corporations and the "Globalization Thesis": An Empirical Investigation', presented at the *European Association for Evolutionary Political Economy Annual Conference*, Eigtveds Pakhus, Copenhagen, Denmark, 27–9 October 1994.

previous chapter. As we shall see, the analysis below supports many of the results emerging from this literature. But as far as we know there has been little systematic work undertaken with company-based data. There is a major advantage to company data over balance of payments data: we are able to see how much MNC activity is conducted on the home territory as compared with abroad.

The appendix describes the sources of information used to construct the data and the mechanics of generating the two data sets. The first of these data sets contains information on the sales, assets, profits, and subsidiaries and affiliates of over 500 MNCs from five countries: Canada, Germany, Japan, the UK and the USA. This is presented for the year 1987. The second set contains information on sales and assets of over 5,000 MNCs from six countries: France, Germany, Japan, the Netherlands, the UK and the USA. This is presented for the year 1992–3. Thus our main aim is to compare the geographical distribution of MNC activities between these two years. The major part of this chapter reports a preliminary analysis of this dual resource. It is supplemented with some other analysis of company-based data, particularly that associated with R&D expenditure and technological activity. In the next section we make some brief remarks about important definitions and compare our approach with other analyses. The main body of the analysis follows, using the two new data sets. Finally, we sum up the indications and potential for this kind of analysis.

The existing approach

It would be impossible to survey the vast existing literature dealing with the geographical distribution of FDI and the activity of MNCs/TNCs. Rather what we do here is pick on three main contemporary sources of information that are representative of this literature. The first is the UN Centre for Transnational Corporations (UNCTC) publication *World Investment Directory 1992, Vol. III: Developed Countries* (United Nations 1993d), which contains an up-to-date country by country breakdown of FDI statistics. The second is a popular textbook on 'globalization' from within the geographical tradition, Peter Dicken's *Global Shift* (Dicken 1992). Finally, we look at John Dunning's monumental study of MNCs in a global economy perspective, *Multinational Enterprises and the Global Economy* (Dunning 1993). Here we give a very brief summary of the similarities and differences between our approach embodied below and what is available from these sources.

Broadly speaking all three sources focus perfectly reasonably on the expansion of FDI and of MNC activities abroad. They tend to rely for demonstrating this on balance of payments flow data, stressing the growth of either investment abroad or inward flows. This is particularly so in the case of the UN study, which gives a very detailed breakdown of these flows for the countries considered in our study below. But there is little or no consideration given to the importance of these flows relative to the activity performed at home by the companies who are responsible for them. What is absent, therefore, is any insight into the relative importance of home and foreign activity for the MNCs from particular countries. This is a gap which the present analysis attempts to close.

The analysis by Peter Dicken contains interesting information on the sectoral and geographical patterns of German and Japanese MNC activity in particular. As will be seen below, we found it difficult to generate robust data from our company sets for these two countries. However, what data we have point once again to the importance of the home territory as a site of economic activity of the MNCs from these countries, something Dicken's analysis does not do. This point also applies to the other countries in our data sets, some of which are also considered by Dicken.

Dunning's consideration of where MNCs conduct their activity is similarly organized around balance of payments flow data and inward and outward investment. In his chapter 2 there are some data on the formation of *foreign* subsidiaries and affiliates for a range of countries, and a consideration of the growth in the number and importance of subsidiaries and affiliates in particular economies. But these are not contrasted with the importance of the number of home territory subsidiaries and affiliates organized by the same companies who operate abroad. Again, this is something we concentrate upon below.

Given that these sources all use balance of payments data, it will be useful to present the latest trends in this. Figure 4.1 shows the recent history of FDI flows for the OECD countries, a sub-section of which are the ones we concentrate on in this chapter. It demonstrates that the decline in OECD FDI activity seems to have 'bottomed out' during 1993, confirming the analysis of the previous chapter. Japanese outflows were still falling in 1993, but USA and UK flows were increasing again. Clearly, the fact that inflows were already on the increase in 1993 (while outflows continued to decline slightly) confirms that the OECD countries were re-establishing their attractiveness as investment locations.

The broad trends on a sectoral basis are that services now attract the largest share of direct investment outflows, though when measured against the GDP size of sector, manufacturing still remains the most important recipient, so that foreign penetration here remains greater than in services. The distribution of manufacturing FDI shows that it is increasingly being directed towards sophisticated manufacturing with high value added, like chemicals, automobiles and electronics, and away from investment in low value-added labour-intensive industries like tex-

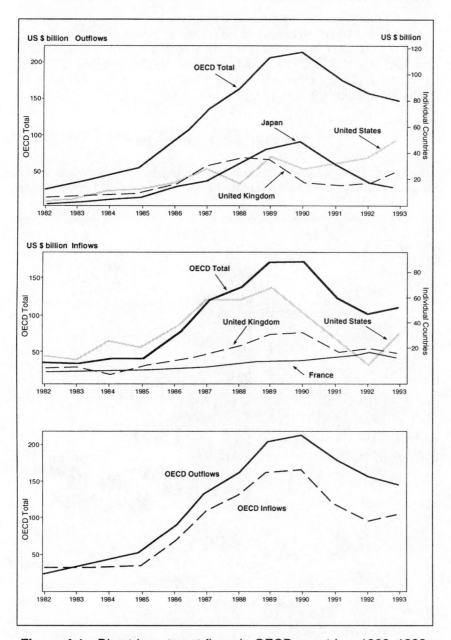

Figure 4.1 Direct investment flows in OECD countries, 1982–1993
Source: *OECD Financial Market Trends*, no. 58, June 1994, p. 18

tiles, leather and clothing, and food processing. Horizontally integrated focused investment strategies are increasingly the order of the day. In 1993 the six most important investors abroad were: the USA ($50,244 million), the UK ($25,332 million), Japan ($13,600 million), France ($12,166 million), Germany ($11,673 million) and the Netherlands ($10,404 million) (OECD 1993, Table 1, p. 16).

The 1987 results compared

In this and the following section the analysis of the two data sets is separately described. Subsequently the common threads between them

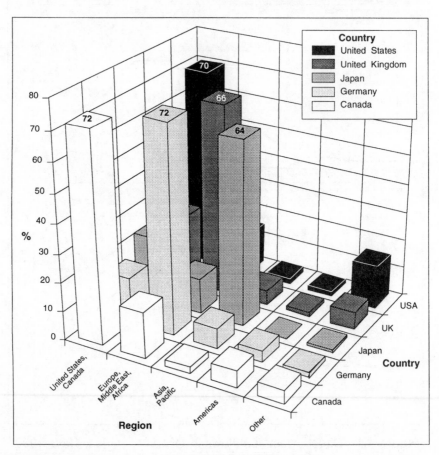

Figure 4.2   Percentage distribution of the sales of manufacturing multinationals by region and country of headquarters, 1987

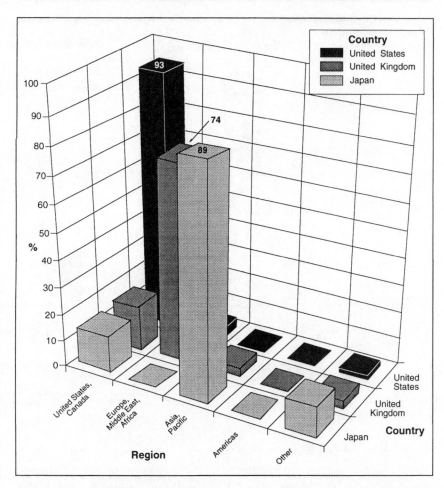

Figure 4.3   Percentage distribution of the sales of service multinationals by region and country of headquarters, 1987

are highlighted and some conclusions drawn. The reason for conducting the initial analyses separately is that the two data sets are not entirely compatible, as is indicated in the discussion below. As explained in the appendix, the first data set pertains to the 'year' 1987 and the second one to the 'year' 1992–3. The results for 1987 are considered first.

We begin with the distribution of sales between countries and regions. It is often claimed that if anything is 'global' in the present era it is the market: thus companies will tend to expand at least their sales activity abroad. Of course the MNC need not necessarily represent a key exam-

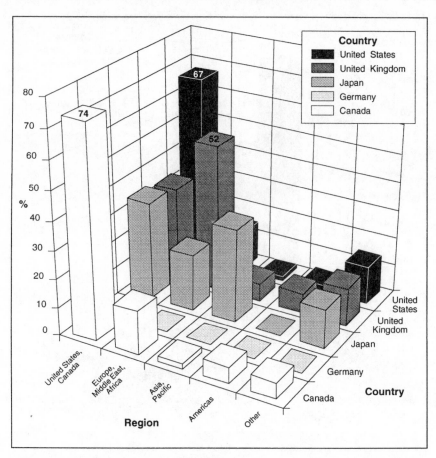

Figure 4.4 Percentage distribution of the assets of manufacturing multinationals by region and country of headquarters, five countries,1987

ple of this trend since it can operate and produce overseas rather than confine itself to a single production site and export from there. Whilst this is so, the results here point to an interesting comment on this issue. Figure 4.2 shows the late 1980s percentage distribution of 'manufacturing' sales for the five country company sets.

What is clear is that 'home country' sales still dominate in MNC activity. In each country case the 'home region/country' sales comprise two-thirds or over of total company sales. In fact, further disaggregation would show that this 'regional' bias amounts mainly to a home *country* bias for Japanese, German, UK and US companies: for UK and German companies, for instance, the Europe/Middle-East/Africa category is

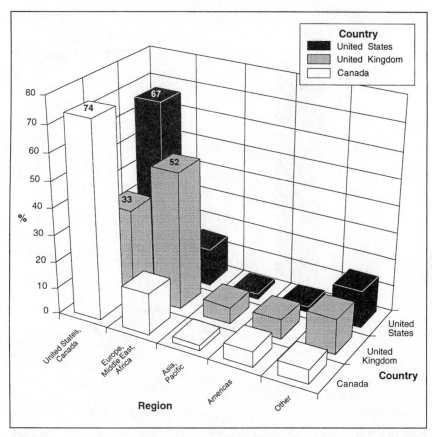

Figure 4.5 Percentage distribution of the assets of manufacturing multinationals by region and country of headquarters, three countries, 1987

dominated by the core European countries, while for Japanese companies the Asia/Pacific category is dominated by Japan itself. (See also the analysis of subsidiaries and affiliates below, which confirms this point – and the subsequent analysis of the 1992–3 data sets, which are entirely disaggregated along home country lines.) But from the way these particular figures are coded and presented, at most it is only the 'regionalization' of markets that is evident.

A similar picture emerges in the case of service sector companies, though, as indicated in figure 4.3, here the 'home region/country' bias is even more extreme. Unfortunately, for the analysis of service sector company sales and assets it was only possible to gather information for three of our five countries. The significance of the category 'other' here

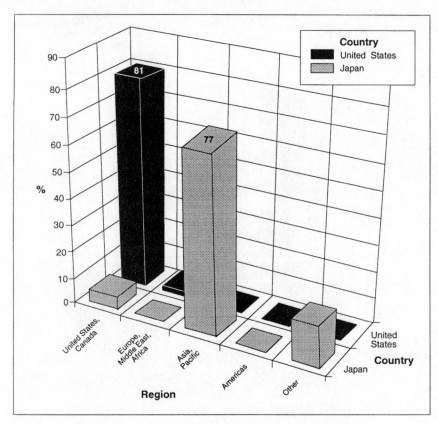

Figure 4.6 Percentage distribution of the assets of service multinationals by region and country of headquarters, 1987

(and in the case of manufacturing: see figure 4.2) indicates the way some service sector and production activity is registered 'offshore': sales can be registered in an offshore area. (Bermuda is an important instance in the service sector for North American companies, because this country was classified as within neither the North American nor the Caribbean zones: see the appendix for the geographical breakdown adopted in our analysis.)[1]

Turning to other measures of company activity, we would expect the distribution of assets to be a clear test of the 'globalization' thesis. As figures 4.4, 4.5 and 4.6 testify, information on this is patchy. Figure 4.4 gives proportions for all five country manufacturing company sets. German companies reported no asset information, while the figures for Japan are based upon four companies only, perhaps undermining their

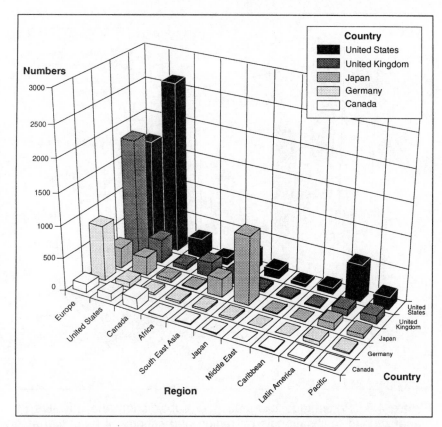

Figure 4.7   Distribution of subsidiaries and affiliates of manufacturing multinationals by region and country of headquarters, 1987

reliability. Thus figure 4.5 restricts the presentation to just the three countries where credible data were available. Here again, the dominance of 'home region/country' is evident, if to a less extreme extent than for sales data. The UK data indicate a more diverse asset base, with North America an obvious site for UK MNC operations. The 'other' category becomes relatively more important here, which relates to difficulties over allocation as mentioned above and in note 1.

The data for service company assets are even more restrictive, but for the two countries where reliable data were available, home country dominance is extreme. These results are shown in figure 4.6.

We now turn to subsidiaries and affiliates (S&A). Here good quality and extensive data were available for both manufacturing and service companies, and for all the countries studied. We were also able to refine

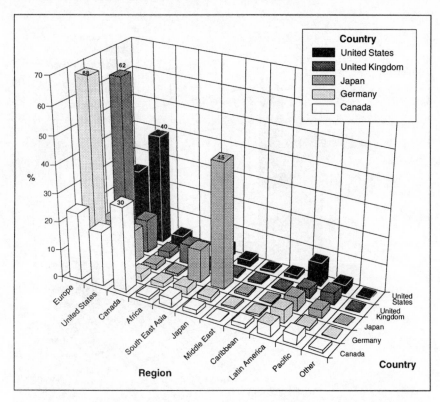

Figure 4.8 Percentage distribution of subsidiaries and affiliates of manufacturing multinationals by region and country of headquarters, 1987

the geographical dispersion of S&A. The results are reported in figures 4.7, 4.8, 4.9 and 4.10. Figure 4.7 presents the absolute numbers of manufacturing S&A, demonstrating the importance of the US and the UK in terms of numbers. But viewed in relation to figure 4.8, where it is percentage distribution that is indicated, some interesting differences between the countries emerge. First, only 45 per cent of Japanese S&A are home based, while 68 per cent of German S&A are located in Europe. Other than this difference, home-country-based S&A are again evident, though for US and Canadian firms Europe is a particularly important site for S&A. The UK is not as well represented in the US. Latin America figures as a relatively important destination for all the countries in this case.

Moving on to service sector companies we find that the distribution,

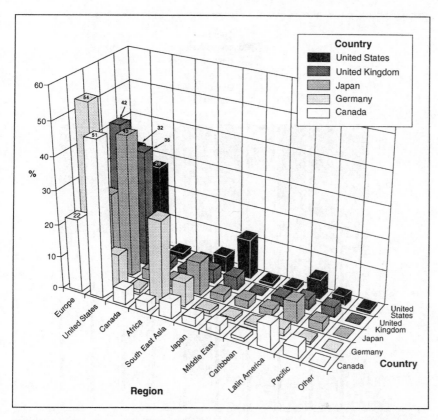

Figure 4.9 Percentage distribution of subsidiaries and affiliates of service multinationals by region and country of headquarters, 1987

though still skewed towards the home-base, is now relatively more dispersed, as shown in figure 4.9. There are some interesting anomalies. German service S&A are important in Africa: in fact, this is mainly accounted for by South Africa. (In general, African activity for all countries is dominated by operations in only two countries: Zimbabwe and South Africa.) Another feature of this evidence is that Japan is not an important site for service S&A, except for US companies. Perhaps this undermines the commonly held belief that Japan is a closed economy for US businesses: it may be that in the case of service activity it is more open to S&A penetration than in the case of manufacturing. As might be expected, Japanese companies were active in South East Asia, but also in Latin America and in Europe. These companies are not particularly home oriented in respect to S&A, one suspects largely because of the

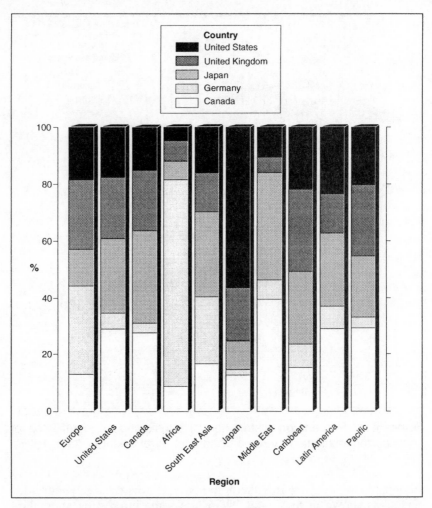

Figure 4.10   Percentage distribution within regions of subsidiaries and affiliates of service multinationals by country of headquarters, 1987

domestic structure of Japanese industries and firms. Germany clearly has the most 'home region/country' oriented companies of the countries shown. Canadian companies are more oriented towards the US than their own country.

Another way of presenting this service sector country data is shown in figure 4.10. It shows the relative importance of each of the five countries in the distribution of service S&A for the regional allocations.

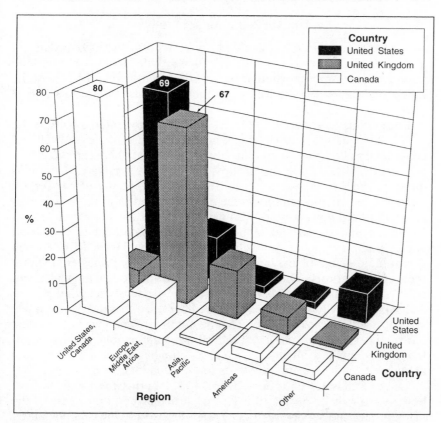

Figure 4.11   Percentage distribution of the gross profits of manufacturing multinationals by region and country of headquarters, 1987

Germany's importance in Africa is apparent, as is the US in relation to Japan.

Finally we can turn to profit data. This is the least satisfactory area from the point of view of data availability, and only the results shown in figure 4.11 could be generated. It provides gross profit distributions for three sets of country manufacturing companies only. Profit distribution follows the pattern established by other indicators: the centrality of 'home region/country' as the site of profit declaration (if not generation: these data do not allow us to distinguish between where profits were generated and where they were declared). Clearly US, and to a slightly lesser extent UK, manufacturing companies are most open to profit declaration in other than the home region/country. The 'other' category for the USA is important here.

The 1992–3 data set analysis

In this section we look explicitly at the results for the 1992–3 data set analysis. This was restricted to sales and asset information only, and the intention is to establish whether the position identified in the case of the fuller 1987 data set is confirmed or otherwise in the case of this 1992–3 data set.

For various reasons one can be less confident about the quality of the 1992–3 data than for 1987. This is mainly because of the difficulty of consistently allocating geographically provided data between the different country-based company groups. Coverage was patchy, definitions differed, and the range of designated areas varied and was often overlapping. The information stored on the original data disk has to be taken as given without knowing exactly how it was first established or coded.

For the analysis included in this section the raw data set described and analysed in the appendix was refined to eliminate all those MNCs which reported no geographical information other than that registered within their home territory. Thus for the purposes of the following analysis an MNC is defined as any company that reported at least one other site for its business activity. It should also be remembered that the two data sets are not strictly comparable because the number of companies, the home base countries, the precise geographical spread of regions, and the population of companies, all differ. Given these qualifications, however, there are some broad comparative trends that can be identified.

Looking at sales data first, figure 4.12 confirms the dominance of home country sales once again. This is particularly so in the case of the primary and the service sectors, though less so for the manufacturing sector, especially in the case of the European nations. The Netherlands is the exception: in the case of its manufacturing sales, the rest of Europe is more important than its domestic economy. This is understandable for a relatively small country, and may be indicative of a wider trend for the MNCs of the smaller economies, particularly in Europe.

Other than the home country dominance, a notable feature is the clustering of sales in a very few geographical areas. An extreme example is Japanese companies, where data are reported only for Japan itself, Europe, the USA/Canada and 'the rest of the world'. Other national data show a wider spread than this with at least some sales in most areas, although not always enough to register a percentage figure. There can be little doubt, therefore, about the massively high concentration of MNC sales as registered by this data set. The Netherlands, the UK and the US show the widest spread in geographical terms, indicating perhaps the relative external openness of these economies.

A further noteworthy feature is the relative unimportance of Japan as a site of sales activity, other than for Japanese companies, if these figures

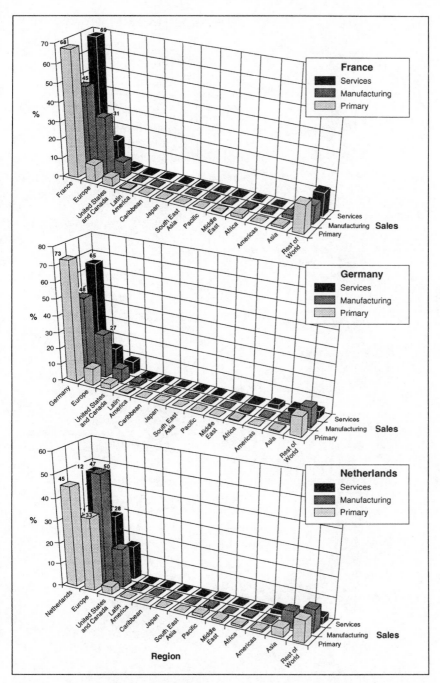

Figure 4.12 Percentage distribution of the sales of multinationals by country, region and sector, 1992–3

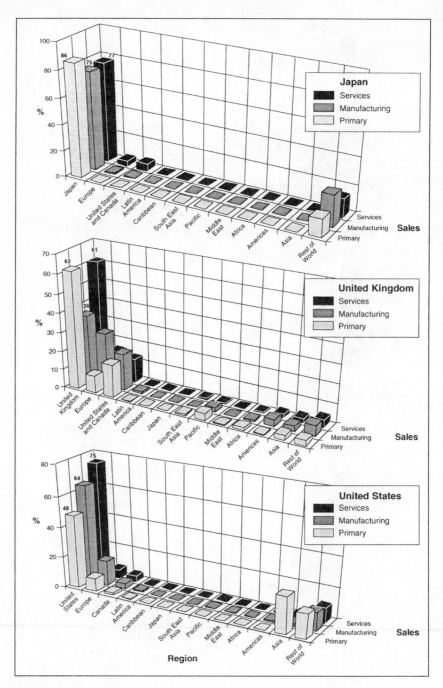

Figure 4.12 *continued*

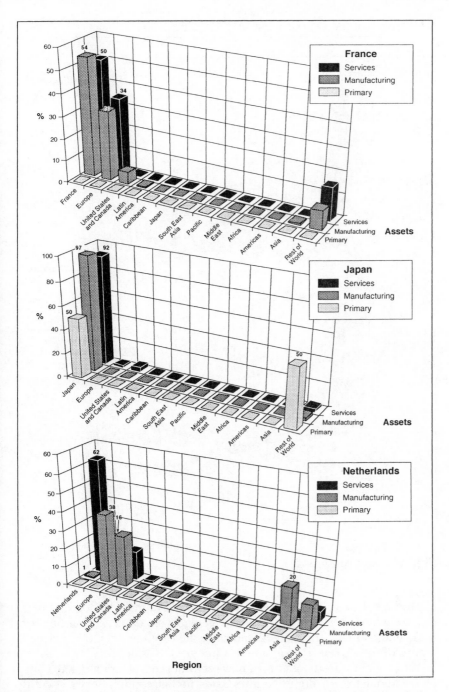

Figure 4.13 Percentage distribution of the assets of multinationals by country, region and sector, 1992–3
No data for primary sector in France and the Netherlands.

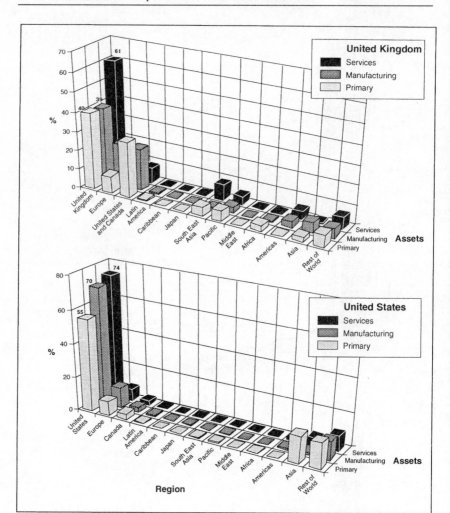

Figure 4.13 *continued*

are to be believed. Whilst it is obvious that there must be some under-reporting here (the 'rest of the world' category no doubt accounting for some of the discrepancy), it still indicates the continued relatively closed nature of the Japanese economy to foreign MNC sales activity.

What about differences in country sectoral specializations? The complete dominance of home country sales for all country service sector companies is evident. The picture for manufacturing is more varied, while the primary sector shows extreme home country bias, but it is not an important sector absolutely. One further point is that US company sales business is concentrated in the US and neighbouring countries (US, Canada, Latin America, and the rest of the Americas categories), with Europe being the only other site of importance. The European powers, while centred on other European states, seem to have a slightly wider geographical spread of activity and are not so obviously regionally locked together.

Finally, let us turn to the 1992–3 asset data. The results here are indicated in figure 4.13. From these data the extreme concentration of assets in the home country for Japan and the US is apparent. For the European countries, other European locations are important, reducing the relative importance of home country concentration. France has the most uniform distribution between the manufacturing and service sectors. The UK has the widest geographic spread of asset locations. Perhaps it is the Netherlands that demonstrates the nearest equivalent to the multinationalization of its manufacturing base, with the home country only accounting for 1 per cent of assets and the rest of Europe 38 per cent (we suspect there may be some home base under-reporting here). But the Netherlands service sector conforms to the more dominant trend of a clear home country bias. Generally, service sector assets are more home country based than are manufacturing assets.[2]

Comparisons and implications

The main conclusion to be drawn from this analysis is an obvious one. The home-oriented nature of MNC activity along all the dimensions looked at seems overwhelming. Thus MNCs still rely upon their 'home base' as the centre for their economic activities, despite all the speculation about globalization. From these results we are confident that, in the aggregate, international companies are still predominantly MNCs and not TNCs as defined by us in chapter 1. There are two aspects to this home centredness. One is the role of the 'home country' and the other that of the 'home region'. As far as the data can be disaggregated, in 1992–3 home country biases were as significant as the home region biases found in 1987. Given that it is only possible to specify an aggregated regional breakdown for 1987, then strictly speaking only two yearly cross-sectional analyses can be compared on this basis.

Table 4.1 provides the relevant figures for sales activity. It compares the percentage distribution of MNC sales for the country company sets for which we have data in both 1987 and 1992–3 (the 'home region' is common for all these data, which includes the home country[3]). Clearly,

Table 4.1   Percentage distribution of MNC sales to home region/country, 1987 and 1992–3

Country	Manufacturing		Services	
	1987	1992–3	1987	1992–3
Germany	72	75	na	na
Japan	64	75	89	77
UK	66	65	74	77
USA	70	67	93	79

Table 4.2   Percentage distribution of MNC assets to home region/country, 1987 and 1992–3

Country	Manufacturing		Services	
	1987	1992–3	1987	1992–3
Japan	–	97	77	92
UK	52	62	–	69
USA	67	73	81	77

although these data should be treated with some caution, they give a reasonable guide to the magnitudes involved. Accepting this, it is probably fair to say that manufacturing sales home biases remained about the same for Germany, the UK and the US between 1987 and 1992–3, whereas they increased for Japan, while in services there was a decrease for Japan and the USA and a slight increase for the UK.

As far as asset data are concerned, the results of a similar exercise are presented in table 4.2. Overall these display a slightly lower home region/country bias than do the sales figures (which is perhaps surprising?). In as much as one can draw any generalizations from these figures it seems that manufacturing assets distribution has become more home region/country biased between the late 1980s and the early 1990s, while for services US companies have become less concentrated (we are not happy about drawing any strong conclusions from Japanese data on services in particular).

Thus from these and the previous set of figures it would not seem unreasonable to suggest that between 70 and 75 per cent of MNC value added was produced on the home territory. This conclusion coincides with the arguments of Tyson (1991) and Kapstein (1991) in their debate with Reich (1990; 1992) about the nature of international business. Both the former authors challenge Reich on his assumption that American business has gone 'transnational', and that this does not matter. By contrast, Tyson points out that: 'Within manufacturing, US parent operations account for 78 percent of total assets, 70 percent of total sales, and 70 percent of total employment of US multinationals in 1988' (p. 38). The analysis reported here confirms this finding for a wider range of countries.[4]

The second major conclusion to be drawn from this analysis is that, despite the common home centredness of our previous findings, the remaining activity of the country groupings is quite diverse. That is, the different country MNCs do operate in different areas to different extents. The MNCs are not all the same in terms of the geographical spread of their extra-home territorial activity. It is difficult to sum this up further other than to point to this diversity and refer to the previous remarks made when discussing the relevant figures.

The relatively 'open' dispersion of S&A seen in figures 4.7 to 4.10, particularly in the case of the service sector, provides an opportunity to discuss a possible slight caveat to these overall findings. One of the strong features of the globalization thesis is that all manner of joint ventures, partnerships, strategic alliances and liaisons are drawing firms into increasingly interdependent international networks of business activity, something we discussed in the previous chapter. A potential problem, then, with the *quantitative* data presented in this chapter is that they do not capture this *qualitative* change in company business strategies. The fact that only 30 per cent or so of company activity is conducted abroad does not of itself tell us anything about the strategic importance of that 30 per cent to the overall business activity of firms. It might represent the key to its performative success both internationally *and* domestically. The fact that we have seen a wider international dispersion of S&A could be taken as an indicator of this 'networking' trend in operation.

We recognized and analysed the increasing international networking being undertaken by firms in the previous chapter, and argued there that this represented no clear indicator of a strong globalization thesis. The analysis in this chapter was designed to supplement that more qualitative assessment, and we see no reason to be more disposed toward the strong globalization thesis as a result of it. Indeed, we would stress the still continued dominance of home country business activity as an *advantage* rather than a constraint on company overall performance. This point is taken up in chapter 8. The overwhelming home centredness of such activity must be taken on its own terms as a clear indicator of the still MNC nature of international firms.

Finally, and in support of the point just made, we can briefly mention another dimension along which the process of company internationalization is proceeding, and which is often used to bolster the argument about 'globalization', namely technological developments and R&D expenditure. Again, there is little systematic company-based evidence about how much of this remains parent country focused rather than overseas, but what evidence there is broadly supports the main conclusion already established in this chapter. In an analysis of the international distribution of R&D laboratories of 500 major firms, Casson et al. (1992) found some degree of interdependency, but it varied greatly between the parent countries of firms. Firms from the Netherlands, Switzerland, West Germany and the UK showed significant foreign orientation (international to home ratio of laboratories all over 60 per cent), while the other nine countries or groupings showed considerably lower ratios (the average ratio was 39 per cent). The dominant country in terms of number of companies and total laboratories, the USA, had a ratio of 31 per cent, confirming it as a relatively 'closed' country on this measure. Countries like Japan and Sweden remain very closed. In addition, papers by Cantwell (1992) and Patel and Pavitt (1992) indicate that on another measure of technological activity, namely patent registration, no more than 10 per cent of patents granted to international firms by the US Patent Office originated from foreign subsidiaries, and that the share of patents coming from foreign subsidiaries did not substantially increase between 1969 and 1986. Thus at most between 10 per cent and 30 per cent of the technological activity of multinationals is likely to be located in foreign subsidiaries.

So where does this leave us in terms of this kind of a company focused analysis? As it stands, what is provided here is no more than a preliminary attempt to establish the legitimacy of one aspect of the globalization thesis. Our conclusion at this stage must be that this is severely exaggerated as far as MNC activity is concerned. International businesses are still largely confined to their home territory in terms of their overall business activity; they remain heavily 'nationally embedded' and continue to be MNCs rather than TNCs. This means that it is not beyond the powers of national governments to regulate these companies. The implications of this we take up and explore in chapter 6.

5

Economic Backwardness and Future Prosperity: The Developing Economies and Globalization

One obvious response to the foregoing arguments is to say that they are backward looking. The current dominance of the First World Triad of the EU, Japan and North America in world trade and foreign direct investment is a consequence of their past success, but it is argued their hegemony is being undermined and the world twenty-five years hence will look very different. It will be much closer either to a model of the world economy proposed by the enthusiastic theorists of globalization or to that of the pessimists.

The enthusiasts predict rapid growth in a substantial proportion of the developing world, in East and South Asia and, possibly, in Latin America. Sustained high rates of growth will transform the share of world output and trade produced by the major developing countries like China, India, Indonesia and South Korea. Thus *The Economist* (1 October 1994) predicts that if present trends continue China will be the world's largest economy in 2020, having already overtaken the United States, and that developing countries will represent over 60 per cent of world output and the rich industrial countries under 40 per cent. Such growth will be beneficial to all successful countries, developing and developed alike. Rising Third World incomes and growing world trade will help to sustain employment and output in the First World. Economic growth will thus create a true world economy. It will also obviate the need for protective policies in the rich industrial countries or general interventionist measures to change the structure of the world economy, such as improvements in the terms of trade for or attempts to direct capital toward the developing countries.

The pessimists predict that capital mobility and free trade will provoke a steady shift of manufacturing investment from the high-wage rich industrial countries to low-wage developing countries (Williams et al. 1995). This will reduce employment in the rich countries, accelerating de-industrialization without compensating advantages for them and at the same time will not bring the benefits of prosperity to the mass of workers in the developing countries. Authoritarian governments and repressive labour laws will hold wages down in the Third World, while public investment in education will produce skilled but cheap labour forces. Most of the Third World will not follow Japan's post-1945 path, but will be export-oriented low-wage countries in an open global economy. Transnational companies will use such low-wage production to penetrate the domestic markets of the rich countries, even as output and employment in the latter stagnates or declines.

These arguments are very different and they require different responses. The case against both, however, is that the majority of Third World economies are unlikely to grow at high rates for twenty-five years, although a minority of NICs are likely to do better than average and achieve First World status, and that rich industrial countries are unlikely to lose such a significant portion of their share of employment and output, either as a side-effect of benign growth elsewhere, or as a direct consequence of the malign effects of capital mobility toward low-wage economies.

It is sobering to look at the past history of growth for both these groups of countries, shown in figure 5.1. The long-term trend has been for both sets to display a downward trajectory in their GDP growth rates since 1961, which does not seem to have quite bottomed out even by 1994. In terms of manufacturing value added (this time excluding China), the downward trend is confirmed. What is clear from these figures is the sharp cyclical character of developing country growth rates: they have swung wildly over the period, so the current cyclical upturn should not necessarily be taken as a long-term shift in the trend. Finally, the figure also shows comparable growth rates for the former Soviet Union and Eastern European economies, which is not comforting as far as long-term growth prospects are concerned. The long-term downward trends collapsed in the late 1980s to reveal dramatically negative growth rates.

Figure 5.1   Growth rates of GDP and MVA in developed and developing regions, 1961–1994
Growth rates are computed using GDP and MVA data expressed in national currencies at 1980 prices and aggregated in terms of 1980 US dollar exchange rates. Broken lines show the long-term trends.
Source: Industry and Development Global Report 1993–4, UN Industrial and Development Organization, 1993

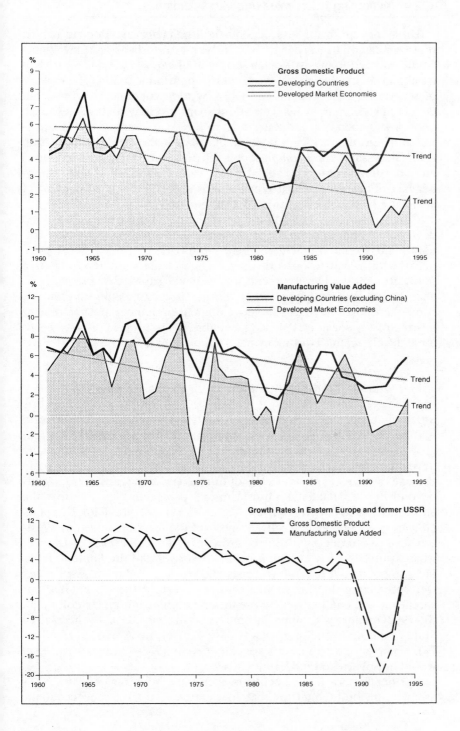

Both the optimistic and pessimistic arguments also depend on the requirement that in order to sustain long-term growth the developing countries need to persist in such strategies of export-oriented industrialization and that this persistence requires political stability. The essence of the optimistic argument for Third World economic growth is that developing economies need to adopt market-oriented strategies in an open world economy and that to do so they need 'good government' – which means democracy if possible but, *sotto voce*, stable authoritarian rule if necessary. *The Economist* puts the point succinctly: 'But so long as most developed countries stick to their reforms and avoid political upheavals, much of the Third World stands its best chance for decades of achieving sustained expansion' (1 October 1994, p. 3).

Can a majority of Third World countries manage the stresses of rapid development and contain the protests of the losers? Can the more fortunate minority among them combine the forced-march search for prosperity with moves towards democracy and at the same time maintain political stability? The arguments for sustained growth depend on one or another political outcome, either the persistence of authoritarian but competent government, or the development of democratic government in spite of the social turbulence inevitable in the process of rapid economic development. How likely are such outcomes?

Accelerated development in historical perspective

Much of the current debate on sustained growth in the developing world is forward looking. At its most simplistic it projects forward current growth rates over twenty-five years in both the developed world and the developing world and sums up the outcomes. This is, of course, to practise one of the most obvious vices of futurology, to extend current trends beyond the calculable. A little historical perspective might sober the enthusiasts who are talking up Third World growth. Paul Krugman (1994c) in a valuable corrective points out the fears expressed by Western analysts about rapid Soviet growth in the 1950s and 1960s, who worried that the Soviet Union might soon overtake the United States. He also points out that futurologists like Herman Kahn and Esra Vogel were predicting that the Japanese would overtake the US in GDP per capita and total output well before the end of this century. He notes that: 'In 1992 Japan's per capita income was still only 83% of the United States', and its overall output was only 42% of the American level' (p. 74). If current growth trends are extended at 1973–92 rates then Japan would not overtake the US until 2047.

Further historical perspective is even more sobering. Today's NICs are not the only countries that have attempted to escape economic backwardness. Consider the cases of Germany, Japan and tsarist Russia. All were 'backward' agrarian countries to varying degrees when they began their process of accelerated industrialization. All had apparently stable and powerful authoritarian regimes, in the German case legitimized by universal suffrage after 1871. Germany and Japan both adopted strategies of export-oriented industrial growth behind tariff walls, the state supporting major companies and industrial cartels. In Russia's case state-sponsored development was strategically oriented and driven by foreign public loans, in the two main phases the 1880s and the 1890s and 1905–14. All these countries experienced extended periods of rapid growth, but none enjoyed the kind of trouble-free extended period of 'take-off' now being predicted for much of Asia by the optimists. All these countries were unable to avoid major and economically dislocating political upheavals. To a considerable degree these political crises can be traced to the effects of rapid modernization in hitherto predominantly agrarian societies. The optimists' argument recalls the excessive claims made by modernization theorists in the 1950s and 1960s. There were powerful challenges to such views then and it is worth reminding ourselves of them again now.

Alexander Gershenkron (1966) and J.M. Barrington Moore (1967) argued persuasively that it was the failure of societies like Japan and Russia fully to overcome the legacies of agrarian backwardness and to transform autocratic agrarian-based power structures that led to rebellion against the consequences of modernization. The discontent of peasant losers was a crucial component of the political turbulence in Germany, Japan and Russia.

Despite radical differences in theoretical approach and political intent, a broadly similar conclusion can be drawn from Lenin's *The Development of Capitalism in Russia* (1899). Lenin argued that uneven development between industry and agriculture, and within agriculture itself, would result in a small but radicalized working class minority and a mass of discontented peasant losers. The former, aided by professional revolutionaries, would lead the latter in revolt against the autocratic regime. Despite considerable differences in ideology, the case of Iran's revolution in 1978 reinforces the point, for it was above all a revolt by the losers against a rapid and highly uneven modernization from above that threatened both traditional urban and poor rural sectors.

Historical analogies are not intrinsically a more effective form of argument than the futurologists' projections forward of current trends. The point is not that modern Third World countries are in the same position as Germany, Japan or Russia. The world economic environment is now very different from that of competing Great Powers each seeking (often at the cost of economic logic) to extend their empires. In each case the strains of a major war were added to those of rapid economic development. Russia and Germany collapsed because they were ruthlessly exploitative of their civilian economies in pursuing the war, leading to the revolutions of 1917 and 1918.

The rise of an authoritarian military regime in Japan in the 1930s owed a great deal to peasant discontent, legitimating and sustaining the ruling military cliques against the old 'liberal' elites. Japanese militarism pursued a policy of imperialist expansion in China in large measure to provide markets and siphon off discontent at home. Aggression in China had the consequence of driving Japan into an unwinnable war in the Pacific, motivated by the economic sanctions imposed by the USA. Japan's defeat in 1945 was thus at least in part a product of its increasing adoption of a strategy of overcoming economic backwardness based on military industrialization and aggressive war, and a drift away from an earlier (partial) strategy of export-oriented economic modernization.

Germany and Japan both ultimately benefited enormously from the defeats that not only shattered their authoritarian regimes but also transformed their existing socio-economic systems. The Japan of 1941 was a highly cartelized and relatively inefficient war-oriented economy that had little prospect of competing with the West and that bore little relation to its post-1945 successor. The ultimate achievement of economic prosperity in both countries has to be seen against a background of immense economic and human cost, resulting in large measure from the ways in which they originally attempted to escape economic backwardness. The conditions for their achieving international competitiveness and political stability also depended to a considerable degree on the forcible destruction of their political systems, on active foreign intervention in promoting reform, and on a quasi-colonial Western political tutelage. We suspect that no existing NIC will achieve political stability by this route.

Tsarist failure in economic modernization and political reform led to no such compensating outcome. It was compounded by the subsequent disasters of forced-march socialist industrialization and the Stalinist terror that accompanied it. Soviet 'modernization' succeeded in converting Russia from an overwhelmingly rural and backward agrarian country into a backward urbanized and industrialized country with a ravaged agrarian sector. In this case prolonged misery and vast loss of human life have not created the conditions for genuine economic modernization, and the new regime is confronted with a form of non-traditional economic backwardness that will require herculean efforts to overcome.

Modern NICs are, however, unlikely to suffer from the super-added stresses of major wars that accentuated the strains of accelerated economic modernization in Germany, Japan and Russia. Moreover, at present the international economy shows little sign that it will reproduce the Great Crash of 1929 and the massive decline in the volume of world trade that resulted from it. In the 1930s the general retreat into protectionism followed from and reinforced the collapse of world trade. It intensified the political-economic competition of the major industrial powers, strengthening tendencies towards authoritarianism and imperialism in the weaker of them. Strategies of compensating for domestic economic crisis by autarchy and political expansion were the direct result of a failure in the international economy.

The analogy is not futile, however, even in a period of growing world trade and an open international economy. There are threats to political stability far short of those provoked by beggar-my-neighbour competition and imperialist war. For major Third World countries to succeed they require consistent and effective long-term economic policies and the ability either to contain or to buy off the losers in the process of modernization. To do this they must not only promote rapid industrialization, producing a shift in employment and output from agriculture to manufacturing and services, but also modernize agriculture and prevent the marginalization of a large class of embittered and impoverished peasants and agricultural labourers.

Failure to modernize agriculture and to even up development between regions and social groups may not lead to successful revolution, but it will require relatively authoritarian forms of government to control peasant discontent and the protests of unemployed and under-employed migrants to the rapidly expanding cities. The point that follows is that authoritarian governments are seldom 'good' governments: rule by unaccountable elites tends to lead to corruption, to protecting the rich, to under-investment in poor regions and to the exploitation of the weak. Such unequal policies perpetuate regional and social inequality, becoming in themselves blocks to modernization and broad social progress. Such failure to modernize blocks growth, keeping incomes down and leading to under-utilized human resources.

Rapid development in certain sectors and regions can be accompanied by relative backwardness and even regression in other regions and sectors. One doesn't have to be Lenin to see that. For example, rapid growth in Latin America in the 1960s and 1970s was accompanied by two processes that help to reproduce backwardness. Firstly, there was the exclusion and marginalization of a large part of the rural economy, accompanied by the relative decline or fall in the incomes of the rural poor and peasantry. Secondly, this promoted flight from the land and the migration of the rural poor to urban areas, producing an unemployed and under-employed class of slum-dwellers who help to hold down urban incomes and retard growth in all but the most advanced sectors by the side-effects of mass urban poverty. Brazil is an obvious example of both processes. These processes make successful policies of uniform education and training, the provision of good mass urban housing, and the development of an adequate infrastructure all but impossible. These policies are essentials for broadly based growth, and the preconditions for them are lacking in large parts of the Third World. Partially developed countries like Brazil, Mexico and South Africa are clearly faced with this growth-inhibiting crisis that follows from uneven development and also with the strains it places on open and accountable government. These strains continue to be evident even when the countries concerned are making some effort to democratize their regimes, as evidenced by the revolt in Chiapas, Mexico and the widespread if formal recognition in Brazil's recent elections by the major parties of the need to meliorate the lot of the urban poor.

Countries that have proceeded furthest on the paths to industrial modernity have in the main managed to avoid excessively uneven development. Economically successful Asian countries like Singapore have managed rapid industrialization because their authoritarian regimes have used their control of political power to promote public investment in education, housing and infrastructure. Singapore has spread the public benefits of modernity, thus creating essential inputs for successful and sustained growth. The regime has claimed legitimacy from broad-based prosperity and has the advantage in promoting relatively even development of being a small city state. However, even here the authoritarian regime is coming under relatively severe strain. Authoritarian 'good government' is the exception, inevitably so as it is almost a contradiction in terms. Regimes like Singapore, Hong Kong, South Korea and Taiwan have all benefited from highly particular circumstances and are all small or relatively small states, in which rapid industrial development could quickly dwarf and contain the agrarian sector or in which there was no rural economy to speak of. They also display unusually low levels of income and wealth inequality. Moreover, these countries have relied on public policies to promote the economy that are very different from the strategies of financial rectitude, avoidance of state intervention, and openness to international competition preached by Western countries and international agencies *pari passu* with their advocacy of 'good government'.

The prospects for growth in the Third World evening up the disparities in the global economy turn on the sustained and successful industrial modernization of large and poor countries like China, India and Indonesia, all with large and backward agrarian sectors. Can such countries combine rapid economic development with the political stability necessary to sustain it? This turns on the question of whether they can prevent or contain the effects of uneven development.

Consider the case of China first. Statistics for economic growth and GDP per capita in China present formidable problems, but, for the sake of argument, let us take official figures. Chinese growth since 1978 has been rapid by any standard: averaging 9 per cent in the 1980s, China matches Japanese growth rates in the 1960s. Chinese growth has strong domestic sources: it is not simply driven by foreign direct investment seeking cheap labour and an unregulated business environment in the special economic zones (though by 1994 China was the single largest recipient of FDI). Moreover, there is evidence that Chinese growth is driven not just by manufacturing but by parts of the agrarian sector, especially in the coastal provinces. As table 5.1 shows, however, overall national growth rates conceal considerable inequalities even in official Chinese statistics. Per capita incomes by province differ by a factor of up to 7.5, and while some poorer provinces like Guangxi are growing at above average rates, others like Anhui show actual falls. Thus the dis-

Table 5.1   Regional inequalities and growth in China

Five provinces with highest and lowest per capita income, 1990–1991

	1991 GDP per capita (yuan)	Multiple of lowest province GDP	Growth 1990–1 (%)
Highest			
Shanghai	6,675	7.5	7.0
Beijing	5,781	6.5	7.5
Tianjin	3,944	4.4	6.0
Guangdong	2,823	3.2	17.3
Liaoning	2,707	3.0	5.5
Lowest			
Henan	1,141	1.3	7.0
Gansu	1,133	1.3	6.5
Guangxi	1,058	1.2	12.7
Anhui	1,052	1.2	−3.7
Guizhou	890	1.0	9.9

Five provinces with highest and lowest growth rates, 1990–1991

	Growth in GDP (%)		Growth in GDP (%)
Highest		*Lowest*	
Guangdong	17.3	Anhui	−3.7
Zhejiang	15.4	Tibet	1.6
Fujian	14.7	Shanxi	3.3
Shandong	13.9	Heilongjiang	3.9
Xinjiang	13.9	Hubei	4.5

Source: *China Statistical Yearbook*, 1993, derived from tables T2.16 (p. 33) and T2.17 (p. 34)

parities within China are as great as those between Germany and the poorer countries of Eastern Europe. Shanghai province has a GDP per capita close to that of some successful Asian NICs, while the poorest provinces are closer to the bottom of the Third World. Economic modernization is also bringing social dislocation, with predictions of large-scale unemployment (figures of up to 200 million are cited). The questions are whether development can be broadened and whether growth in the most successful regions can avoid being choked off by local inflation, labour unrest, and the influx of migrants from poorer regions. Harsh administrative measures are capable of repressing labour discontent and containing mass migration from poorer regions while an authoritarian central government continues to exist. More problematic will be to divert private capital and public investment towards some of China's poorest regions and not just to those adjacent to the rapidly growing coastal provinces and Beijing.

Growth and continued foreign direct investment depend on political stability. China may avoid political turbulence and major conflicts between its regions. However, the future of the political succession, the character of the regime, and its sources of legitimacy are all matters of uncertainty. China has a dual economy, part rapidly modernizing Asian NIC, part semi-stagnant state socialist system, and with every variant of rural economy from prosperous capitalist farms to grinding peasant poverty. But it cannot have a dual state. If the state neglects the less successful minority, the result is likely to be social unrest and political conflict, but if it attends to their needs there must be some division of income and investment from the fastest growing regions, slowing growth in the course of distributing its benefits more widely. Whatever happens China is unlikely to become a democracy, given its vast regional and income differentials. Can it remain a stable and competent authoritarian regime? The question must surely be moot, and it raises serious concerns about the political conditions for continued rapid growth. No sensible person would wish continued economic backwardness on China, not least because a prosperous and outward-looking China would be both a major growing market and a source of peace and stability. Equally, there are grounds for scepticism about assuming a quarter century of rapid and uninterrupted economic progress.

The cases of India and Indonesia are even more problematic and subject to scepticism. India has an impressive record of maintaining democratic institutions since independence in a very poor country with strong centripetal forces and acute differences in living standards between regions and social groups. Hitherto, however, national integrity has been sustained by a strongly protectionist regime, by national strategies for import substitution and strategic industrial development and a history of strong state intervention and regulation. India's turn toward economic openness and a less interventionist strategy will weaken those foci of national unity, undermining the functions and economic power of the central state. Uneven development will accelerate regional disparities and strengthen strong localist and communalist tendencies. India may survive as an integrated and democratic country but the pressures undermining central control and making for politico-cultural antagonism are intense. Indonesia is an even more obvious example, an authoritarian state holding together an extremely heterogeneous society. The odds against both countries maintaining national integrity and the political cohesion to sustain very rapid economic growth in spite of the claims of the losers must be very real. Only if several large countries like China and India can escape economic backwardness on a broad front will a major redistribution of output and trade in the world economy take place.

In a consideration of the prospects for the major Third World economies, there is also the issue of population growth. It is not our purpose either to advance or to evaluate the highly pessimistic prognostications that link widespread famine and ecological damage with excessive population growth. They may or may not be correct, but, even on relatively optimistic assumptions, rapid population growth affects both the prospects for political stability and sustained high rates of economic growth in the developing countries.

We know that two quite distinct population regimes tend to inhibit economic growth. On the one hand, a stagnant or declining and ageing population forces a diversion of resources to care for the economically unproductive elderly and also reduces the population of economically productive adults to support them. On the other hand, a rapidly growing population, where the majority is under twenty, consumes a great deal of resources in supporting and educating economically unproductive children, and also requires a very high rate of investment to create jobs for the steadily growing mass of young workers. If economic growth and investment in new jobs fail to keep pace with the population growth then societies face a far more immediate and potent threat than Malthus's spectre of famine: they are confronted with masses of unemployed and under-employed youngsters without hope who are a ready recruiting ground for disaffected political groups.

This process can be seen today, contributing to undermining the regimes in countries like Egypt and Algeria with very rapidly growing populations. The most successful Asian NICs like Singapore and South Korea have deviated from this pattern of rapid population growth widespread in the Third World. They are experiencing a different population revolution, one like that which occurred in developed countries like Britain after the industrial revolution. For example, South Korea has reduced its overall fertility rate from 4.5 per 1,000 in 1965–70 to 2.0 per

1,000 in 1985–90 (Kennedy 1993, p. 30). As it turns out neither China nor India has spectacularly high population growth rates by Third World standards (1.5 and 2.1 per cent respectively, compared with Iran's 3.7 per cent, for example: table 5.2). Yet it is estimated that their populations could both grow to about 1.5 billion by 2025. China has managed by considerable efforts and much authoritarianism to control its fertility rate. Yet as the population 'bulge' of the 1960s passes through the generations and as a paradoxical consequence of restrictive population policies, China may by 2025 have 300 million people over sixty and the same proportion of older and unproductive people as Europe is expected to have in 2010 (Kennedy 1993, p. 168). Thus even if China could reduce population growth to zero, it would still need to grow very rapidly to raise overall living standards, to continue to raise education levels to match competition from other Third World countries like Malaysia, and to care for its growing numbers of unemployed and economically inactive aged. China could thus be a Third World country with a First World problem of caring for substantial numbers of old people. It needs simultaneously to escape poverty, to absorb a growing workforce (many of whom will be unemployed in any case and will require resources to be diverted to their welfare), and, increasingly, to provide pensions and health care for the elderly. This is a daunting prospect, even for a people as industrious and resourceful as the Chinese.

These difficulties will be dwarfed by the simple problems of too many people faced by India if its population really does virtually double from 883 million in 1992 to 1.5 billion in 2025 (Kennedy 1993, p. 163). It will have to dramatically increase its current rates of economic growth simply to maintain the very low existing GDP per capita. As for rapidly growing populations like those of Nigeria, Iran or Egypt, they threaten to swamp any attainable rate of economic growth, leading inexorably to collective impoverishment.

Table 5.2 Populations and growth rates, 1985–1992

	Population 1992 (million)	Growth rate 1985–92 (%)
China	1,166	1.5
India	883	2.1
EU	346	0.3
USA	255	0.9
Brazil	154	1.8
Japan	124	0.4
Iran	60	3.7
Argentina	33	1.3

Source: *World Bank Atlas*, 1994 pp. 8–9

The purpose of this argument is not to retell tales of Malthusian gloom: since the notorious Club of Rome Report in 1970 these have often proved to be wrong and alarmist. The world will probably find the means to feed its population, even if this does involve developing synthetic foodstuffs and genetically manipulated plants and animals, and if a substantial proportion of the poor depend on charity. What such projected population growth figures do mean, however, is that even if output and employment do manage to keep pace with the increase in human numbers in the majority of developing countries (which is by no means certain), Third World incomes are unlikely to rise in the way predicted by the optimists. The share of total global output represented by the developing countries could rise relative to the advanced countries without there being much in the way of improvements in welfare in the Third World. Some shift of output share is inevitable because the vast majority of the 8–9 billion people in the world in 2025 will be in the poorer countries.

The optimistic case and its limits

The optimistic case actually rests on the recent performance of a relatively small number of Asian NICs and the belief that a number of other and bigger countries like China are about to follow them. It also assumes in projecting future performance and shares of world GDP that the key Asian NICs will go on growing about as rapidly as they have in the past. Thus the argument turns a great deal on the reasons for the apparently spectacular past performance of NICs like Singapore, South Korea and Taiwan, and their likely future rates of growth.

Sceptics like Paul Krugman (1994c) and Alwyn Young (1994a; 1994b) have recently begun to challenge the conventional wisdom on the past and future growth of the Asian Tigers. This intervention suffers from the limitations of the econometric manipulation of aggregate economic statistics, but these are no more disabling than the often ill-digested qualitative reflections on case studies and journalistic reports that make up a sizeable portion of the literature on the Tigers. Where Krugman and Young are valuables in talking down the excesses of enthusiasm for and fear of Asian competitiveness on the part of Western commentators based on raw growth rates from the 1960s onwards: Singapore growing at 8.5 per cent per annum between 1966 and 1990, and South Korea growing at 9.5 per cent from 1970 to 1980 and 9.7 per cent between 1980 and 1990. The case made by both Krugman and Young is that these growth rates are actually less spectacular once their sources are known.

Thus Krugman (1994c) argues that Singapore's increases in output are dramatic but are overwhelmingly due to the dramatic increases in inputs.

Consider the following three examples: labour participation increased dramatically, the employed portion of the population rising from 27 to 51 per cent; education standards were dramatically improved by public policy, for in 1966 half the workforce was without formal education whilst in 1990 two-thirds had completed high school; and investment as a proportion of output rose from 11 to over 40 per cent (pp. 70–1). These improvements are clearly unrepeatable. Hereafter, Singapore's economy will have to grow not by further increased inputs but by increases in the efficiency of use of capital and labour productivity. There is little evidence that Singapore has grown by such efficiency in addition to heroic increases in inputs.

Similar arguments are advanced about South Korea and Taiwan. Young (1994a) compares total factor productivity growth in Hong Kong 1966–91 (2.3 per cent per annum) and Singapore, South Korea and Taiwan 1966–90 (−0.3, 1.6, and 1.9, respectively) with that of other countries during similar periods of rapid growth: Canada (1947–73 1.8), France (1950–73 3.0), Germany (1950–73 3.7), Italy (1952–73 3.4), Japan (1952–73 4.1), the UK (1955–73 1.9) and the USA (1947–73 1.4). The results of Asian growth are thus unspectacular. The Asian Tigers have advanced by mobilizing hitherto under-utilized human resources and combining them with a massive employment of public investment and private capital. This process having been accomplished, their growth rates will tend to fall, and, as incomes rise towards those at the bottom end of the advanced world, any competitive advantage they had hitherto enjoyed from low wages will vanish. Further economic progress will, therefore, depend crucially on improvements in overall efficiency and labour productivity – a much harder task.

But as Krugman has pointed out, there are significant difficulties in drawing too many strong conclusions from comparisons of 'national competitiveness'. For instance, Germany exported 32 per cent of its GDP in 1990 while the UK exported 25 per cent. But the EU as a whole only exported 9 per cent of its aggregated GDP outside its borders, a very similar amount to the US (10 per cent) and Japan (11 per cent) (see chapter 6 and figure 6.2). The export to GDP ratio of China was already 20 per cent in 1991, for Korea it was 29 per cent and for Malaysia 81 per cent. The point here is that if only 10 per cent or thereabouts of GDP is exported, then a key issue for domestic prosperity and welfare is the productivity of the remaining 90 per cent, which is domestic productivity *per se* and not relative to other nations (Krugman 1994a).

Clearly, there are good reasons to be suspicious of all the implications of this kind of argument. International trade has very important 'demonstration effects' on home-oriented production and 'learning effects' for exporters (Prestowitz 1994, p. 188). The point is, however, that most of those nations identified as potential Asian challengers to the position of the advanced industrial countries already have high export to GDP ratios, as shown above (furthermore, for Hong Kong the ratio was 141 per cent and for Singapore 185 per cent in 1991, indicating the re-export nature of their economies). In fact it is the very high-ratio countries that are the vulnerable ones since they have become almost totally dependent upon their 'international competitiveness' for the prosperity of their citizens (they have become rather like firms, who 'export' close to 100 per cent of their output) (Thompson 1995b). This is even more so where these countries are relatively small players in terms of their overall GDP levels (thus China is a potential exception here). Those in the most comfortable position are the Triad bloc countries since, if properly managed, they have a vast domestic cushion of GDP to fall back on, and are only 'lightly' implicated in the international economy in terms of exports. They retain a serious option to retreat into autarchy if pushed. The heavily export-oriented economies, by contrast, could easily become trade policy hostages to one or all of the Triad group.

But the successful Asian NICs have prospered because they did not follow the route for the developing world in fashionable modern economic advice, for that places great emphasis on foreign direct investment and openness to foreign trade. Had they been seduced by *laissez-faire* policies as advocated by some of the enthusiasts for globalization, who believe that world free markets and capital mobility can solve all development problems given the right regime and mass attitudes, then they would not have developed either as rapidly or as relatively evenly as they have.

The analyses of Krugman and Young imply that Asian growth rates in the successful countries will slow and cannot be projected forward at 1970s and 1980s levels for another twenty-five years. That seems most likely to be the case. A dose of econometric scepticism is a healthy corrective to much of the ill-considered hype about the 'Asian miracle'. But Krugman's rather churlish conclusion is hardly fair about the Tigers' past successes:

> The newly industrializing countries of the Pacific Rim have received a reward for their extraordinary mobilization of resources that is no more than the most boringly conventional economic theory would lead us to expect. If there is a secret of Asian growth, it is simply deferred gratification, the willingness to sacrifice current satisfaction for future gain. (1994b, p. 78).

It is one thing to demystify Asian growth, it is another to disparage it. One has a distinct feeling of the excluded middle here: Asian growth is basically pure effort and it does not prove that free-market economies like the USA have much to learn or to fear from it. There is nothing in this view between successful *laissez-faire* and industrious but rather inefficient development based on high rates of saving, lots of investment, and state intervention. Surely Asian policies still have much to teach us and *laissez-faire* is by no means an obviously successful route to economic development, either in newly industrializing economies or in failing advanced economies.

Indeed, in criticizing the World Bank's (1993) analysis of the East Asian economic success, Rodrik (1994) emphasizes the crucial role of the governments in these countries in engineering a rise in investment: this involved a range of strategic interventionary measures including investment subsidies, administrative guidance and the use of public enterprise. Far from validating a *laissez-faire* approach, the experience of Asian NICs shows how necessary are determined public policies and a substantial measure of social consensus in promoting growth through large-scale public and private investment if developing countries are to succeed. What is exceptional are the *political* sources of a mobilization of resources, not the boring conclusions of economic theory. All these Asian NICs have benefited from public investment to dramatically improve human resources, from state support for high rates of saving and capital investment, from active state industrial policies in the cases of South Korea and Taiwan, and in most cases from protectionism to support developing industries and reserve domestic markets to them. Without these policies such countries would not have reached the edge of industrial modernity so rapidly, if at all.[1]

The routes to economic modernization taken by the successful Asian NICs do not predetermine their future. They may be able to switch from investment-driven growth to a new regime based on increases in overall efficiency and labour productivity. For example, Singapore attracted one-sixth of the total for the ten largest recipients of FDI in the developing countries in 1988–92 ($21.7 billion: *The Economist* 1 October 1994, p. 29). Asian developing countries are expanding their share of R&D as a percentage of GDP close to European levels and they are continuing to upgrade the skills of their workforces. Thus there is no reason why some of these countries, and most obviously Singapore, should not become part of the advanced world. Indeed, GDP per capita in Singapore is comparable with that in the poorest regions of some advanced countries (like West Glamorgan in the UK). Such changes will not alter the balance overall between the advanced and the developing worlds that much: Singapore is a small city state. It does show that one should neither dismiss the specific reasons for the Tigers' success nor simply extrapolate that success to the rest of the developing world.

However, in spite of Krugman's blithe dismissal, developing and advanced nations can still learn valuable lessons from the sources of Asian success. These lessons may not be encouraging, but they show the value of determined national economic management and solidaristic public policies in producing international competitiveness. This is the exact opposite of what most globalization theorists argue: success in the international economy has *national* sources. If the sources of Taiwan's success are unsurprising, they are sobering for countries like the UK, which practises *laissez-faire* policies to excess and whose government has set its face against both public investment and social solidarity. If Taiwan can grow by mobilizing investment resources, the UK can decline by not doing so. A society like the UK, which devotes too high a proportion of its national income to consumption rather than investment and whose financial markets steer capital away from long-term investment in manufacturing, faces the reverse of societies like Singapore: the collapse of public infrastructure, progressive de-industrialization, and economic stagnation. The UK, moreover, is dominated by politicians who believe that national-level policies to promote industry are futile in the face of globalization. The problem for other developing countries now is that these Asian strategies are hard to copy, especially as the new GATT regime will make protectionist policies far harder to sustain in future.

The pessimistic case and its limitations

The pessimistic case for the malign effects of globalization depends crucially on the lure of low wages to TNCs and their capacity to mobilize capital to follow them. We have already argued in earlier chapters that the great bulk of FDI continues to be concentrated in the advanced world, with China and Singapore as significant exceptions, that true TNCs are rare, and that most companies are not footloose but still have distinct national bases. Nevertheless, circumstances could change, and it is worth considering whether low wages will confer a significant competitive advantage leading to a large-scale shift of output and employment from the developed to the developing world.

Economic growth in developing countries driven primarily by foreign capital (whether in the form of loans or FDI) is by no means unknown. The evidence suggests that it is highly volatile and that it tends to result in highly uneven development. As we have seen, the successful Asian NICs developed primarily because of domestic capital formation and public investment, with foreign direct investment in a subsidiary role. The Latin American countries, on the other hand, have depended considerably on external sources of capital since the late nineteenth century. If we compare performance with the same period of rapid growth as in the Asian NICs, the 1960s to 1990, then we can see that Latin American countries have experienced violent fluctuations in both capital flows and growth rates. As Ajit Singh (1993) argues in a comparison of Asian and

Latin American performance, the massive influx of foreign capital, especially in the 1970s, opened Latin American countries to violent externally generated shocks that their socio-political systems and means of economic governance were unable to master in the early 1980s. Heavy dependence on foreign loans led to subsequent high inflation and to savagely deflationary policies imposed on local governments by the international financial system. The result was that Latin American growth fell from a peak of over 8 per cent per annum in 1973 to below −2 per cent in 1983, and has fluctuated violently thereafter (figure 5.2). In the same period the successful Asian economies grew steadily.

It is, of course, possible to be open to foreign capital flows, and to FDI in particular, and not reproduce the excessive boom and bust cycle of Latin America. But it is difficult to see how sustained growth of an Asian type would be possible. The more open a developing country is to FDI and the more dependent its modernization is on foreign capital sources, the more likely its growth is to be driven by exogenous forces, by cycles

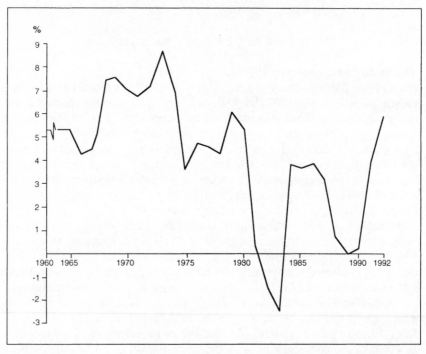

Figure 5.2   Latin America GDP growth rates, 1960–1993 (per cent per annum)

Source: *UN National Accounts Yearbooks*

of demand in the developed world, and by fluctuations in the supply of capital and the cost of borrowing. Investment levels will thus tend to fluctuate with international conditions. However, for this strategy to succeed, domestic policies have constantly and successfully to be retuned to solicit foreign capital and MNC investment. This will inevitably mean bowing to the nostrums of the international financial community, even if this places curbs on public investments necessary to growth and starves domestic enterprises of cheap capital. Such policies may be good for attracting foreign manufacturing enterprises in periods of growing First World demand, but they impede broad-based development in Third World countries, and are unlikely to lead to rapid rates of growth overall.

The level of FDI in the developing world is closely tied to the economic cycle in the advanced countries, with depressions in the First World stimulating a flow of capital to key developing countries. The recent surge in FDI into the developing countries from $31 billion in 1990 to $80 billion in 1993 is closely correlated with the widespread downturn in the advanced world. Investment is also highly concentrated in certain favoured locations: of the total of $126.1 billion of FDI going to the ten largest recipients of investment among the developing countries in 1988–92, $47.3 billion went to just two countries, China and Singapore, and $78 billion of the total was absorbed by the four top countries (*The Economist* 1 October 1994, p. 29). China's share of FDI may be substantially over-stated as an effect of government tax breaks for local businesses if they go into partnership with foreign investors – leading to large-scale fictitious reporting (Krugman 1994c, p. 75). FDI to the developing world is, moreover, even in periods of peak flow, a tiny portion of the capital stock of the developed world: Krugman (1994b, p. 119) contends that the entire net outflow of investment since 1990 has reduced the advanced countries' capital stock by a mere 0.5 per cent. FDI has yet to prove it could transform a major part of the developing world.

If capital mobility is far from being a panacea for a developing country, might it still not be a menace for the developed world? The question here ultimately boils down to how much of an incentive to First World firms the low wages in poor countries represent. Labour costs in the manufacturing sector in Indonesia are less than 2 per cent of those in Germany: in 1993 $0.5 per hour as against $25 per hour (*The Economist* 1 October 1994, p. 16). However, as labour costs typically represent no more than about 20 per cent of the cost of the final product in manufacturing in advanced countries, the benefits of cheap labour are unlikely to dominate all the strategies of firms for whom R&D costs or marketing costs are as significant or more so than labour costs, or those of firms for whom quality of the final product (and, therefore, its close supervision) is a primary concern. Low wages alone are thus unlikely to be decisive in the location of production in all but the most labour-intensive products or phases of production (such as highly repetitive final assembly by hand). These labour-intensive operations will typically be low tech and low value. The tendency to locate in or lose jobs to low-wage countries in certain industries must continue to put pressure on low-wage and low-skill employment in the advanced countries, but it does not mean that output in manufacturing will switch wholesale to less developed countries.

The loss of jobs to low-wage countries is much less significant in generating structural unemployment in the advanced countries than is the ongoing process of steady improvement in productivity in both manufacturing and services in most of these countries. Moreover, we may be on the verge of another major revolution in productivity through advances in robotics and information technology that will make possible the widespread substitution of human labour not only in the less generically skilled areas of manufacturing, but also in far more routine jobs in the financial and marketed services sectors. This will eliminate many of the supposed advantages of relocating services to Third World countries, such as routine information processing, and will devastate much of the mainstays of unskilled work in advanced countries, such as supermarket checkout clerks or shelf stackers. This will be a far more serious threat to the employment structure of the advanced countries than Third World competition, and it threatens to undermine wages-based economic systems. Unless employment in labour-intensive personal services for which there will be a continuing demand – such as nurseries, care for old people, etc. – can be substantially expanded and funded in the advanced countries, they will be forced to restructure both income and work, for example by providing a guaranteed citizen's income as of right and sharing work. Otherwise they will face social turbulence and a collapse in demand. This seems a threat which dwarfs any changes likely to result from a switch of work to low-wage economies.

A major counter-tendency towards sourcing from low-wage economies is the adoption by Western retailers of strategies based on returns from electronic point of sale (EPOS) systems, requiring of manufacturers short delivery times and very responsive production methods, and the widespread adoption by Western manufacturers of just-in-time strategies for components, which put similar pressures for short delivery times on sub-contractors and suppliers. In both cases this tendency inevitably favours sourcing from the advanced countries, and as locally as possible. The widespread adoption of flexibly specialized production strategies in many industrial sectors – that is, the production of a changing range of customized or semi-customized goods – favours broadly skilled and well-educated labour, able to use general purpose machinery and act autonomously without much detailed direction, rather than low-wage low-skill labour. In both the advanced and the developing countries alike the adoption of such flexible manufacturing strategies will also act against giving priority to low-cost workers, who will enjoy competitive advantages only in unskilled handwork or in repetitive mass production where specialized and dedicated machinery can compensate for labour skill. Adopting strategies of industrial development in the Third World that favour mass production with relatively low-skill labour may, however, be risky in all but the most stagnant and low-tech sectors. Otherwise competition by product and process transformation is likely to overtake them as research-driven companies in advanced countries seek competitive advantage. For example, the adoption of new materials, such as carbon fibre structures, may transform the automobile and dramatically change its nature, eliminating the need for assembly plants.

There is one final point to consider: should the above arguments prove fallacious, and a general drift of manufacturing employment to the Third World actually begin to take place, then we should not assume First World states will remain passive in the face of this threat. Confronted by the prospect of the collapse of employment and output, they could reintroduce tariff barriers and exclude Third World products: GATT would be swept away by political necessity. In the case of the EU, its semi-autarchic status and large agricultural surpluses would make such a protectionist strategy relatively easy and also quite successful in the short term. Such inward-looking strategies are advocated by disenchanted rightists like Ross Perot and James Goldsmith. They remain quite unnecessary at present, but they could exclude Third World manufacturers and inhibit the growth of overall demand, although protecting European output and employment in the short term.

In the past, states threatened with economic failure and its national-political consequences have readily turned towards protection, especially in the 1930s. While medium-sized nation states would find it difficult to practise such strategies today, continental-scale economies like the EU and North America could do so if they had the political will. Japan could not go it alone so easily since it has fewer options for diverting trade to near neighbours and is export dependent in a narrow range of sectors to a degree that neither of the other two major trade blocs are (see chapter 6). This might make a unilateral US policy of protection more difficult, Japan having the means to sanction the USA through its large holdings in American companies and its capacity to undermine the dollar. A common policy by the three major trade blocs against over-successful low-wage countries like China or Malaysia would not prove impossible, if Japan were included in a general protectionist scheme and given import quotas in Europe and the USA. If this scenario developed, Japan would have as much to fear from low-wage competitors and capital flight by its major companies as Europe or the USA.

The threat of collapsing employment and output in the First World as jobs fly to the Third World is at present quite unreal and there are good reasons to suppose it is unlikely to materialize (Krugman 1994a). Moreover, it rests on some rather thin macroeconomics. Can we envisage a collapsing First World to which Third World economies are exporting their super-competitive products based on low wages? How can First World countries continue to sustain demand if their employment and output are both falling under competitive pressures? How can Third World economies continue to grow if First World demand is held down by economic decline and yet their own populations are unable to afford many of the products of their more advanced industries because of the very low wages that make these industries competitive? The optimistic case has a certain logic, since it is based on a win–win scenario, in which rising Third World incomes contribute to maintaining output in the advanced world. The pessimistic case in its extreme form continues to assume that wages in the developing countries will remain low, and be held down by authoritarian governments if need be. But that makes no economic sense: the result must be either lose–lose and relatively slow growth in the Third World, or a more punctuated decline in the advanced countries and growing incomes in the Third World, a variant of the optimistic case less favourable to the advanced countries. Either way, the pessimistic theory is deeply problematic, whilst the strong version of the optimistic theory requires too many virtuous circles occurring at once to make it probable. The odds are that neither of these theories that predict a radical shift in global wealth and output will prove to be accurate. In that case something like the present dominance of the advanced countries will continue, and the great bulk of the developing countries will remain poor. This is not, we must emphasize, a desirable outcome. The optimistic case would result in a fairer world in economic terms, although the environmental effects of such massive and basically market-driven industrialization are difficult to imagine or tolerate. The conclusion of this analysis is that if we want a fairer world, a better distribution of global output and income, we cannot as the optimists argue leave it to market forces, but must intervene to restructure the world economy by public policies that generate more public aid, that encourage ethical private capital investment in the poorer countries, and that improve their terms of trade.

6

Economic Governance Issues in General

This chapter concentrates on existing mechanisms for economic govern-ance in the open international economy and also considers the possibili-ties for future enhanced economic governance, particularly with respect to international financial markets. In chapter 8 we shall consider the broader political aspects of international governance and the continuing role for the nation state in such regulatory mechanisms. Here we outline the five levels at which governance can operate, from that of the world economy to that of regional economies within nation states. We argue that at each of these levels there are possibilities for the enhancement of the scope of governance and the development of more effective regula-tory mechanisms. These five levels are:

1 Governance through agreement between the major nation states, particularly the G3 (Europe, Japan and North America), to stabilize exchange rates, to coordinate fiscal and monetary policies, and to co-operate in limiting speculative short-term financial transactions.
2 Governance through a substantial number of states creating internat-ional regulatory agencies for some specific dimension of economic activity, such as the WTO to police the GATT settlement, or possible authorities to police foreign direct investment and common environ-mental standards.
3 Governance of large economic areas by trade and investment blocs such as the EU or NAFTA. Both are large enough to pursue social and environmental objectives in a way that a medium-sized nation state may not be able to do independently, enforcing high standards in labour market policies or forms of social protection. The blocs are

big enough markets in themselves to stand against global pressures if they so choose.

4   Governance through national-level policies that balance cooperation and competition between firms and the major social interests, producing quasi-voluntary economic coordination and assistance in providing key inputs such as R&D, the regulation of industrial finance, international marketing, information and export guarantees, training, etc., thereby enhancing national economic performance and promoting industries located in the national territory.

5   Governance through regional-level policies of providing collective services to industrial districts, augmenting their international competitiveness and providing a measure of protection against external stocks.

These five levels are interdependent to a considerable degree. Effective governance of economic activities requires that mechanisms be in place at all five levels, even though the types and methods of regulation are very different at each level. Thus the forms of coordination of world financial markets are very different from the processes of balancing cooperation and competition in specific industrial sectors at the regional level. The upshot of this interdependence of levels is that those national and regional economies that are not well regulated by appropriate means would benefit least from extended international economic governance such as effective stabilization of world financial markets and the management of world trade through international agreements and the practices of supra-national trade blocs. However, interdependence is relative: strong mechanisms of national and regional governance can compensate for volatility at the international level and provide reinsurance for specific economies against shocks caused by weak governance of world markets. National and regional economies remain significant as we shall see later in this chapter.

In this chapter we concentrate firstly on levels 1 and 2, and then go on to consider levels 4 and 5. We consider level 3 to a lesser extent here and give it greater emphasis in chapter 7 when we examine the EU as the most developed trade bloc. Levels 1 and 2, and 4 and 5, are closely interwoven into two linked couples. We begin with a discussion of the relationship between the G3 and the G5/G7 economies, and move on to level 2 as soon as we consider the wider range of countries assembled into the various groupings and institutions that have been formed to manage aspects of the international economy. Likewise effective regional governance depends very much on the policies of national states, and the degree to which they recognize the need for effective local knowledge in promoting coordination and cooperation between firms and between economic actors more generally.

A central plank of this argument, applying to all five levels, is that market economies need to be appropriately governed if they are to perform effectively in meeting the substantive expectations of a wide range of economic actors. Markets are an effective means of economic allocation if the conditions in which they operate are controlled, and the degree of that governance and the specific mechanisms of achieving it vary with the character and scale of the markets in question. Most markets need to be embedded in a context of non-market social institutions and regulatory mechanisms if they are to produce effective outcomes. This social embeddedness of markets is complex and changes as conditions change. It is thus not amenable to a simple elegant general theory and must be revised constantly to meet changed circumstances. The dogmatic advocates of economic liberalism deny this need for market institutionalization. They use a simple elegant general theory of markets to advocate that markets be freed from the interventions of other social institutions, for economic liberals' sales and purchases can function as an effective mechanism of economic coordination in and of themselves. The problem is that the relative internationalization of economic relations since the 1970s has appeared to strengthen the economic liberals' case, giving rise to the widespread belief that global markets are ungovernable. As we shall see below, this is far from being the case, and, even in a period of economic liberal ideological dominance, structures of market regulation have been built up or maintained at the international level.

However, appropriate concepts of economic governance, capable of recognizing the five interdependent levels of activity from world markets to regions, have hardly begun to develop. One reason for this is that the best established effective argument for governed and socially embedded markets, the theory of the 'mixed economy', was developed for national-level economic management. We need a new equivalent type of theory which recognizes that many aspects of economic activity are no longer under direct national control and that a changed international environment needs new strategies and institutions. The concept of a polycentric economic regulation that relies on a number of loci and a variety of mechanisms is a necessary successor to doctrines of national economic management developed in the 1930s and put into practice in a number of advanced economies after 1945.

The *international* institutions appropriate to and complementary to the era in which national economic management was the dominant form of regulation, centred on managed multilateralism between the major advanced economies, also need rethinking and adaptation. Whether a new polycentric version of the mixed economy will emerge remains to be seen. We now move on to consider the general governance of the international economy as it currently exists.

Governing world markets

What are the current prospects for a more orderly international economic environment in the relationships between world markets, countries
and trade blocs? As indicated in chapter 2, there is still a great deal of
volatility and increased uncertainty in the international economy relative
to the stability of the period between 1950 and 1972. Nevertheless, the
indications are that not all the adverse trends giving rise to those uncertainties are set and robust. Counter-trends do exist: thus the inaug-
uration of the EMS, and particularly its exchange rate mechanism
(ERM) component, in 1979 initially decreased the volatility of the member states' exchange rates. It also led to some convergence of underlying
monetary conditions. Although the EMS was substantially undermined
by market pressures in late 1992 and early 1993, the EU still represents
an arena of potential stabilization for the international economy, as well
as for its member countries. In addition the G5/G7 summit system of
policy coordination has seen some successes, particularly in its early days
and in 1991 (Artis and Ostry 1984; Putnam and Bayne 1987).

These instances of policy coordination have so far only been of limited
scope. They have involved monetary issues almost exclusively, although
in recent years the monitoring of real variables like growth rates if not
their active management has been added to the deliberative agendas of
such bodies. However, 'monitoring' is still far from active cooperation to
change policy. By and large the G5/G7 countries have each gone their
own way on domestic economic policy issues, and the divergence of their
basic philosophies and approaches has been evident over the last ten to
fifteen years. This is further registered by the recent divergence in the
business cycles of the advanced countries indicated in chapter 2. We
should not dismiss outright these attempts at limited exchange rate and
monetary coordination, but neither should we over-exaggerate their
importance or success.

The problem inhibiting further coordination at present is the divergent interests that still characterize an international economy where,
despite the claims of the globalization enthusiasts, the major nation
states of the advanced countries and increasingly the emerging trading
blocs are the dominant players. If nothing else the very different underlying economic conditions of the Japanese economy and the American
economy should testify to a divergence of interests that limits active and
positive cooperation between them. Similar remarks can be made about
the difference between the interests of Germany and those of the majority of other European countries.

This is not to suggest that complete non-cooperation will develop
between the major players in the international economy. Rather the
probability is that cooperation will be either minimal – cooperation to

manage periodic international crises – or by default as policies in the stronger economies dictate those in the weaker ones. To this must be added the very obvious continuing differences in economic policy frameworks and outlooks that typify the main international trading countries and that will inhibit coincidental agreements on more developed cooperative ventures. In the case of some national states the domestic institutional frameworks are lacking to implement ambitious policies agreed within an international negotiating structure, even if they were more actively canvassed there. Coordinated fiscal policy initiatives are an obvious example. For instance, it is unlikely that a properly functioning fiscal federalism could be rapidly constructed even within the EU, as we shall see in chapter 7.[1]

But these necessary caveats should not blind us to the ways in which the international economy has become integrated to the degree that an outright return to overt protectionism between the major trading blocs, while still a possibility, remains unlikely. The case of the financial balances between the major blocs illustrates this point, something already referred to in chapter 2. Figure 6.1 shows that the EU was in rough balance on its savings and investments ratios over the period between 1960 and 1994. This was also the case for the USA and Japan until the early 1980s. Then the US went into a dramatic international 'deficit' as its savings collapsed while inward investment remained high (to support its balance of payments and budget deficits). This twin deficit was financed by the Japanese, and to a lesser extent by the EU in the mid 1980s. Thus despite some volatility in the overall trends, which show large swings in GDP to investment and savings ratios, the three main bloc powers appear to be locked together in a reciprocal relationship. In particular, the Japanese economy could hardly continue to exist in its present form without the US markets for its manufactured goods, while the US currently needs Japan as a source of finance for its domestic spending. Japan and the US need one another, because their economic fates interlock despite divergent interests in manufacturing and in monetary policy.[2]

These points are reinforced if we look at the structure of trade *within* the major trading blocs (Lloyd 1992; IMF 1993; Kirkpatrick 1994). The percentage of total trade that each bloc leader conducted with its immediate partner countries in 1990 was 74 per cent for the EU countries within Europe, 33 per cent for US trade with America, and 30 per cent of Japanese trade with Asia. Thus the most integrated bloc as regards trade is the EU: neither the US nor Japan trade to such an extent with their natural 'bloc associates', where intra-bloc trade is small. Rather the US and Japan must still look to the wider international environment for their trading partners. This should reinforce their mutual commitment to a more 'open' trading environment. The US may have much to fear from Japanese import penetration in its manufacturing sector, but it remains a

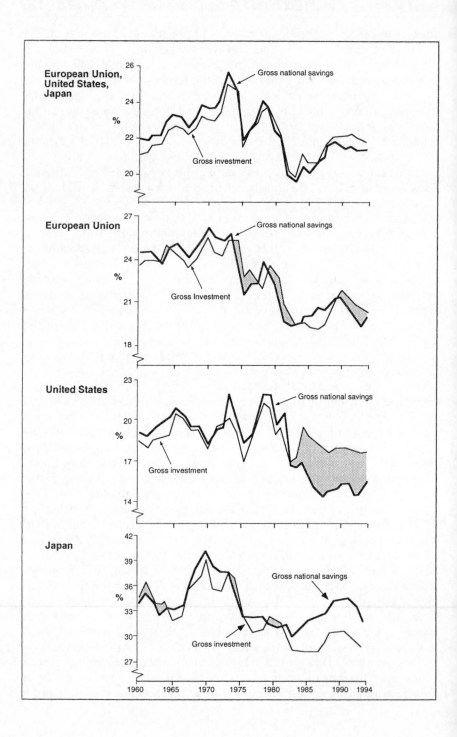

European Union,
United States,
Japan

%

Gross national savings

Gross investment

European Union

%

Gross national savings

Gross Investment

United States

%

Gross national savings

Gross investment

Japan

%

Gross national savings

Gross investment

1960   1965   1970   1975   1980   1985   1990   1994

major exporter both of manufactured goods and services and of primary products, and it relies upon a liberal regime of world trade to be so. Japan may be a virtual trade policy captive of the US, but the US is still committed to free trade and will remain so until Japanese or other foreign competition threatens a catastrophic collapse of its domestic manufacturing base.

Figure 6.2 gives an indication of the importance of trade to the three main economies/blocs between 1960 and 1994 (expressed as a percentage of GDP). What is remarkable is the way the proportion of both exports and imports for all three sets of economies moved closer together in the late 1980s. Since then there has been a slight divergence in the case of imports, but over the period 1970–94 the importance of trade to the three has been relatively stable and similar. This similarity in levels of trade to GDP ratios for the three main players indicates a symmetry in their external relations that could lead to a broader agreement between them (see also chapter 5).

The most vulnerable economy, however, remains that of Japan. This is signalled by its consistently higher exports to GDP ratio than that of the other two groups (except for the very recent years), indicating its export orientation, and by the recent fall in its import penetration ratio, which makes it vulnerable to pressures for 'market access'. Whilst discriminatory trading blocs have been formalized in Europe and North America, Japan has no such formal arrangements with its neighbours, and the prospects for this developing in East Asia with Japanese involvement seem slim (Kirkpatrick 1994; Panagariya 1994). Thus Japan has a more restricted natural hinterland for its trading than the other two main players, even though they all share a similar combined aggregate total of trade to GDP ratio. Japanese export trade in particular is concentrated in a small number of sectors (motor vehicles and consumer electronics, for example), which would make it highly vulnerable to US and EU trade policy.

Finally, the three country groupings also display a growing similarity in the ratio of externally held assets to GNP. Between 1981 and 1988 the ratio of the share in currency portfolio of world financial wealth to GNP fell from 1.94 to 1.59 for the US, while it rose from 0.21 to 0.34 and from 0.44 to 0.71 for Japan and the EU respectively (Commission of the European Communities 1990, table 7.5, p. 187). These trends have continued since, so that more even external asset to GNP ratios are developing amongst the big three.

◄──

Figure 6.1   Evolution of savings and investment in the EU, USA and Japan, 1960–1994 (percentage of GDP)

Source: European Commission services

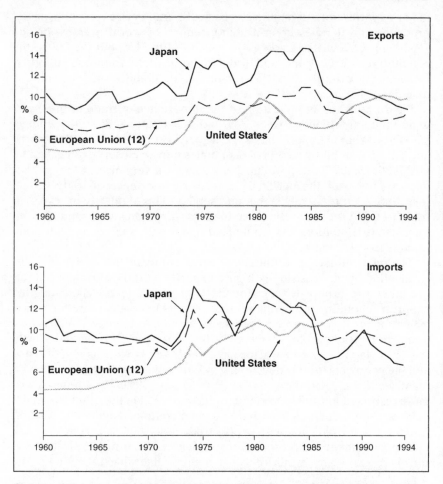

Figure 6.2   Importance of trade for different economic blocs, 1960–
1994 (percentage of GDP at current prices)

Source: *European Economy*, no. 58, derived from tables 38, 41, 42, 45

The point of this account is to confirm the emergence and continuing dominance of the three main players in the international economy. They are roughly of the same economic size and standing, and the degree of diversity in their aggregate external relations is decreasing. Thus at least potentially this offers the prospect of the active management of the international economy by the three leading economies cooperating. It is easier to achieve agreement between three players than it would be for the G5 or G7, if for no other reason than that there are fewer actors involved. This does not mean, of course, that new agreements will necessarily be forged. That depends upon the economic issues and circumstances that arise and require management. The immediate prospects for extended cooperation are not auspicious, as we saw earlier. There remain significant policy differences on the form and style of economic management between the three main players, for instance, which could inhibit even a serious attempt on their part at international policy coordination or cooperation. In addition, a more active practice of international management requires that the blocs will form into coherent managerial/regulatory entities themselves. The current state of affairs is not altogether encouraging in this respect. In part this is an issue of political will and momentum. In none of the major blocs are the political leadership or prevailing economic ideas conducive to an ambitious extension of international economic governance. In the next chapter we consider the internal evolution of the EU and draw relatively pessimistic conclusions. The gap between the potential for extended governance and the perceptions and policies of the major actors remains substantial. But this could change, particularly under the pressure of events.

At this stage the analysis suggests a minimal modified-multilateral international governance structure will prevail in the immediate future. It will be modified as against the previous regime of multilateralism under US hegemony, in the form of a trilateral regime based on the three main blocs. To this will be added bilateral negotiations that are emerging between the three main players on important issues, and between them and other minor parties as well. This latter phenomenon is termed *minilateralism* and is discussed below. Quite what the full consequences of this configuration for the management of international economic affairs might be remains an open question. It does, however, seem that overt and widespread inward-looking protectionism on the part of the major blocs is immediately unlikely. Such a minimal level of modified-multilateral cooperation would seem to be enough to ensure the continued 'openness' of the international economic system, even as that system continues to move further away from the traditional post-war type of full liberal multilateralism.[3]

Specific aspects of international financial governance

Having introduced the general background to issues of international economic governance it is useful to develop its various features more fully. In this section we examine the first two levels outlined at the beginning of this chapter together since, as will become apparent, they overlap significantly in terms of institutional evolution.

The international financial regime

That part of the international economy attracting most attention from commentators – and the one that seems to have internationalized to the greatest extent – is the financial system. This is also the most controversial area, particularly since the great regime shift of the early 1970s heralded the transition from what Padoa-Schioppa and Saccomanni (1994) have characterized as the government-led international monetary system (G-IMS) of the Bretton Woods era to the market-led international monetary system (M-IMS) of today. Padoa-Schioppa and Saccomanni list six main features that characterize the M-IMS (p. 246): (a) the internationalization of financial portfolios consequent upon the widespread domestic liberalization of capital movements; (b) the decline in the importance of banks relative to markets as agencies of financial intermediation (signalled by the rise in importance of securitization, bond issues, etc.); (c) the financial market determination of exchange rates in the light of the growth in the scale of international financial transactions relative to trade transactions; (d) market volatility – the amplification of shocks across the system – which they attribute largely to the growth of information and communications technology; (e) market concentration, where a relatively small group of institutions trade simultaneously across international markets employing similar conventions of analysis and behaviour; and finally (f) the paradoxical emergence of non-insulation of countries from exchange rate pressures at the same time as this did not lead to the 'disciplining' of them in terms of their domestic economic policies.

As a response to these changes in the international financial system there have been developments in three distinct areas of regulation. The first concerns the general relationship which coordinates and regulates the monetary, fiscal and exchange rate relationships between mainly the key players of the G3. Broadly speaking, in practice, this has been restricted to the determination of the global money supply and exchange rate manipulation, since the coordination of fiscal policies has not been in the forefront of economic policy thinking since the late 1970s. As discussed in chapter 2 the attempts to multilaterally manage international liquidity collapsed after 1979. This led to the principal mismatch in governance characterizing the present period: that is, an institutional gap between the increasingly international nature of the financial system and the still predominantly 'national' remits of the major central banks and the wider nationally located regulatory mechanisms for financial markets and institutions.

How might this institutional gap be closed? The G3 to G7 summit meetings, whilst providing an arena in which these broad issues have been addressed, still lacks a proper institutional base: there is no permanent secretariat attached to these summits; they are conducted in an informal atmosphere without tight procedural rules or functionally specified agendas; there is no proper external accountability for decisions taken; and few if any sanctions can be applied to national actors if implementation is not forthcoming. The upshot is that in terms of controlling international liquidity, the summits have had only a partial success, often as much by chance as design. The 'exchange of views' that they embody has led to a number of *ad hoc* monetary initiatives of an interventionary kind (as mentioned in chapter 2) rather than a permanent regime of institutionalized management. But while a formalized international central bank is absent from the M-IMS, as argued in chapter 2, the task could still fall to a particular country and its central bank. Thus the US Federal Reserve Board has been instrumental in developing initiatives in respect to governance and regulation, as we shall see below.

More developed institutional arrangements are characteristic of the second important governance aspect of the M-IMS – international payments mechanisms. Clearing and settlement systems for international financial transactions may not seem a particularly significant aspect of the international monetary regime but they are crucial for the continuance of all types of financial activity, whether it be organized as banking or securities markets. This activity is redolent with 'public goods' features: it begs to be organized in a collective manner but suffers from severe free-rider problems. At the national level, central banks play an important role in the creation and supervision of payments mechanisms, the provision of 'final money' services being a key part of the central banks' 'lender of last resort' obligations. While this central banking function remains unfulfilled at the international level the risks of default increase and disturbances threaten to become magnified across the whole system.

Amongst the international banking community the growth in international financial transactions has been recognized as raising important issues for efficient payment services and has been addressed in a number of G10 reports (Angell Report 1989; Lamfalussey Report 1991; Noel Report 1993). The result is a growing network of cooperative and coordinative institutionalized mechanisms for monitoring, codifying and regulating such transactions (centred on the BIS and headed by the Group of Experts on Payment Systems). These G10 central bank initiatives have been paralleled by similar developments within the EU, which now has the promise of an effective cross-border clearing system. This could quite easily be extended to encompass Central and Eastern Europe when necessary (Padoa-Schioppa and Saccomanni 1994, pp. 255–7).

The third area of regulation of the newly internationalized monetary system concerns supervision of those organizations conducting banking and financial market business. Here the landmark policy initiative was the G20/G30 1975 Basel concordat that established the BIS's leading role in the supervision of international financial institutions. Following on from this the Basel Committee's 1988 Capital Accord was probably the most significant international agreement to date in the field of bank supervision. This established both a framework for further developments and a set of rules for measuring capital adequacy and fixing minimum standards of business conduct for banks involved with international activities. Recently this credit risk approach has been extended to include market risk and derivative assessment procedures, amongst a range of other matters (*OECD Financial Markets Trends*, no. 54, February 1993, pp. 13–26). Again, the Basel agreement structure has been mirrored by developments within Europe, where the EU approved a comprehensive Capital Adequacy Directive for banks in 1989.

Much like the monetary summits of the G3 to G7 the Basel Committee was initially designed as a forum for the exchange of ideas in an informal atmosphere with no set rules or procedures, let alone decision-making powers. But, although it maintains this original informal atmosphere, its evolution has been toward much more involvement in hard-headed rule-making and implementation monitoring. The Committee does not take as its brief the further liberalization of capital and banking markets; that is left to the policy of national governments. What it has done is respond to the effects of this liberalization on organizations conducting the business of international finance and the central banks involved with them. It has been led by the demands of the banks, security houses and governments for a more codified and ordered international financial environment, rather than initiating discretionary action on its own part. The Basel Committee's activity with respect to the banking community is paralleled by the International Organization of Securities Commissions (IOSCO), a younger and less robust body dealing with other aspects of international financial transactions, notably security market supervision. This was established in 1986 and, although in a dialogue with the Basel Committee framework, has yet to mature to the same extent.[4]

The issue that the emergence of these bodies (and other similar ones discussed in a moment) raises is why and how they came about in an era of increased ideological emphasis on market-led solutions to international economic relationships. Why create new coordinative bodies to regulate and manage markets and transactions when such regulation and management are supposed to be increasingly frowned upon by policy-makers? We outline an answer here, and one strand of it was suggested above. The Basel Committee responded to demands made elsewhere – by both governments, through their central banks, and commercial companies involved in the financial intermediation activity itself. One paradoxical consequence of the financial innovation unleashed by the national liberalization and deregulation of financial markets in the 1980s, and of the technological development of information and communication systems that were introduced in its wake, was a sense of organizational 'loss of control' experienced by both central bankers and the managers of the financial institutions themselves. The development of fee-based 'off balance sheet' activity (options, swaps, forwards, futures, etc.) by banks and other organizations undermined well-established and understood practices of commercial management within those firms and countries. Paradoxically, a technology introduced in the expectation that it would provide up-to-date information and so help managers, actually led to them feeling a loss of control. These institutions had previously thought of their commercial environment as a 'level playing field' in terms of competitive activity between companies and countries. But this was undermined by the developments just described. The players no longer quite understood what their 'capital base' was or how it functioned in terms of credit and market risk. This knowledge had been disrupted by the innovative financial engineering of the 1980s. The rapidity of the introduction of new financial instruments, the very pace of trading activity itself, and the necessity of 'on the spot' decisions having to be made by floor dealers or in the OCT markets meant that even managers of commercial banks became unsure of their risk exposure and the real worth of their firms. Bank officials, along with their traditional national supervisors, the central banks, thus had an interest in re-establishing greater transparency in the light of the new circumstances they faced in international dealings.[5]

As a number of commentators have pointed out (Helleiner 1994; Kapstein 1994; Padoa-Schioppa and Saccomanni 1994), this attitude amongst central bankers, governments and mainstream commercial banks was first fostered (and later reinforced) by a number of banking crises/failures of the 1970s and 1980s (Bankhaus Herstatt in Germany, Franklin National Bank in New York, and British-Israel Bank in London, all in 1974; Banco Ambrosiano in 1982–3; BCCI in 1992). These banking crises were successfully 'managed' by the judicious intervention and cooperation of national governments. So the trend was set for *national governments* to cooperate more fully over a wider range of supervisory and monitoring tasks in this field.

Indeed, the central role of the policy of national governments in the creation of the M-IMS and its continued relevance for international financial governance is stressed by both Helleiner and Kapstein in their analyses. These authors dispute the view first that the turn from the G-IMS to the M-IMS was the result of inexorable economic or technological forces rather than policy changes, and secondly that it has thereby undermined either the will or the ability of national governments to manage the present system.

The move to a nationally liberalized financial system in the 1980s was the result of deliberate political decisions taken in the face of a range of definite choices available to policy-makers (Helleiner 1994). Similarly, the subsequent development of a new regulatory regime was equally driven by national governments, and according to Kapstein (1994) it is national governments that remain central to the nature of that regime. For instance, it was the US that took the lead in securing the Basel Accord. Within this framework, home country supervision of financial institutions came to dominate that of host country supervision – what Kapstein calls the principle of 'international cooperation based upon home country control'. This was then gradually accepted by all the participant states and remains the dominant characteristic of the system. Although there have been tensions between home country and host country control, and between both of these and multinational organizations with a stake in the regulation and supervision of financial institutions, the central role of the home nation state in the process remains.[6]

What is more, according to Kapstein (1994), those countries not directly involved with the Basel Accord process have been keen to attach themselves to its regulatory framework. This was pressed upon them by the banks operating within those countries. The dynamic of the system is fostered by a market-led desire to achieve a certain 'credit status' commensurate with that of the G20 sanctioned banks – a status dependent upon operating within the Basel Accord guidelines.

One further consequence of this process is that the 'informality' of the system's decision-making processes actually fosters an emphasis on the *trust* between the parties involved. It is a question not just of formal rules and procedures amongst them – important though these undoubtedly are – but also of the informal nature of the decision-making process. In many ways, the success of this process speaks against the idea of substituting for it by creating a new formal multinational body to regulate and supervise all capital market activity under one roof – such as the capital markets supervisory authority suggested by Bergsten (1994, p. 361). The present system of national cooperation based upon home country control is firmly in place in the case of banking supervision, and in embryonic form in the case of securities markets. It would seem potentially disruptive to undermine this with a more multinational initiative under present circumstances.

What we have then is not totally unregulated markets but an elaborate system for the detailed management of international financial transactions. National governments have not proved powerless in the face of an overwhelming 'globalization' of international finance. Indeed, they have joined together to organize an effective supervision of the new situation. This remains, nevertheless, the limited *supervision* of a market-led international economy. Regulation does not attempt to alter price fixing by markets or the direction of financial flows. Currency markets are left to operate broadly unhindered and exchange rates to find their own levels. Thus massive short-term speculative capital flows can still wreak havoc with well-founded national economic management objectives.

What is not considered by the current supervisory organizations is ways of checking the unhindered operation of these market processes. Here the development of 'acceptable' exchange rate bands – commensurate with Williamson-type 'economic fundamentals' – within which currencies are allowed to fluctuate would seem highly desirable (Atkinson and Kelly 1994, p. 33; Holtham 1989). This is clearly preferable to completely floating rates in the degree of certainty and stability it offers, is more attainable than completely fixed rates, and is less likely to trigger speculative activity in periods of crisis or transition (as is the case with EMS-type adjustable-peg rates). This could be considered as a new strategy of governance of markets along with the introduction by the states with major financial centres of a tax on short-term (speculative) foreign exchange trading – thereby reducing the possible gains from simply specializing in the recycling of money.

As suggested by Tobin (1978; 1994) and Eichengreen et al. (1995), a small transactions tax on the purchase and sale of foreign exchange would 'throw sand in the wheels of international finance' without necessarily preventing long-term investment or indeed all speculative activity. As has been emphasized by Holtham (1995, pp. 244–5) and Kenen (1995, p. 189), some speculation is warranted since it genuinely works to reduce risks, stabilizing currencies and reducing volatility. The issue is to prevent speculative activity for its own sake, and while 'target zones' might be useful in conjunction with a tax, other measures can also be considered to isolate the purely 'super-speculative' element in foreign exchange dealing. One way to tackle this would be for national authorities to legally limit the financial institutions allowed to engage in such activity, so that the smaller number of players can be more easily monitored. In addition, this raises the connected issue of how to prevent 'spillovers' from one market into another. An increasingly interdependent financial system can mean the rapid 'lateral' spread of problems from one financial arena into another, e.g. as with the relationship between foreign exchange markets and securities markets, as well as an increasing momentum to panics and crises. The policy response here is to erect 'fire walls' between different arenas so as to prevent spillovers, and to introduce or extend 'stops' or interruptions in trading activity to allow cooling-off periods.

These moves would go a long way to 'cool the casino'. However, their introduction is not without serious technical difficulties (Akyuz and Cornford 1995; Garber and Taylor 1995), and would require agreement between at least the G20 (but perhaps just the G3 in the case of some of these measures): this is difficult to envisage in the immediate future, but is by no means impossible in the longer run. The more thoughtful international monetary experts and central bankers are beginning to talk about a limited managed monetary multilateralism under the slogan of a 'new Bretton Woods'. Fundamentally, these issues are not 'technical' but 'political': they require a political will on the part of the leaders of the major nations. This is discussed further in the concluding chapter.

Governing trade

After the major financial markets, the second most important area of the international economy is that of trade. Here an already highly tuned regulatory regime has been firmly in place and it is not our intention to describe the development of this in any detail as it is well known. But there are a number of issues that arise in the context of the GATT treaty framework which are worth considering separately in this section.

First, the traditional liberal multilateralism of the initial phase of GATT came under increasing pressure after 1965 from two sources. One was a move towards *bilateralism* in the form of a set of negotiations and agreements between pairs or smaller groups of countries, conducted outside the formal GATT multilateral framework. The second source of tension arose with the creation of regionalized trading blocs, and particularly the 1980s and 1990s development of supra-national dispute settlement mechanisms between the EU, NAFTA and Japan. Both of these trends constitute what Yarbrough and Yarbrough (1992) have called a move towards *minilateralism*. While minilateralism does not hold to the cherished GATT cornerstone of non-discrimination and 'most favoured nation' status, neither does it necessarily abandon 'openness' in trade relationships. Thus it would be perfectly possible to have an open and liberal trading regime, but not one based upon multilateralism.

The tensions between multilateralism, bilateralism and minilateralism in international trade have yet to fully work themselves out. However, the current *modus operandi* for world trade was formalized by the second important development considered here – the conclusion of the Uruguay Round of GATT negotiations in 1994 and the formation of the World Trade Organization (WTO) in 1994–5.[7] We have discussed the issues involved in this particular set of negotiations in chapter 3. The points to emphasize here are the relative revival in the fortunes of multilateralism with the conclusion of this round, but the still lingering importance of bilateralism and minilateralism in both the way it was concluded and the difficulty experienced in the process of ratifying the

agreement. The key to bringing the negotiation to a successful conclusion, for instance, was a deal struck between the US, Japan and the
EU over agricultural issues and at the time of writing there was still no
final ratification of the Act by every one of the parties involved.

Meanwhile, in anticipation of final ratification, the WTO was formed
during 1994 to become operative sometime in 1995. The Final Act established the WTO as a fully fledged international governing institution
recognized in international law (GATT Secretariat 1993; Jackson 1994).
It brings together and supersedes the previous diverse and sometimes
ambiguous agreements, articles, codes, clauses and treaties of the entire
post-1947 GATT process, binding them into a single package. At the
same time it incorporates the agreements and articles of the Uruguay
Round: these have become mandatory on all members of the WTO by
imposing binding legal obligations on them. The result is a comprehensive bureaucratic administration of the 'rules of conduct' for undertaking
international trade, the establishment of an enlarged and streamlined
disputes mechanism, and a unified framework for future rounds of negotiations. Although this is an international organization its structure remains essentially 'representational': the members make the decisions as
representatives of their governments, and decision-making is on the
basis of various forms of majority voting (still with a number of 'escape
clauses'). Thus 'national sovereignty' would seem to be no more compro-
mised than under the old GATT procedures.

The conclusion of the Uruguay Round leaves almost as many problems for regulating world trade as it has solved. Three of the most
pressing involve agriculture, environmental standards and the protection
of Third World interests. All these in turn involve the future of the
protectionism versus free trade debate. In many ways the three issues are
interlinked through the problems confronting some of the less developed
economies in the face of the Uruguay Round. There will continue to be
legitimate objections to the appropriation of genetic engineering outputs
from agricultural experiments by advanced country firms. The potential
for distortion of Third World agricultural output towards providing for
standardized First World market demands remains. The general viability
of an environmentally sustainable agricultural system as integrative
trade pressures grow needs careful thought. In addition, the question of
continued subsidization of First World agricultural output and trade has
not been properly solved by the Uruguay Round, and this regime of
subsidy continues to characterize all the G3 players to greater or lesser
degrees.

The issue of sustainable agricultural development under the new post-
GATT regime can be seen as part of the wider problem of global environmental governance. The Uruguay Round, by strengthening the
liberalization of trade under the notions of non-discrimination and

mutual treatment, could make it harder for different and higher environmental standards to be maintained by particular nation states. The pressure could mount for these standards to be watered down or cut back altogether, under the rules for fair and non-discriminatory trade treatment (Lang and Hines 1993). More rigorous standards increase the cost of goods and services originating from a single country, and prevent the discrimination of imports from those countries that undercut in standards and costs. The environmental code of the WTO has come under considerable attack on this score, from US environmental interests in particular (though much criticism is also directed at the NAFTA agreement with Mexico). It should be remembered, however, that many Third World countries argued against the imposition or maintenance of high standards, fearing their inability to compete if these were imposed upon them.

These dilemmas have rekindled the protectionist and anti-free-trade argument (Lang and Hines 1993; Nader et al. 1994; Goldsmith 1994). There are legitimate concerns raised in this debate, which spans the political spectrum including both left and right. These concerns should not be ignored, but the solution is not, as we pointed out in chapter 3, the generalized restriction of trade, even in the name of a 'new protectionism'. Rather prosperity and growth of the world economy are more likely with an open and broadly liberal trading order. Environmental concerns can better be addressed by diverting the revenue of a growing and prosperous international economy than of a stagnant one, which would be a real danger if widespread protectionism ensued. The lessons of the 1930s are that widespread protectionism not merely helped to prevent recovery from the Depression, but promoted antagonistic and self-defeating competition between states, hardly a suitable scenario in which to protect the environment or benefit poorer and weaker economies.

The agricultural issues mentioned above would not necessarily be any better dealt with by protection either. What is needed is sensible new negotiations on terms for trade, rather than abandoning them in the name of localist autarky. Protection of specific sectors over definable periods may be justifiable at times, and this would be less damaging for individual economies in a world where trading blocs took sole responsibility for deciding this as relationships between them evolve. But, as far as possible, an open liberal trade regime is the most desirable. And it is still possible, though the revitalization of multilateralism with the setting up of the WTO may have closed off some options. Minilateral negotiations are still possible, however (and if circumstances dictate, nation states will make them possible by overriding the strict multilateralism of the WTO). Minilateralism may provide a better basis upon which to tackle some of the problems identified above (e.g. the case of agricultural subsidies, where negotiations between just the big three could produce results). Trilateral and bilateral forms of open economy negotiations have provided powerful levers for a wider trade liberalization in the past (Oye 1994, pp. 156–61).

Finally in this section a caveat needs to be introduced on much of the above discussion. The way the issue is set up corresponds to the traditional notion that international trade takes place 'in the open' as it were between national states. However, as was pointed out in chapter 3, up to a third of international trade is actually carried out within the boundaries of MNCs: it is intra-MNC trade. This raises a whole new set of problems, associated as much with the general regulation of international businesses as with international trade itself. The issues explored in this sub-section are not necessarily made redundant by this observation: they remain vitally important even in an environment where it is companies that are conducting trade internally. It is issues like 'transfer pricing', international accounting conventions, tax and profit declaration procedures that arise in the new context. Such issues are probably better tackled in a multilateral negotiating environment like the General Agreement on International Business (GAIB) framework discussed in the next section.

The regulation of FDI and of labour migration

The international management of FDI was raised and discussed in chapter 3. There we considered two possible approaches to governance: either the development of a multilateral and multinational approach via something like a parallel organization to the GATT/WTO, a GAII or a GAIB; or a progression along more functionally specific lines to negotiate over specific aspects of international direct investment in separate forums. In addition, the minilateralist option of bilateral or trilateral (G3) bargaining was also raised in chapter 3.

This is an area where strengthening the international public policy regime is most pressing, given the dramatic growth of FDI and its increasing strategic importance for the future shape of the international economy. Much of the recent policy moves here have been designed to increase market access and further liberalize FDI flows, particularly in the case of service sector investment (e.g. the OECD Code on Liberalization of Capital Movements). One possibility would be to push this trend further by explicit public policy of the major states – to extend the range and cover of FDI liberalization moves. This would mean the further extension of essentially *ad hoc* initiatives, developing the existing patchwork of bilateral and trilateral agreements while attaching any remaining genuine multilateral issues to the WTO framework (Julius 1994). On the other hand those who see the problem of inconsistency in the regulation of FDI emerging, who are worried about partial coverage, and who see the need for a deeper coordination on specifically FDI matters – which is not necessarily associated just with further liberalization – have pressed for the multilateral option and the development of a new institutional structure (Bergsten 1994). However, neither of these approaches sees the problem as one of redirecting FDI flows on a global basis, so that it not only moves toward those countries at present disadvantaged in terms of flows and amounts, but is also directed toward investment in specific sectors at present starved of such funds.

This discussion of FDI regulation has so far concerned only possible international cooperative moves. We have left out of account policy initiatives that might be made at the purely domestic level. There exists a generalized feeling among political radicals and extreme globalization theorists that little can be done here: the left in particular sees TNCs as predatory and beyond the control of any particular government. However, as we saw in chapter 4, this attitude is unnecessarily pessimistic; it is also politically disarming and needs to be challenged. The bulk of the business activity of international companies remains specific to country of origin. One modest but realistic possibility is the institution of a system of national monitoring of the activity of home-based MNCs (Bailey et al. 1994). Countries like the UK have no such monitoring structure, though to a greater or lesser extent it is common in other comparable advanced countries. Bailey et al.'s suggestion is to institute, develop or strengthen these forms of enquiry across the advanced world, so that they at least provide good quality information and analysis on what the exact impact of both inward and outward investment is on an economy.[8] Their proposal is to set this in an elaborate social accounting framework, which could be extended to incorporate the general business issues mentioned above in connection with intra-MNC trade. This would then form the basis for developing consensus policy measures, both between the major nation states and domestically, to tackle any adverse effects so identified. Given our results in chapter 4, the option for regulating MNCs in this way remains a distinct possibility, particularly since they are unlikely to quit their national bases. It would provided a further example of Kapstein's (1994) 'international cooperation based upon home country control'.

Another approach towards dealing with MNCs at the national level – an approach that attempts to neutralize any of their adverse consequences – is to try to 'by-pass' them by stimulating an alternative domestic-oriented sector, via the use of favourable fiscal and other incentives. The 'mutual sector', broadly conceived, fits this bill. The restrictions put on 'discrimination' in trade or investment matters by international treaties of the WTO/OECD Liberalization of Capital Movements type can be circumvented by a policy aimed solely at domestically oriented activity of a cooperative form. This type of measure would involve corporate reforms, and is best considered below in the context of stimulating local industrial initiatives, regional economic networks and the like.

Another area of economic governance that potentially at least straddles the international and the national as the appropriate level of regulation involves labour and migration matters. This is often neglected as a governance issue, but it is likely to become an increasingly important one, as the analysis of migration in chapter 2 showed.

Amongst the proposals to deal with this in an international context would be to create a new international regulatory function and to institutionalize it through an existing body like the UNHCR's International Organization for Immigration or the International Labour Organization (ILO). Such a body would then take responsibility for negotiating common standards and procedures for the migration and entry/exit of labour, dealing with questions of illegal entry, family and refugee movements, establishing fair and efficient disputes procedures, etc. The aim of such common criteria would be to avoid racism and promote at least some mobility into the First World, especially for those threatened by oppressive regimes. It could also extend the main work of the ILO, laying down common standards of employment conditions, industrial relations, etc. The existing structures in this area are extremely weak, so the attempt to build a new international migration/labour regime along these lines would prove very difficult. These are also particularly sensitive areas of economic policy-making. Until now international cooperation has been aimed more at restricting migrant movements than liberalizing them.

An alternative is to think along rather more regional or sub-regional lines. This would build on current trends and emerging arrangements, which are increasingly mirroring the regionalization of trade and investment. But even here, one suspects that handing over further policy formation and control to inter-governmental bodies would prove politically difficult. Within the EU, the most advanced of the regional configurations, developments along these lines have progressed very unevenly, particularly in respect to immigration into the Union. Thus for the foreseeable future we suspect that national governments will continue to retain their prerogative in these sensitive matters. The result will be a patchwork of differing criteria and procedures, with the likelihood of more draconian measures to try to control migration of all kinds.

Managing economic development and economic transition

The final area considered in the context of the first two of our five levels of governance involves the traditional institutional arrangements for dealing with economic development, and also the way these have expanded to deal increasingly with societies in transformation from authoritarian regimes.

Here it is the World Bank and the IMF that have been centrally involved. The Bank set the pattern for multilateral development lending to governments in the Bretton Woods era, involving its own activity and that of a set of regional development banks for Latin America, Africa and Asia. The IMF concentrated upon shorter-term assistance, mainly associated with liquidity for balance of payments crises and stabilization policies. Although the IMF was heavily involved with managing the 'petro-dollar' shocks of the 1970s, with the spread of floating exchange rates its specific role in liquidity provision has diminished, and the rationale for the IMF has been somewhat undermined. The role of the World Bank has also changed since the related 'debt crisis' period – which saw the rise in importance of commercial banks in the financing of official Third World government debt. The emergence of somewhat inward-looking regional economic configurations like the EU has also undercut many of the World Bank and IMF functions.

Both organizations have responded to these developments by looking for new policy approaches and for new areas in which to offer 'assistance'. The new approaches are signalled by a move from the centrality of the criteria of 'conditionality' in their dealings with client states to that of 'good governance', by which the World Bank basically means good public administration (World Bank 1994). The new areas were rather fortuitously offered in the form of the 'economies in transition' after 1989 (or more properly 'economies in transformation': see Thompson 1995), and the Bank and the IMF eagerly embraced these areas for the deployment of their advice and activity.

Along with the emergence of 'good governance' as a criterion for assistance, other 'softer' targets and criteria have risen in importance. Thus human development and poverty alleviation, the production of knowledge and the provision of technical assistance, and the protection of the environment have all entered the vocabulary of these organizations, alongside their traditional concerns with project finance and external resource transfers. To some extent these softer criteria have made the organizations and the activity they are there to monitor more difficult to manage. With strict 'conditionality' criteria at least the objectives of policy were clear and precise (however perniciously they were applied at times), but 'good governance' and 'human development' are imprecise, loose criteria which vary significantly between situations and are thus difficult to monitor consistently as constraints. Indeed, such criteria may give international organizations wider discretionary powers and may be more invasive of the sovereignty of member states than were the old examples of strict monetary and fiscal objectives.

The other important change in the case of the World Bank is to insist on 'trade regime neutrality' in its dealings with the newly emergent economies in transformation. Thus there has been a move away from support for either import substitution or export-led growth strategies, both of which are thought to implicate discretionary interventionist policy-making on the part of governments. This is all part of a further move towards market-led solutions to the economic problems faced by these economies.

However, formally at least, it is this new 'softer' monitoring regime that will guide these organizations in the conduct of their main business with the economies in transformation. One question posed by the change in the circumstances of their operation is whether the World Bank and the IMF should be merged into a single organization. Interestingly, in not a single area considered above has there been a proposal for the closure of an existing organization or institution, only the call to strengthen existing ones or create new ones. However, there remain real problems with the proliferation of different organizations and regimes in terms of the overlap between their jurisdictions and the coordination of their various activities: potential conflicts could develop and a mismatch of ineffectual overall governance result. The merger of the IMF with the World Bank would seem rational and would at least close one potential source of overlapping policies.

National economic governance

There can be no doubt that the combined effects of changing economic conditions and past public policies of dismantling exchange controls have made ambitious and internationally divergent strategies of national economic governance far more difficult. Also reduced has been the capacity of states to act autonomously on their societies. This is because the range of economic incentives and sanctions at the state's disposal has been restricted as a consequence of this loss of capacity to deliver distinctively 'national' economic policies.

Most obvious is the case of macroeconomic management. The case of the current impossibility of ambitious national-level Keynesian strategies hardly needs making, particularly after the failure of the French Socialist government's ambitious reflationary programme in the early 1980s. But nationally distinctive monetarist policies of an ambitious nature have proved hardly more viable. Thus the UK was saved from accelerating losses of employment and output in the early 1980s by international impacts that reduced the value of sterling against the dollar and brought down interest rates, but that had nothing to do with national policy.

If macroeconomic management is problematic, so too is that supply-side alternative, a centralized state-directed industrial policy. Technologies are currently changing too rapidly for the state, however competent and well informed its officials, to 'pick winners' on a national basis. Moreover, the population of firms that the state would have to bring into such a policy is less stable and easy to interact with than it was in the 1960s. Many major products are now the result of complex inter-firm partnerships. Changed economic conditions favour risk-sharing between firms, diversification and flexibility, and put a premium on specialist and local knowledge. These are factors that traditional state institutions and uniform systems of industrial administration find it hard to cope with.

Despite the foregoing, national governmental policies to sustain economic performance remain important, even if their methods and functions have changed. This is true even when states are part of a supra-national entity. In the EU the free movement of capital, labour, goods and services from the end of 1992, monetary union as provided by the Maastricht Treaty, and greater political integration as envisaged after the next inter-governmental conference scheduled to begin in 1996, must obviously restrict some hitherto important areas of specifically national economic management. But they will make others more important – giving a new significance to non-monetarist fiscal and supply-side policies, for instance.

While national governments may no longer be 'sovereign' economic regulators in the traditional sense, they remain political communities with extensive powers to influence and to sustain economic actors within their territories. Technical top-down macroeconomic management is now less important. However, the role of government as a facilitator and orchestrator of private economic actors has become more salient as a consequence. The *political* role of government is central in the new forms of economic management. As we shall see in chapter 7, neither the financial markets nor the Commission officials in Brussels – to take the case of the most developed supra-national economic association, the EU – can impose or secure the forms of social cohesion and the policies that follow from them in the way that national governments can. National governments can still *compensate* for the effects of internationalization and for the continued volatility of the financial markets, even if they cannot unilaterally control those effects or prevent that volatility

Before going into more detailed political orchestrational features of national policy, let us look at the more overtly economic character of (non-monetarist) fiscal policy. Fiscal policy has been in the shadow of monetary policy ever since the demise of Keynesianism. During the late 1970s and the 1980s it became very difficult to argue for an 'independent' fiscal policy, one that was both nationally autonomous and independent of monetary policy. However, things may be now about to change.

One thing closer economic and monetary union within Europe (and more generally, the relative 'cooling of the casino' internationally) could do is to help 'disengage' fiscal from monetary policy once again. Take the case of the EU. The closer monetary union becomes, the more individual countries could engage in independent fiscal policies. This does not mean that they will be totally free to do as they wish on the fiscal front. The post-Maastricht guidelines for government fiscal balances, for instance, were quite tight (around 3 per cent of GDP). But these are only meant to be guidelines and in practice they may be quite flexible (more flexible than monetary guidelines for instance, which are to be under the direction of an 'independent' European central bank). Thus, as decisions on monetary policy are increasingly taken elsewhere, i.e. centrally, individual governments will be able to decide their own fiscal policies relatively independently of monetary policy. This could enable some quite innovative fiscal responses as a result. Any new fiscal regime will also be operating in an environment of increasing financial and labour market integration, and this would need to be taken into account by policy-makers.

The problem this will pose is how to develop tax systems that minimize both the incentives to avoid individual national taxes and the ability to do so. Broadly speaking the need is to think in terms of factor mobility in relationship to taxation. Capital and money markets will probably integrate most rapidly and thoroughly, so there may be little scope for nationally differential corporation taxes or taxes on savings (via taxes on savings institutions). Nationally differential taxes on domestic consumption may also be difficult, but here it depends upon how internationally mobile purchasers are in the face of tax rates. Will they be prepared to travel long distances just to save tax differences? Thus there may be more scope here.[9] In the case of income taxes again this depends upon how integrated labour markets become. Clearly there are likely to be degrees of integration. A lot of work overseas is temporary. But in general the highest paid and the lowest paid tend to be the potentially most internationally mobile. In the case of indigenous EU workers, cultural and linguistic barriers may still be high in terms of labour mobility, and a lot will depend upon how quickly and efficiently mutual recognition of professional qualifications and standards develops. In general there may still be some scope for differential income taxes before (dis)incentive effects become rife and undermine the effectiveness of these. The most immobile factor is likely to remain property of one kind or another. People cannot just up and away with their houses for instance. Thus there may be some innovative scope for new forms of property taxes as this becomes an increasingly attractive source of tax revenues for governments.

One other significant area where new revenue-raising strategies may be available to national states and to subsidiary governments is energy consumption and environmental pollution (Hewitt 1990). Taxes on non-renewable energy consumption and the widespread adoption of the 'polluter pays' principle through taxes on industrial emissions, vehicle use, etc. may well be the major sources of revenue of the future. Such taxes have three advantages: they have less of a stigma for international financial markets than direct taxation (mainly because they have not yet been factored into the market-makers' calculations); they appear to be more acceptable to citizens than taxes on income; and they serve the dual purpose of raising revenue and forcing both firms and final consumers to internalize the environmental costs of their actions. Thus energy taxes seem to offer one of the best ways of decoupling fiscal and monetary policy and attaining a measure of autonomy in revenue raising.

Returning to the general theme of the nation state in regulating the economy, there are three key functions it can perform which stem from its role as orchestrator of an economic consensus within a given community. States are not like markets: they are communities of fate which tie together actors who share certain common interests in the success or failure of their national economies. Markets may or may not be international, but wealth and economic prosperity are still essentially national phenomena. They depend upon how well national economic actors can work together to secure certain key supply-side outcomes. National policy can provide certain key inputs to economic performance that cannot be bought or traded on the market. Markets need to be embedded in social relations. Political authority remains central in assuring that markets are appropriately institutionalized and that the non-market conditions of economic success are present. National governments thus remain a crucial element in the economic success of their societies – providing cohesion, solidarity and certain crucial services that markets of themselves cannot (Hutton 1995).

The three key functions of states are as follows. First, the state, if it is to influence the economy, must construct a *distributional coalition*: that is, it must win the acceptance of key economic actors and the organized social interests representing them for a sustainable distribution of national income and expenditure which promotes competitive manufacturing performance (amongst other things). The major components of such a coalition are: the balance of national income devoted respectively to consumption and investment; a broad agreement on the level of taxation necessary to sustain state investment in infrastructure, training and collective services for industry; and a framework for controlling wage settlements, the growth of credit and levels of dividends such that inflation is kept within internationally tolerable limits.

Second, for such a distributional coalition to be possible the state must perform another function, that is, the *orchestration of social consensus*. Such coalitions only work when they emerge from a political culture that balances collaboration and competition and in which the major organized interests are accustomed to bargain over national economic goals, to make ongoing commitments to determine policy by such bargaining, and to police their members' compliance with such bargains. Industry, organized labour and the state can be related in various ways, perhaps much less rigidly than the highly structured national corporatism practised in states like West Germany and Sweden into the 1990s. The point is to ensure that the key components of the economic system are in dialogue, that firms cooperate as well as compete, and that different factors of production relate in other than just market terms, i.e. labour and management and capital providers and firms. Such systems will not be devoid of conflict, nor will interests be wholly compatible, but there will be mechanisms for resolving such differences. Such an overall consensus can only work if it is also keyed in with the effective operation of more specific resource allocation mechanisms, such as the system of wage determination and the operation of capital markets.

Third, the state must achieve an adequate balance in the distribution of its fiscal resources and its regulatory activities between the national, regional and municipal *levels of government*. The centralization of EU policy is promoting the increasing importance of effective regional government. The regional provision of education and training, industrial finance, collective services for industry and social services is gaining in importance. Regional governments are more able to assess the needs of industry because they possess more localized, and therefore accurate, information and because they are of a scale where the key actors can interact successfully. Regional government must be seen not as something inherently opposed to national economic management, but as a crucial component of it. It is the national state which determines the constitutional position, powers and fiscal resources of lower tiers of government. Those national states which allow a considerable measure of autonomy to regional governments tend to have the best and most effective supply-side regulation at the regional level. In a European context Germany and Italy offer obvious examples. The most prosperous *Länder*, like Baden-Württemberg and Bavaria, or the most successful Italian regions, like Emilia-Romagna, have achieved a high level of devolution of the tasks of economic management (Sabel 1989).

The main problem about the ways in which nation states continue to have a salience as a locus of economic management is that such activities now depend on social attitudes and institutions that are not equally available to all states. The new mechanisms of economic coordination and regulation give primacy to the high level of social cohesion and cooperation that the state can both call upon and develop. The new methods of national economic regulation in a more internationalized economy are not, for example, like Keynesianism, that is, a technique of macroeconomic management that was in principle available to every substantial and competently administered modern state if it chose to adopt such a strategy. Rather the new methods rest on specific ensembles of social institutions and these are more difficult to adopt or transfer by deliberate choice. States are thus in considerable measure trapped by the legacies of social cohesion that they inherit. Countries like the USA cannot just decide to adopt the more solidaristic and coordinative relations between industry, labour and the state that have hitherto prevailed in Germany and Japan (Albert 1993).

This means that between blocs and within blocs there will be fundamental differences in the ability to respond to competitive pressures and changing international conjunctures. Those societies that have emphasized short-term market performance, like the UK and the USA, are threatened by the competitive pressures of societies that have concentrated on enhancing long-term manufacturing competitiveness and have had the social cohesion to achieve it, like Germany and Japan, and also by newly industrializing societies following similar strategies like South Korea or Singapore. The political process and the interest group culture in societies like the UK and the USA do not favour rapid adaptation in a more cooperative direction: rather they emphasize competition and the dumping of social costs on those who are both least organized or influential and least able to bear them. This tends to push such societies away from effective international or bloc cooperation. The USA, unlike its role between 1945 and 1972, will refuse to bear any substantial level of cost to secure a more stable international environment: it will pursue narrow and short-term considerations of national advantage. The UK will seek to minimize European integration and to trade down standards of social welfare and occupational protection to a lowest common denominator.

It might appear in one sense as if the less solidaristic and more market-oriented societies like the UK or the USA may actually have an *advantage* in a more internationalized economy where national-based economic governance is less effective. British and American firms are used to putting competition before cooperation and to fending for themselves in the face of narrowly self-interested financial institutions. Not only are activist macroeconomic management and a centralized state-directed industrial policy increasingly obsolete, but also a range of social and economic changes, and not just the internationalization of major markets, are making national uniform systems of corporatist intermediation more difficult to sustain. Industrial structures and divisions of labour are becoming more complex and differentiated throughout the advanced industrial world. Large, highly concentrated national firms with stable and highly unionized manual workforces are becoming less salient (Kern and Sabel 1994). Thus countries like Japan and Germany will find that their (very different) national systems of corporatist coordination are less and less representative of industry and, therefore, less effective.

There is a good deal of truth in this argument, but it does not go to sustain the conclusion that less solidaristic countries will actually *benefit* from the changed conditions. It is difficult to see how the future of complex social systems, including investment in manufacturing, training, and public infrastructure, can be left in the hands of firms that compete but cannot cooperate and to the workings of weakly regulated markets alone. In fact, societies like Japan and Germany will continue to enjoy major competitive advantages even if their national systems of corporatist representation decline, precisely because their forms of non-market economic governance are diverse and multi-layered. In both countries strong patterns of cooperation and solidarity *within* firms and effective forms of governance through regional institutions or patterns of inter-firm cooperation continue to give them advantages in supplementing and sustaining market performance. The general functions performed by political authority in promoting competition and coordination remain important, even if some of the means by which they have been delivered heretofore are changing.

Regional economic governance

The growing importance of regional economies and industrial districts and the contribution to their continued success of public and private forms of local economic governance are now well recognized (Sabel 1989; Zeitlin 1992). It is not our purpose here to discuss such regional economies and their diverse forms of governance in and of themselves. Rather we consider why such forms of local regulation have become important in a more internationalized economic environment, and how they can help societies to cope with the competitive pressures and market shocks of a more open economic system.

The major reason for the re-emergence of regional economies at the very point when many markets and manufacturers internationalized is the changing structure of industry, especially the increasing importance of more diversified and flexible production, and, as a consequence, the continued survival and growth of small and medium enterprises. Flexible forms of production can cope with shifting and volatile patterns of international demand. Populations of smaller firms sharing work and collective services, or in partnership with larger ones, are more able to resist market shocks and adapt to rapid changes than are large hierarchically organized firms. Large firms themselves are changing: entering into partnerships with other firms, diversifying internally, reducing hierarchy and layers of management (Moss Kanter 1989; Sabel 1991). In the period of national economic management large firms could expect to supply growing national markets with standard industrial goods. Such management was supposed to smooth out the economic cycle and promote full employment and industrial growth. Firms could, therefore, at least in theory, plan for long runs and adopt relatively inflexible mass production methods (Piore and Sabel 1984). The new production strategies and the increasing importance of regional economies are thus in part a direct response to the internationalization of markets in manufacturing goods and the complex and changing patterns of demand bought about by servicing diverse markets in a period of volatile trading conditions and uncertain growth. The point to emphasize is that both large and small firms are less exposed and more secure in cooperative relationships: partnerships that share expertise and risk in the case of small firms, industrial districts that provide the cost advantages of collective services and the benefits of cooperation with other firms, for example in work sharing (Lorenz 1989; 1992).

Public governance of an appropriate kind clearly reinforces the advantages of a closely integrated population of firms in a region or district. An industrial 'public sphere' (Hirst and Zeitlin 1989) provides an industrial district or region with the means to anticipate and respond to change, to reconcile cooperation and competition, and to restructure both production and common services in a way difficult for a less organized and articulated population of firms. Public governance, especially in partnership with private governance institutions like trade associations, is thus important in protecting regions against external shocks and in responding to major changes in trading conditions. It is clearly the case that some national states are better able to sustain such regional governance institutions and some regions are more capable of responding to the needs of their local economy than others. In this respect societies like the UK are singularly disadvantaged (Zeitlin 1994).

Another significant aspect of regional economies in the context of an internationalized economy is as a means of responding to the perceived threat of capital mobility. One way of responding to remote financial institutions that invest across the globe as economic advantage dictates is to build up a financial sector dedicated to industrial finance and governed by public policy. Such low-cost finance is unlikely to be well founded unless its disbursement is based on local knowledge; nor is the public likely to invest in such institutions unless the investment both carries low risk and brings a distinct advantage in work and output to their own locality. For these reasons such an alternative financial sector is likely to be closely linked to regional economic governance and to local economies. Such alternative institutions, combined with other forms of public governance at the regional level, and a population of firms strongly rooted in and oriented to the locality, could result in very robust decentralized economic systems relatively independent of wider capital markets, but capable of trading effectively. This model has much to recommend it both as a means of reversing industrial decline and as a way of protecting successful industrial districts from the full ravages of international competition (Hirst 1993). The regional level of governance is capable of a good deal of development, and, for the wider national society, such experimentation at local level is less risky than ambitious centralised state-sponsored investments in a few key main technologies or major initiatives of national institutional reform. Provided the national state is not actively hostile to such local governance then, of the five levels outlined above, the regional is probably capable of the most rapid enhancement. Such extensions of effective regional economic governance would, in consequence, secure advanced industrial societies at the local level against at least some effects of increased international openness.

7

The European Union as a Trade Bloc

This chapter is a bridge between the general discussion of the possibilities of economic governance in the preceding chapter and the consideration of the wider political issues in the one that follows. The role of the European Union is central because it is at one and the same time the most developed and the most complexly structured of the major trade blocs. The evolution of the EU's capacities for coordinated common action by its member states will determine to a considerable degree whether the governance of the world economy is strong or minimalist.

As we have seen, trade blocs represent a vital intermediate level between general institutionalized governance mechanisms for the world economy as a whole, such as the WTO, and the economic policies of the nation states. The Triad of the EU, Japan and NAFTA currently dominates the world economy, and it is likely to account for a majority share of the world manufacturing output, world trade and FDI for a long time to come. The Triad could, therefore, effectively control the direction of the world economy if it chose to act in concert. Loosely organized trade blocs with mutually incompatible interests will inevitably lead to minimal (if still vitally necessary) governance, patching up the existing world institutions and engaging in periodic crisis avoidance measures. The strong governance of the world economy towards ambitious goals (such as promoting employment in the advanced countries and raising output and incomes in the developing world) requires a highly coordinated policy on the part of the members of the Triad. If they did embrace such ambitious goals and devise the governance mechanisms to fulfil them, then they could impose a new tripartite 'hegemony' on world financial markets, international regulatory bodies, and other nation states comparable to that exercised by the USA between 1945 and 1973. It is just not the case that any attempt to further regulate the international financial system by the means discussed in the previous chapter, for instance, would immediately be undermined by the 'flight' of that business to new 'offshore' locations because those locations could be quickly put out of business if there were the political will to do so. The preconditions for such coordination are that the three component parts of the Triad remain roughly equal with one another in their share of world GDP, that they find a common doctrine of governance, and that each bloc develops the internal consistency needed for external action.

There is a significant degree of asymmetry between the three components of the Triad. The EU is the most ambitious project of multinational economic governance in the modern world, but it is still far from being completed. It has major problems of internal articulation and different perceptions of its future evolution that currently restrict its capacity for concerted external action. NAFTA is dominated by the USA, and Japan is a bloc-sized economy within a nation state: both are thus less ambitious in their governance strategies and more like traditional political entities. Given that Japan and the USA could agree on a common agenda and each obtain internal support for it, then they could coordinate policy in much the same way as nation states have done in the past. The EU's problem is to reconcile divergent interests within itself and to settle the course of development of its own institutions.

The European Union as a political entity

The European Union's capacities for effective economic governance are closely tied to the further development of its political institutions. Such development is confronted with two serious difficulties. One of these is that the EU is a new venture for which pre-existing political models are of little use in guiding its evolution. The other and most important is that there are substantial differences in economic performance, social standards and, therefore, political interests between the component countries.

The Union is not and will not.become a nation state writ large. Its development cannot be modelled on a continental-sized centralized federal state like the USA. Rather the Union is a new kind of political entity to which the conventional constitutional categories do not readily apply. Such categories have been derived from the institutions of the nation state: at the most basic level, the sovereignty of the principal legislature and the accountability of the central executive to that legislature. In contrast to this, the Union has no single and sovereign source of law, nor does it possess a central multi-functional executive that is democratically accountable through a single channel to representatives of the people (Harden 1994).

The Union is far from resembling the constitutional forms of a nation state. Many of the Union's powers derive from treaties between the member states. Much of its legislation depends on incorporating common framework initiatives at the level of the member states, and it also depends on the executive branches of those states to carry out common policies. The system of common decision-making still depends to a great degree on agreements between national governments and the relatively secret and nationally unaccountable deliberations of the Council of Ministers. Europe's nation states retain many distinct and important governmental functions and the nations have distinct languages, cultural traditions and legal systems that will continue to make complete European integration impossible. Even if a common foreign and security policy is developed after 1996, it would depend on the majority decision of the representatives of the member states and would require the donation of nationally controlled and funded military units to support common policies. The Union, even if considerable further political integration takes place after the next inter-governmental conference in 1996, will never become a political entity that remotely resembles the old national states.

Yet it would be wrong to over-emphasize the political weakness of the European Union. The Union *has* displaced the national states in a number of areas of governance. The states are no longer 'sovereign' entities, as they once claimed to be. The European Parliament, especially after the Maastricht Treaty of European Union, does exercise certain important legislative and accountability functions. The Commission plays an important role in creating legislative initiatives, consulting on major policies across Europe, and directly exercising certain regulatory powers and supervising others as carried out at national level. Those aspects of European legislation giving implementation to the single market take precedence over national legislation and thus radically abridge national legislature sovereignty with respect to certain functions. Europe's peoples are, after the Maastricht Treaty, common citizens of the Union and enjoy certain supra-national rights guaranteed and overseen by a superior judiciary.

The Union thus fits into no established constitutional schema. It is not like a unitary, a federal or a confederal state: rather it could best be called an ongoing association of states with certain functionally specific governance functions exercised by a common public power. Thus it is *not* a state. It should be seen as a complex polity made up of common institutions, member states, and peoples. There is both strength and weakness in this newly evolved, very distinctive and slightly cumbersome structure: strength because it minimizes the conflicts that occur when one set of institutions is to have primacy, as when an attempt is made to build a unitary state from diverse political institutions; and in the short term, serious weakness because such a complex association limits the rapid development of certain very necessary common governance functions.

The point is that Europe's political evolution will have to build on and make a virtue of this complexity. One cannot, as some enthusiastic 'federalists' imagined in the late 1980s, scale up to the European-level national forms of government and accountability. The European Parliament cannot be expanded into a superior legislature and national assemblies reduced to the role of subordinate authorities in a national state: it is just not an omnicompetent sovereign body and it lacks the common legitimacy to exercise such functions. Likewise the Commission cannot evolve into a European Executive, primarily answerable to the Strasbourg Parliament and taking precedence over national governments. Political development is most likely to be successful if it concentrates on enhancing the common decision-making procedures of the association of states, rather than by seeking to supplant national-level political institutions. Both Union and national levels can gain in authority and governance capacity if they can cooperate and coordinate; as we shall see in chapter 8 it is by no means the case that 'sovereignty' is a fixed quantum and that what one agency gains in governance capacity must be at the expense of another. It is time the old Bodinian view of sovereignty was buried, along with the conceptions of exclusive governmental powers on which it is based (Bodin 1576).

The European Union's national states continue to have a vital role. They remain a crucial locus of political legitimacy and democratic accountability without which the Union would find it impossible to function. National-level politics and citizen identification remain compelling in a way that, for the foreseeable future, European politics and a common European identity will not be. But this strength of the Union's member nations can be turned to positive advantage in the governance of the Union. Too rapid a development of Europe's central institutions might in fact threaten their legitimacy, leading to justified fears of remote, technocratic and unaccountable government.

National politicians too readily see their role, if they are democrats, as protesting at the institutional defects of the EU and, if they are pragmatists, as bargaining for the best narrowly self-interested deal for their nation within its councils. Democratic radicals, especially MEPs and their advisers, raise the spectre of a 'democratic deficit' at the centre of the Union. This criticism has some force to the degree that bureaucratic and technocratic conceptions of policy-making have predominated among Europe's elites. But this view is mistaken when such critics see the problem as being *like* that of a lack of accountability within the nation state but on a bigger scale, and as being capable of remedy by political mechanisms derived from the national level and scaled up to the European. On the contrary, democracy and accountability can best be bolstered by seeing the EU as a polity in which the nation states are the most significant sources for the representation of the people *at the European level*. Some of this enhanced accountability can be quickly achieved, without large structural changes, but providing there are significant changes in attitude on the part of Europe's politicians. Thus greater majority decision-making by representatives of the member states in the common councils of the Union will require both MEPs and national ministers to perceive and to exercise their roles as 'continental electors' in a wider polity (a notion we will develop further toward the end of chapter 8).

To facilitate this the role of the Council of Ministers and the scope of majority decision-making within it needs to be enhanced and made constitutionally explicit as the principal thrust of political union. The decisions of the Council and the deliberations of the Parliament need to be made transparent to Europe's citizens. The actions and votes of national ministers in the Council need to be more fully debated and made known to the Parliaments of the member states so that they are directly accountable to national elected representatives. Ministers have to recognize that their actions when they speak and vote in Brussels are no longer inter-governmental, but *governmental*. They have to think and act as national representatives in a supra-national forum, shaping policy in a constitutionally ordered association of states.

This is not a Euro-sceptical argument. The EU could not long remain a weakly structured association of nation states and not suffer the consequences of weak and partial governance of a continental-scale economy (Hirst 1995). Strong government is not, however, necessarily centralized and exclusive government. Strength can be had by consultation, coordination and division of labour in governance functions. The great danger in Europe is of competition between nation states and conflict between them over common policy. This will lead to both overlapping and conflicting competencies and 'gaps' in the scope of governance. Capacities for governance vanish into these gaps and diminish the competing powers, weakening exclusively self-interested governments at the *national* level because of failures of effective control at the European level. The creation of a single market and the continuing concentration and integration of production at the European level have created phenomena that can be neither governed by national-based policies nor left to the working of unregulated markets. Weak common and cooperative governance by the national states at the European level will lead to bitter and divisive struggles between unevenly performing and competing national economies over those dimensions of policy that states acting alone can no longer control. Euro-sceptics who want to reduce the Union to a loosely structured free-trade area and localist dissenters who seek to reduce the governance powers of the Union by turning the doctrine of 'subsidiarity' against Brussels thus threaten not only the project of the Union but the powers of their own national states over large areas of economic life. European economic governance needs to be extended, and it cannot be done by creating a super-state. Instead such extension will involve a division of labour across national and regional governments, cooperating with Union institutions with considerable power but limited functions.

One of the main problems of responding coherently to these issues is the paucity of political thinking to span the gap between the global and the national. The extreme theorists of globalization are particularly pernicious in this respect because they argue that there is no need to try: they deny both the need for strong supra-national governance and the possibility of national-level action. They are pessimists of the intellect and of the will. The need to develop a balance of powers between the regional, national and Union levels of governance in Europe highlights the fact that there is no commonly accepted theory of the art of government required to practise such distribution, and therefore no compelling model of an institutional architecture to replace those derived from nation states. This is one reason why the debates on the political future of Europe are so difficult and the terms so confused, and why so many people are arguing at cross-purposes.

In fact such a theory is not that difficult to develop, once the issues are clearly recognized, nor do Europe's states lack some common grounds for action despite conflicting national interests. But cooperation between states in the Union, necessary to make it an effective polity of states, can only be refocused if there is some strong common basis for action. The most obvious one is that of Europe's relations with the rest of the world. As a common voice shaping an emerging agenda of international governance Europe would have a basis for cohesion, balancing cooperation and competition between its component national interests in the course of pursuing a strategy that attempted to promote cooperation between the major players in the world economy towards common goals. Its role in the GATT negotiations shows that this international orientation as a source of internal unity is by no means well developed, but also that it is possible. The easiest way for Europe to be united externally is as a competing and protectionist trade bloc, opposed to NAFTA and Japan. Such a focus of unity would be negative, would favour conservative forces in Europe, and would be highly destructive of any project for extended international governance. A more open and extended agenda towards the external world, promoting stability in an open international economy, will be more difficult to pursue but it is essential. Europe would ultimately gain from such re-regulation of the international economy and could also gain internal coherence by such external concerted action.

Centripetal and centrifugal forces in Europe

We must now turn to the substantive sources of conflict and the potentials for extended governance in the Union. It was clear even before the prolonged ratification crisis of the Maastricht Treaty and the beginning of a period of intense turbulence in the ERM in 1992 that European integration was at a point of balance between powerful centripetal and centrifugal forces. The centrifugal forces are recent and significant. They are to be found in the collapse of a unifying external adversary, the decline of political homogeneity, and the faltering of prosperity. The European Community was created in the shadow of the Soviet threat. This set limits to the political divergence of European states. The Community was not coterminous with NATO – it had its neutralist members like Ireland, and France had withdrawn from military commitments to NATO – but the Soviet threat both unified Western Europe and linked it to the USA. Until 1989 the EC had clear political limits: it was a *Western* European entity. Now the future of 'Europe' is an open question, and the European Union's development is threatened by a potentially fatal conflict of interests between those who wish to deepen its institutions and those who wish to widen its boundaries.

The second of the centrifugal forces is the most ominous from a liberal internationalist perspective. Since the late 1940s Europe has been dominated by a political spectrum from centre right to centre left. The exclusion of and containment of the far left will continue. The threat to political homogeneity comes from the right and from new non-ideological regionalist parties. The latter are often no great challenge except to their national states, since they are centrist in policy – like Britain's separatist Scottish National Party (SNP). The far right are another matter. Their nationalism has two faces. It is anti-immigrant, and currently predominantly directed against non-EU migrants. But it also defines the benefits of membership of the European Union in 'national' terms and therefore limits the scope of possible European cooperation by such parties to a free-trade area. Europe is for them an economic convenience, not the source of a new kind of political identity or a new level of political legitimacy. Legitimacy for Le Pen, for example, as he made clear in the 1992 French referendum on Maastricht, is a matter of adherence to 'national' interests. Such ultra-nationalist forces must in practice be hostile to the goal of ever closer union, whereas some of the regionalist parties or smaller nationalist parties like the SNP are, by contrast, strongly in favour of European integration.

The fundamental factor sustaining the rise of the far right, and therefore the decline in political homogeneity, is unlikely to diminish in importance in the next decade. That factor is immigration. These pressures against immigrants are likely to intensify if economic failure in Eastern Europe and continuing poverty in Africa lead to strong tendencies toward attempted economic migration to Europe. A new 'wall' to keep the poor out would be a wretched irony after the collapse of the old fortified frontiers in the East. Such a tight immigration policy may be the price the political centre will be faced with and be willing to pay to contain the far right and exclude them from office.

The most serious of the centrifugal forces is the prospect that Europe has lost its greatest unifier and pacifier, economic growth and prosperity. Until the recession which began in earnest in 1991 the European Community as a whole has not suffered a serious and prolonged interruption of growth since the founding Treaty of Rome was signed in 1957. Integration of member states into the Community has been achieved without serious national costs. All states have experienced rising output and rising real incomes, and some, like Italy and Spain, have made spectacular leaps toward the first rank of the advanced industrial countries. However, if growth slows across Europe for structural rather than conjunctural reasons, and if the divergences in economic performance within the Union become even more marked, then the pressures toward national protective measures would grow. These pressures are unlikely to be for tariff barriers *within* Europe. Within the Union there may be competitive devaluations, pressures toward reversing the common competition policy (which is to reduce state aids to industry) and aspirations for greater independence in fiscal policy than the process of monetary union would allow. If Europe does suffer from relative economic failure this may lead to pressure for the creation of protective tariff walls against major and threatening competitors outside the Union, like Japan and South Korea. In fact if Japan, in particular, remains far more competitive and resistant to European imports, Europe might actually *gain* in the short run from exclusionary measures and strengthening its role as a trade bloc. The far right might have a certain economic logic to bolster their chauvinism. The nationalist far right is not wedded to economic liberalism, and should another major crisis occur, its advocacy of national protective measures will press centrist politicians toward divergence from the common European objectives outlined at Maastricht and from the new GATT regime.

Europe is still at the point where a great deal of institutional work needs to be done to complete effective economic integration. Yet at a primitive economic level, as a single market, integration *is* virtually irreversible. It will also be almost impossible to unscramble the effects of common citizenship of the Union and extremely difficult to reimpose national limits on work and residence. The creation of common economic citizenship as part of market openness has thus eroded a central component of national sovereignty. Those British Conservative politicians who support the notion of Europe as a 'free market' but oppose the erosion of 'national sovereignty' are caught in a fundamental contradiction: the measures needed to ensure the free movement of goods, capital and labour will inevitably remove crucial powers from Europe's nation states.

There are also centripetal forces in Europe, as well as sources of strain and divergence. Crudely put, the Union's national states have lost the effective capacity to serve as regulators over certain vital dimensions of economic activity, for which regional governments are even less effective. But the central institutions of the Union have not acquired the political capacity to exercise those economic functions. This functional imbalance will put continuing pressure on both national policies and the institutions of the EU. How such an imbalance can be resolved is another matter.

Hitherto it was assumed by most pro-Europeans that economic integration would inevitably draw political union in its wake. Now, on the contrary, it is becoming clear that effective economic governance of the EU depends on major institutional reforms. It is now clear that there is no inevitable and automatic economic logic that will unite Europe. The creation of the single market has not yet given the boost to growth across Europe that some enthusiasts hoped, nor will market openness in itself reduce inter-regional inequality. It is also the case that the reverse is not true. The construction of new forms of political legitimacy for European institutions would not of itself ensure effective economic governance. Rather that legitimacy, even if it could be achieved, will be wasted unless political union *does* transform the European economies. Effective political union cannot ultimately be built out of a series of states and regions with radically divergent economic performances. A Europe of 'tiers' cannot be either economically integrated or politically united. The differences over substantive policy issues will in that case tear the political union apart. Political union will be blighted from the start for the economic losers if it promises to do nothing for them and if the existing forms of economic integration simply expose them to the competitive pressures of the winners. Such economic divergence, if it continues, will threaten to fragment the Union into a united prosperous core and a poor and marginalized periphery.

The issue is not just the integration of markets or the transfer of national regulatory functions upwards to EU institutions, but the creation of new mechanisms, objectives and policies of economic governance appropriate to the level of the Union as a whole. The EU is an agency of economic governance of continental dimensions. It has, therefore, the potential to do things medium-sized nation states like France and Italy cannot, but also it cannot effectively and efficiently perform certain governance functions that nation states traditionally have done.

The question remains one of a balance between regional, national and EU economic regulation.

The issue of monetary union

Monetary policy provides a striking example of this contradiction between the need for integration and the impossibility of merely scaling up national policies and institutions. The Maastricht Treaty envisages that the outcome of European monetary union (EMU) will be a politically independent central bank that will direct monetary policy and operate without direct accountability to national economic policy-makers. It would in effect pursue the same economic priorities as the Bundesbank: exchange rate stability and an anti-inflationary policy. The problem is such that a central bank and a single currency can only exist after a period of real economic 'convergence'. It is now widely recognized that many of the Union's national economies cannot meet the convergence criteria. The last thing Europe will need as it approaches the new century and comes out of a recession is a widespread deflationary dose of Euro-monetarism in order to create a single currency.

Germany's economy survived the policy objectives of the Bundesbank, once it acquired full autonomy in monetary policy after 1972, because its export-oriented manufacturing sector was strongly competitive by international standards and because its unions tended to practise wage restraint and thus put less pressure on the central bank's anti-inflationary policy. Even so, and especially in the 1980s, Germany traded lower growth and higher unemployment as the tariff for price stability. These conditions do not apply in Europe as a whole. Manufacturing output grew substantially in the 1980s in most European states except Britain, but it is doubtful if much of Spanish or Italian industry, for example, could be competitive under a combined regime of Euro-monetarism and relatively open trade with the world outside.

The implications of this are twofold. Firstly, the process of 'convergence' must be slower and its criteria looser if it is to be less painful. Rapid monetary integration as envisaged in the framework of the Maastricht Treaty is, therefore, likely to be an unworkable policy for all eleven states and, in fact, may damage European integration. As a result of the radical weakening of the ERM this fact has become clear even to many committed 'Europeans' and may provoke a fundamental rethink on the part of policy-makers. The alternative is either a slower process with looser targets and wider objectives, or a two-stage process with a fast and a slow stream. The danger with the latter option is the creation of a partial monetary union and the virtual exclusion of some of the weaker currencies from the possibility of convergence – creating a semi-permanent first and second 'tier' of European countries.

Secondly, the idea of an 'independent' central bank at the EU level is absurd. Unlike the Bundesbank, the broadly representative council of which both protects its substantial degree of independence and ensures its accountability, such a bank will lack legitimacy (Kennedy 1991). That lack will be reinforced by its divorce from wider economic policy-making and by its tendency to set constraining conditions for the latter. The effect of the 'independence' of a European central bank would be to allow virtually unaccountable officials to dictate economic policy, at a time when the central organs of the EU will still lack legitimacy and citizen identification. The result could all too easily be a disaster for the process of building support for EU economic and political integration (Grahl and Thompson 1995).

The problem of divergent regional economic performance

The wider policy dimensions of the regulation of the new European single economic space and of European-level economic and social policy also raise serious questions about both the need for such common programmes and the difficulty of attaining them within existing institutions. How, for example, can Europe have a 'single market' unless it also has not only rules to ensure market openness but also effective mechanisms to compensate for some of the regional effects of that market's workings? Such a market has the danger that it puts firms and capital markets beyond effective national control, and thus enables them to impose social costs and to avoid paying for them. Most European politicians are not happy with this economic liberalism and subscribe to Christian democratic or social democratic principles. They aim for the highest measure of market liberalization consistent with long-run social efficiency. That means common European standards and regulation where they are necessary – in environmental protection, in company law and regulation of capital markets, in social and health and safety legislation. Existing European Union institutions currently already perform many of these regulatory functions and enjoy legitimacy in doing so. The EU creates a common 'framework' legislation – a common structure of rights and regulations that enables all economic actors to operate with a measure of certainty throughout Europe.

The problems begin to occur at the point where programmes of regional harmonization involve major spending, for example, on common standards of environmental protection or compatible social benefits. Not all nations and regions can afford to comply with the emerging 'first-tier' conceptions of a healthy environment, nor can there really be a single labour market until there are common basic social benefits. The current Social Chapter is a minimalist document for this very reason. A more ambitious social programme would imply serious redistribution of revenue within the EU, to bring economically weaker states and regions up to common higher standards without a crippling fiscal burden. The EU's current approach is, on the contrary, to dilute common standards down to a minimum.

The same difficulties will occur in other areas of policy: in particular there will be great resistance to a European regional policy that seeks to improve the efficiency of weaker regions by further substantial investment in infrastructure and in crucial supply-side factors like education and training. Policies to promote economic revitalization are essential on narrow economic grounds and are ultimately of benefit to the richer regions too. Widespread success and growth are needed to maintain a base of effective demand to sustain an extensive growing and productive advanced industrial sector. Baden-Württemberg or Rhône-Alpes cannot ignore their sister regions in Europe. The idea of a Europe of 'tiers' where capital can profit by exploiting low-wage zones is ultimately self-defeating. Such zones will also be low-demand peripheral areas and thus limit the scope and competitiveness of the 'first-tier' core of regions by restricting the growth of their markets. Moreover, no European Union region can compete in this respect with the vast low-wage 'third tier' of countries that has opened up in Eastern Europe.

The drive to regional harmonization and social homogeneity makes sense in the long run and from the perspective of the whole Union. The problem is that richer regions and states, like wealthier social groups within a nation state, will not spend on fiscal redistribution and social harmonization if they can avoid it. Europe needs to challenge its own version of the 'culture of contentment' (Galbraith 1993) if it is ever to develop into a fully integrated economic zone. If it does not then the differences in real economic performance between centre and periphery will begin to lead to disintegration.

Continental Keynesianism

The issue is not merely one of harmonizing income levels between EU regions. The European Union still faces, despite failing to take prompt action in the early 1990s, a situation in which it has the possibility of reconstructing the whole continent, if it were to take a decisive lead. It would be possible to stave off depression in Western Europe in the course of aiding the East – a form of 'continental Keynesianism'. Such a programme would most productively take the form of large-scale infrastructure investment aid, and long-run trade credits for Eastern Europe.

Such Western infrastructure investment would enable those states to support their citizens' living standards in the course of transition to a market economy, offering the unemployed jobs on public works, and trade credits would allow them to obtain essential capital goods in order to reconstruct. The effect of such trade credits on Western firms' order books would be immediate, stimulating in particular the depressed capital goods sector. Rising employment in Western Europe would increase both domestic effective demand and the tax base for European social harmonization measures. If the East could be started on the path to rapid economic recovery, then its markets would offer to the EU the best prospect available of re-creating the long economic boom after 1945.

The scale of the European economy makes possible policy options of this kind that no medium-sized national government can contemplate. The problem is that such options cannot be realized within the existing structures of governance of the EU. The national governments of the member states rejected Jacques Delors's proposals greatly to expand the central EU budget and to spend a sizeable chunk of that revenue on an aid programme for Eastern Europe.

The EU can best ensure its security by promoting prosperity in the East and increasing living standards in its poorer Southern states. Internal harmonization and external action to promote growth in its neighbours are related rather than contradictory objectives. Seeking *military* security in the East and countering threats from its Southern Mediterranean littoral constitute an expensive and economically ineffi- cient option, maintaining high levels of unproductive defence expendi- ture when promoting prosperity in its neighbours and its weaker members is a more effective security strategy. The problem is that the EU currently finds it difficult to act externally and internally in this way and is forgoing, through caution and because it cannot overcome institu- tional obstacles, policies that stem from its position as the world's largest trading bloc (Hirst 1994b).

Our point in drawing attention to this issue is not that we expect such a continental Keynesian option to be followed, given existing attitudes and structures. It is simply to point out that this option is in principle possible and that the EU is potentially capable of far more effective action as a trade bloc than it is currently delivering. In terms of its future development only success in substantive areas can secure the long-term legitimacy of the European Union as a political entity. It is in essence an association founded on *economic* objectives, not cultural homogeneity or collective security (it can rely on all the military force it requires through its member states, NATO and the WEU to ensure its survival). Promot- ing growth within and rising and widespread prosperity among its neigh- bours, conditional on its own policies, are preconditions for its successful evolution and internal institutional development.

Problems of political cooperation and the limits to integration

Unfortunately, the Union needs to make *rapid* progress toward concerted common policies on Eastern and Southern Europe in the later 1990s if it is to seize the opportunities of the moment and ensure the prosperity of both halves of the continent. The odds against rapid progress toward such very necessary common objectives are high. But even if such progress were to be made, the European Union as a political entity would still for the foreseeable future be a complex amalgam of overlapping powers and responsibilities. For the most ambitious policy goals to be realized there would have to be a substantial measure of political coordination at the European Union, national and regional levels. Even if the central institutions of the EU were to gain considerably in citizen support and political legitimacy they could not substitute central social coordination for the more complex processes of the orchestration of consensus and consent at national and regional levels. Nations and regions are the sites of social solidarity, and some of these entities have a far stronger capacity to coordinate their social interests than do others.

If one considers the sort of policies that could become possible, given the continental scale of the EU, the necessity and the difficulty of achieving this complex division of labour become obvious. Thus the Commission – even with an expanded budget – is not in itself a large enough fiscal actor in relation to total EU GDP to provide the stimulus for 'Euro-Keynesian' policies without coincident fiscal and monetary policies in at least the majority of the member states. Assuming that the EU could orchestrate such a policy on the demand side, then it is even more the case that its central institutions could not create the complementary non-monetary policies to contain money wage growth and prevent inflation. Such income restraint would fall to national governments. Some like Germany might still be able to deliver because of the continued, if weakened, presence of corporatist structures and a relatively disciplined union movement. Others like France would probably be able to comply because unions are weak. In a category of its own is Britain, which is manifestly incapable of constraining wage growth during periods of rapid expansion without highly restrictive macroeconomic policies. A European-level policy of boosting demand and output would, therefore, lead to patchy results: those states most able to restrain wages growth would benefit, and those unable to do so would lose out through accelerating unemployment or nationally imposed deflations.

It is difficult to see how the discrepancy between the different national experiences and institutional legacies can be eliminated. There is no prospect, for example, of a strong 'Euro-corporatism' that brings the social partners from different countries together to make binding agreements at Union level (Streeck and Schmitter 1991). Business will not present itself at this level as a single 'social partner'. It is too divided by national and sectoral interests, and it would prefer to lobby for those interests with national governments and the Directorates of the Commission on an issue-by-issue basis. Its national collective bodies are divergent in their degree of organization, in their objectives and their willingness to enter into partnership with labour. German industry remains highly organized on the employers' side with strong sectoral and peak employers' associations, the member firms of which follow collective policy in a disciplined manner. German employers, despite a growing internationalization of outlook, still retain strong commitments both to industry-wide bargaining on wages and working hours and to the codetermination system of consultation with labour at enterprise level. British employers' associations are, by contrast, almost exclusively concerned with representing the most general perceived interests of their members to government, and have few powers to discipline their members or get them to take part in coordinated consultation with labour. Wage bargaining has undergone massive decentralization in Britain since the 1970s, with very few industry-wide agreements (Hirst and Zeitlin 1993). British employers are actively hostile to the idea of an extended dialogue with organized labour to build consent for national policies: this is 'corporatism' and has no place in the modern British manager's lexicon. This stark contrast shows that the European Union will find it difficult to create institutionalized means of orchestrating consensus for macroeconomic policy at federal level. European labour, through its federal-level organizations, may well wish to try to enter into a dialogue with the Commission about policy coordination and the orchestration of consent across the Community. It will have problems if it alone is interested and the employers refuse to cooperate, but even greater problems on its own side too: for European-level consultations will not be able to deliver disciplined continental commitments by member unions in the nation states in such key areas as labour market policy and wage restraint.

This tells us that *some* nation states will remain the crucial actors in constructing a *political* basis of consent for the macroeconomic policies of the Community and for their own fiscal, regulatory and industrial policies. Only at the national level can effective *distributional coalitions* be built: that is, as we saw in chapter 6, broad-brush agreements between the major parties and social actors about the conditions for and the sharing of the necessary costs of economic success. Social Democrats and Christian Democrats in Germany both continue to agree on a wide range of policies and institutions which sustain the economy, for example, but also enter into intense and open political competition. Such coalitions may be tacit or more orchestrated: what matters is that cooperation and competition between the major interests are in a rough balance. In either case it involves the commitment by social actors and the organized social interests representing them to a sustainable distribution of national income between consumption and investment, and to a pattern of expenditure that promotes manufacturing performance. For example, a critical mass of the German financial community still accept the priority of investing in German firms at terms and conditions that protect their competitiveness. The mainstream political parties, organized labour, and employers' organizations all accept the need for public and private investments in education and training. In other countries such commitments and their orchestration would require explicit government action: the UK is the prime example, and since 1979 Conservative governments have seen this as no part of their task. It will be more difficult to extend such national distributional coalitions to cover the costs of ensuring competitiveness at federal level.

If the European Union were to try to move in a 'Euro-Keynesian' direction it would, as things stand, be better off without Britain or with it confined to a semi-detached 'third-tier' status. Britain is, quite frankly, a menace to the Union. Britain's institutions of economic and social governance deviate so far from the continental norm that, without major structural reform, the UK is a liability to Europe.

The role of regional economic governance in Europe

Nation states will remain crucial in a uniting Europe in that, among other things, it is they who provide the domestic constitutional framework and policy support for effective regional governments. States differ massively in size, and the categories 'nation state' and 'region' have no ultimate coherence: Bavaria is a 'region' but could easily be a 'state'; Ireland and Luxembourg are states with smaller populations than many regions. As we saw in chapter 6, regional governments are now key agencies of economic governance, in that they are more able to assess the needs of industry because they possess more localized and, therefore, more accurate information and because they are of a size that enables the key public and private actors to interact and cooperate successfully. Regions are small enough to possess 'intimate knowledge' and yet sufficiently large to aid and regulate local economies through a significant revenue base. The regional provision of education and training, industrial finance and collective services for industry is gaining in importance in Europe. It is also a vital component of the new 'supply-side' policies that promote industrial efficiency and reverse the trend of European economies toward declining competitiveness.

The most successful national economies are those that have allowed the measure of local autonomy necessary to regional regulation and have developed strong industrial districts. The UK has failed most conspicuously in this regard. Its governments have relentlessly promoted centralization since the 1960s. The Conservatives have since 1979 reduced local government to client status (and UK local authorities are too small to be regional governments). Also recent Conservative governments have denied the need for local industrial policies or public–private partnerships to provide collective services. Business has also concentrated massively through mergers and acquisitions, turning local firms into subsidiaries of remote headquarters and severing regional cross-linkages between firms. The UK will thus lose out most in any further move toward the regional governance of economic activity: it will suffer both from the competitive pressures of the single market and from those competitive pressures which stem from the enhanced efficiency available to foreign firms through their use of regional economic cooperation and collective services.

In other states regional governments have compensated for ineffective national policies. Italy is the obvious example, with the more successful industrial districts and regions in the north and the 'third Italy' providing effective economic assistance to firms. One should note that the very weakness and paralysis of the Italian state aided this process in the 1980s. Italy did not fall prey to fashionable monetarist doctrines, and lax government allowed a strongly expansionary (and inflationary) policy. This benefited the more 'post-Fordist' enterprises and industrial districts at the expense of Italy's large firms, big cities and the south. Italian growth in the 1980s thus benefited those areas and social groups that are in favour of greater autonomy and look on the central state as a liability. The political failure of the Italian state in the 1990s has so far had remarkably little effect on the economy. Italian social governance in the more effective regions remains robust and seems able to compensate for political paralysis at the centre.

However, a 'Europe of the regions' remains rhetoric and at present has no precise shape. Most of continental Europe's nation states may accept the need to facilitate regional government. France has at least partially decentralized, for example. But they are not about to sponsor their own dissolution, even if they are strongly regional-federal like Germany. The European Union could not conceivably create central institutions fast enough and with enough legitimacy to achieve an effective federal-regional division of labour, marginalizing national governments in most economic regulatory functions. The danger is that a 'Europe of the regions' will emerge not as a result of an equitable balance of power between federal, national and regional levels, but from the reverse. Europe will be divided into successful and failing regions, in conflict within their nation states and the Union over the direction of policy and the distribution of resources. National states will differ considerably in their capacities for economic management and for effective cooperation with their own regional governments. Strife between rich and poor regions, violent divergences, the direction of the EU's economic governance, could then help to ensure the unsettled character of European institutions and prevent a generous policy toward the East. The future of Europe may as a whole be decided by differences within the European Union that prevent it from acting to unite the continent.

The worst and quite possible prospect for the beginning of the next century would then be a bleak one: a divided and weakened European Union, with aspects of its economic affairs beyond the control of either the member states or Brussels, faced with the Eastern half of the continent predominantly plunged into poverty and strife, and confronted with a tide of refugees and economic migrants that will promote ever more repressive measures against immigrants. Only if European politicians see the need for policies that link the rich and poor regions in the EU, and that link the rich states of the EU with the poor ones of Eastern Europe in a common search for prosperity, can there be any hope of evading such a future. The problem is that politicians in the national states and in the richer regions of the Union can currently see only the costs and dangers and not the hopes and benefits in such programmes. 'Self-protective' policies at national level will most probably prevent progress towards the economic and political integration of Europe. Europe will only develop if its national leaderships and its central institutions are able to exploit the advantages that the pooling of sovereignty and the resources of the largest trade bloc in the world make possible.

8

Globalization, Governance and the Nation State

So far we have been primarily concerned with the economic aspects of globalization, and have considered governance primarily in terms of its economic necessities and possibilities. In this chapter we consider the wider political issues raised by globalization theorists, and consider in particular whether the nation state has a future as a major locus of governance.

We begin with a reminder that the modern state is a relatively recent phenomenon, and that 'sovereignty' in its modern form is a highly distinctive political claim – to exclusive control of a definite territory. We emphasize the *international* aspects of the development of sovereignty: that agreements between states not to interfere in each other's internal affairs were important in establishing the power of state over society. We go on to consider the development of the nation state's capacity for governance and how these capacities are changing in the modern world, especially after the end of the Cold War.

While the state's capacities for governance have changed and in many respects (especially national macroeconomic management) have weakened considerably, it remains a pivotal institution, especially in terms of creating the conditions for effective international governance. We shall make the following main points in our discussion of the possibilities of governance and the role of the state:

1   If, as we have argued in earlier chapters, the international economy does not correspond to the model of a globalized economic system, then nation states have a significant role to play in economic governance at the level of both national and international processes.

2   The emerging forms of governance of international markets and other economic processes involve the major national governments but in a new role: states will come to function less as 'sovereign' entities and more as the components of an international 'polity'. The central functions of the nation state will become those of providing legitimacy for and ensuring the accountability of supra-national and sub-national governance mechanisms.

3   While the state's exclusive control of territory has been reduced by international markets and new communication media, it still retains one central role that ensures a large measure of territorial control – the regulation of populations. People are less mobile than money, goods or ideas: in a sense they remain 'nationalized', dependent on passports, visas, and residence and labour qualifications. The democratic state's role as the possessor of a territory in which it regulates its population gives it a definite legitimacy internationally in a way no other agency could have in that it can speak for that population.

The rise of national sovereignty

Political theorists and sociologists commonly assert, following Max Weber, that the distinctive feature of the modern state is the possession of the monopoly of the means of violence within a given territory (Weber 1968, vol. 1, p. 56). In the seventeenth century the modern states system was created and mutually recognized by its members. Central to that recognition was that each state was the sole political authority with exclusive possession of a defined territory. The 'state' became the dominant form of government, accepting no other agency as rival. The Middle Ages had known no such singular relationship between authority and territory. Political authorities and other forms of functionally specific governance (religious communities and guilds, for example) had existed in complex and overlapping forms that made parallel and often competing claims to the same area (Gierke 1900). Some would claim that the period of the domination of the nation state as an agency of governance is now over and that we are now entering a period when governance and territory will pull apart: different agencies will control aspects of governance and some important activities will be ungoverned. This is questionable, but the nation state's claim to exclusivity in governance is historically specific and by no means foreordained.

The modern state did not acquire its monopoly of governance by its own internal efforts alone. After the Treaty of Westphalia in 1648 governments ceased to support co-religionists in conflict with their own states. The mutual recognition by states of each other's sovereignty in the most important contemporary matter, religious belief, meant that states were willing to forgo certain political objectives in return for internal control and stability (Limm 1984). By exploiting the autonomy from external interference sanctioned by this mutual and international agreement, states were thus able to impose 'sovereignty' on their societies. The agreement of states changed the terms of conflict between territorial authority and confessional groups in favour of the former. Thus to a significant degree the capacity for sovereignty came from *without*, through agreements between states in the newly emerging society of states.

The rise of the modern state, as a territorially specific and politically dominant power, thus depended in part on *international* agreements. The doctrine of the 'sovereignty' of states in the new international law and the mutual recognition of their internal powers and rights by European states thus played a central part in the creation of a new relationship between power and territory, one of exclusive possession (Hinsley 1986). These international understandings made possible an 'internalization' of power and politics within the state. States were perceived as the primary political communities, with the capacity to determine the status of and to make rules for any activity that fell within contemporary understandings of the scope of legitimate authority. States were sovereign and hence each state determined within itself the nature of its internal and external policies. The society of states was thus a world of self-sufficient entities, each acting upon its own will (Bull 1977). International relations could be conceived as 'billiard-ball' interactions, limited by mutual recognition and the obligation to refrain from interfering in the internal affairs of other states (Morse 1971). The anarchical society of external interactions between states, their autonomy one from another, was thus a precondition for an effective monopoly of power within. In the nineteenth and twentieth centuries liberal and democratic regimes inherited these claims of absolutism to sovereignty within a coherent and exclusively governed territory, and brought to them new and powerful legitimations.

Thus to this fundamental sovereignty postulated by seventeenth century states could be added, without excessive contradiction, most of the other features of modern politics. States were autonomous and exclusive possessors of their territory, and this fact did not alter whether they were dynastic or national, autocratic or democratic, authoritarian or liberal. The notion of a 'nation' state actually reinforces the conception of a sovereign power having primacy within a given territory. Nationalism is in essence a claim that political power should reflect *cultural* homogeneity, according to some common set of historically specific political understandings of the content of the nation.

Nationalism thus extends and deepens the scope of 'sovereignty': it requires certain kinds of cultural conformity for citizenship.[1] In this respect the advent of nationalism did not alter our understanding of states as 'sovereign' bodies, rather it required it. The concept of a culturally homogeneous and, therefore, legitimately sovereign territory could justify both the formation and the breakup of states. The result of the various waves of nationalism from the early nineteenth century onwards has been to increase the population of the anarchical society of sovereign states, rather than change its nature. Indeed, if anything, nationalism rendered international cooperation more difficult, reinforcing the notion of the national community as the master of its fate.

Democracy had no greater effect on the fundamental characteristics of the sovereign state, a political entity created in a pre-democratic era. Democracy, in the sense of representative government based upon universal suffrage, has become a virtually universal ideology and aspiration in the late twentieth century. Non-democratic regimes are now signs of political failure and chronic economic backwardness. The notion of a sovereign people could easily replace the 'sovereign', annexing the latter's claims to primacy as the means of political decision within a given territory. Similarly, democracy and nationalism can, at a price, be made compatible. Democracy requires a substantial measure of cultural homogeneity (or publicly recognized cultural difference within some overarching political identity) if it is to be tolerable (Hindess 1992). Bitterly divided communities cannot accept the logic of majority rule or tolerate the rights of minorities. National self-determination is a political claim that derives its legitimacy from the notions of democracy and cultural homogeneity in equal measure: its essence is a plebiscite on independence in a territory claimed to have a degree of distinctive cultural coherence (Nairn 1993).

Modern political theory – that is, the theory of government and political obligation in a sovereign state – evolved before mass democracy, but adapted relatively easily to it. This is not just because it was possible to substitute the people for the monarch. It is also because the nation state is simply the most developed form of the idea of a self-governing political community, with which the very possibility of a distinctive 'political' theory has been bound up (Hindess 1991). Democracy is a source of legitimacy for government and a decision procedure within an entity seen to be self-determining. From the Greek *polis*, through the civic republicanism of the Italian city states, to seventeenth century ideas of government by consent, the notion of the community that controls its social world through collective choice has been central to our understanding of politics. Modern democratic theory blended together what had hitherto tended to be the contradictory ideas of the sovereignty of the community (that power ultimately derived from the people and that government must be by consent) and ruler sovereignty (that state and society were separate entities and that the sovereign was an uncommanded commander, not bound by prior agreements) (Hinsley

1986). Democratic elections legitimated the sovereign powers of state institutions, and thus provided a better foundation for a state viewed as the organ of a self-governing territorial community than did the will of a prince. Democratic sovereignty *includes* citizens and binds them through a common membership that is denied to others.

The notion of the self-governing community has ancient sources, but in the form of the modern nation state it acquired a distinctive credibility. First, in its pre-democratic guise, the state (as a distinct entity separate from society) monopolized violence, imposed uniform administration and provided a form of the rule of law. States claimed to guarantee a substantial measure of security to citizens from external enemies and internal tumults. This claim, advanced as the justification for enlightened autocracy, only became fully credible when states became representative democracies and matters of war and peace ceased to be determined by princely ambitions and dynastic considerations. Since Kant's *Perpetual Peace* (1991), the proposition that liberal states will not attack one another has been the foundation for the hope that a world of nation states could be a peaceful one, that democracy within would temper the anarchical relations between states (Doyle 1983). Second, the modern representatively governed state could govern its territory with a degree of completeness and comprehensiveness unavailable to previous regimes. Representative government reinforced and legitimated the state's capacities for taxation and, given this fiscal power and the removal of competing and subordinate authorities, it could create a uniform national system of administration. On this basis it could extend social governance, for example, creating universal systems of national education or public health measures. Third, but only in the twentieth century, states acquired the means to manage or direct national economies, either through autarchy and state planning, as with the state-directed economies in Britain and Germany in the two world wars, or through Keynesian measures, using monetary and fiscal policy to influence the decisions of economic actors and thus alter economic outcomes.

Thus by the 1960s the state appeared to be the dominant social entity: state and society were virtually coterminous. The state governed and directed society in both the communist and Western worlds, albeit in rather different ways. Communist states represented a distinct variant of the objectives of national economic management, achieved through permanent central planning. In the 1960s the excesses of forced socialist construction seemed to be over and reformers like Khrushchev were promising greater prosperity and peaceful coexistence rather than open conflict with the West. In the advanced Western industrial states it was widely believed that national economic management could continue to ensure both full employment and relatively steady growth.

Industrial states, East and West, were ramified public service agencies, omnicompetent to supervise and to provide for every aspect of the life of their communities. In Western societies still shaped by the industrial revolution, in which the majority of the employed population remained manual workers even into the 1960s, uniform and universal national services in health, education and welfare remained popular. Populations that had only recently escaped the crises of unregulated capitalism continued to welcome collective state social protection, even as they began to enjoy the new mass affluence created by full employment and the long boom after 1945.

This perception of the state has changed out of all recognition and with surprising rapidity. The revolutions of 1989 in Eastern Europe and their aftermath have led to a widespread perception of the modern world as one in which nation states are losing their capacities for governance and national-level processes are ceding their primacy to global ones. What 1989 ended was a specific structure of conflict between allied groups of nation states, the Cold War. The driving force of this conflict was mutual fear between two armed camps: it was then exploited on both sides for ideological purposes but it was not primarily a clash of ideologies. The Cold War reinforced the need for the nation state, for its military capacities and for the national-level forms of economic and social regulation necessary to sustain them. The states system was frozen into a pattern of rigid passive confrontation at the centre, with conflict by proxy at the margins. The state remained necessary, even though its powers remained in reserve in a suspended conflict. Until 1989 it remained possible, although unlikely and mutually suicidal, that the two superpowers and their allied states might go to war. This eventuality, the fear of a mobilized and immediate enemy, made nation states necessary. If they weakened or lost their capacity to control their societies then the enemy might overrun them, and, depending on one's viewpoint, destroy the gains of socialism or impose communist tyranny. This blocked conflict preserved the saliency of the national level of government in a way that delayed or masked the changes that would subsequently weaken it.

The political rhetoric of globalization

We have seen that it has now become fashionable to assert that the era of the nation state is over, and that national-level governance is ineffective in the face of globalized economic and social processes (Horsman and Marshall 1994). National politics and political choices have been sidelined by world market forces which are stronger than even the most powerful states. Capital is mobile and has no national attachments, it will locate wherever economic advantage dictates, but labour is both nationally located and relatively static, and it must adjust its political expectations to meet the new pressures of international competitiveness. Distinct national regimes of extensive labour rights and social protection are thus obsolete. So too are monetary and fiscal policies contrary to the expectations of global markets and transnational companies. The nation state has ceased to be an effective economic manager. It can only provide those social and public services international capital deems essential and at the lowest possible overhead cost.

Nation states are perceived by authors like Ohmae (1990; 1993) and Reich (1992) to have become the local authorities of the global system. They can no longer independently affect the levels of economic activity or employment within their territories: rather, those are dictated by the choices of internationally mobile capital. The job of nation states is like that of municipalities within states heretofore: to provide the infrastructure and public goods that business needs at the lowest possible cost.

This new political rhetoric is based on an anti-political liberalism. Set free from politics, the new globalized economy allows companies and markets to allocate the factors of production to greatest advantage, and without the distortions of state intervention. Free trade, transnational companies and world capital markets have liberated business from the constraints of politics, and are able to provide the world's consumers with the cheapest and most efficient products. Globalization realizes the ideals of mid nineteenth century free-trade liberals like Cobden and Bright: that is, a demilitarized world in which business activity is primary and political power has no other task than the protection of the world free-trading system.

For the right in the advanced industrial countries the rhetoric of globalization is a godsend. It provides a new lease of life after the disastrous failure of their monetarist and radical individualist policy experiments in the 1980s. Labour rights and social welfare of the kind practised in the era of national economic management will render Western societies uncompetitive in relation to the newly industrializing economies of Asia and must be drastically reduced.

For the radical left the concept of globalization also provides release from a different kind of political impasse. Confronted with the collapse of state socialism and of Third World anti-imperialist struggles, the left can see in globalization the continued reality of the world capitalist system. It can also see the futility of national social democratic reformist strategies. The revolutionary left may be weakened but the reformists can no longer claim to possess a pragmatic and effective politics.

Left and right can thus mutually celebrate the end of the Keynesian era. National economic management, full employment and sustained growth, standardized mass production with large semi-skilled manual labour forces, corporatist collaboration between industry, organized labour and the state: these factors, central to the period of the post-1945 long boom, created conditions that favoured the political influence of organized labour and that confined credible political policies to a centrist and reformist path. The dominance of volatile international markets, the change to flexible methods of production and the radical reshaping of the labour force, fitful and uncertain growth in the advanced countries, the decline of organized labour and corporatist intermediation have all, it is claimed, rendered reformist strategies obsolete and reduced the centrality of national political processes, whether competitive or cooperative.

There is some truth in the proposition that national politics in the advanced countries is increasingly a 'cool' politics (Mulgan 1994). It is no longer a matter of war and peace, or of class conflict. It is no longer a matter of mass mobilization for common life or death national efforts. For the globalists, national-level politics is even less salient because it cannot greatly alter economic and social outcomes, unless foolish interventionist strategies are adopted that undermine national competitiveness.

Hence national politics is held to become more like municipal politics, a matter of providing mundane services. Thus energy drains out of conventional politics, away from established parties, and first-rate people cease to be attracted by a political career. Energy flows into the politics of morality – into issues like abortion, gay rights, animal rights and the environment. Activist or 'hot' politics can be played as primary politics without fear that this will distract or divert attention from vital 'national' issues – for these are now mundane.

The decline in the centrality of national-level politics, of war, of class conflict and revolution, of effective economic management and social reform, frees political forces from the need to cooperate against enemies without or to collaborate within to maintain national prosperity. Subnationalities and regions can assert their autonomy with less fear: being, for example, an active advocate of Breton culture and interests will no longer have the effect of weakening France in its life or death conflicts with Germany. Equally, cultural homogeneity at the 'national' level is less central in advanced states linked to world markets, since the nation state as a political entity can offer less. Hence religious, ethnic and lifestyle pluralism can expand within such states and groups within national states can grow in significance as alternative foci of allegiance for their members.

These arguments have some force. There is no doubt that the salience and role of nation states has changed markedly since the Keynesian era. States are less autonomous, they have less exclusive control over the economic and social processes within their territories, and they are less able to maintain national distinctiveness and cultural homogeneity.

The changing capacities of the nation state

There are certain areas in which the role of the state has changed radically, and its capacities to control its people and domestic social processes have declined as a consequence. The first of these is war. The state acquired a monopoly of the means of violence within, the better to be able to mobilize the resources of a territory for external conflict. From the sixteenth century to the present the primary defining capacity of the modern state has been the power to make war, and to draw on the lives and property of its citizens in order to do so. As we saw, the Cold War kept this power alive. Mutual enmity between East and West reinforced the need for permanent mobilization against an ever present threat of war. The development of nuclear weapons, however, has the effect of making war impossible, in the traditional sense of the use of force to attain some objective. Classically war was seen as a means of decision, victory settling an issue between states that could be resolved in no other way. Clausewitzian war was purposive, and to that degree rational, the continuation of policy by other means. Nuclear war between roughly equal combatants could only end in mutual destruction and the negation of any rational policy pursued by the officials of the participating states. As Bernard Brodie (1946; 1965) perceptively observed (immediately after Hiroshima), the sole function of nuclear weapons was deterrence: the greatest military force could no longer be employed to reach a political decision but could now only be effective if it prevented its use and thus gave politicians time to devise means to bring it under political control by the mutual agreement of the nuclear states.

Brodie was right, even if it took a half century of extreme risk and the danger of extinction before such political measures finally became possible. The Cold War was insupportable, deterrence unstable, and nuclear stalemate bought at ever higher cost. Periods of intense competition between the superpowers, seeking technological advantage through arms races, were followed by periods of *détente*. The major nuclear states have forgone 'sovereignty': they have created a world civil order by their treaties, not merely limiting wars, but granting to other states powers of inspection and supervision, of notification of military manoeuvres etc., of a kind that render effective war mobilization extremely unlikely.[2] States have had to accept a hitherto intolerable level of interference in their internal affairs to make peace credible. The ultimate force that nuclear arsenals represent is useless, for it cannot make war; and political agreements, if they can be institutionalized, will make deterrence unnecessary.

War between nuclear states became impossible, whether they were liberal or illiberal, provided their leaders were possessed of minimal rationality. Non-nuclear conflicts could only occur in peripheral regions, conflicts by proxy where the defeat of one side would not lead to the threat of nuclear war. The possession of nuclear weapons thus also ended the possibility of conventional war between nuclear states.[3] Nuclear weapons drove war out of international relations between advanced states: they were no longer an alternative means of decision but the threat of a terrible mutual disaster that needed to be negotiated away.

Armed forces are thus virtually an irrelevance for the major advanced states in their dealings with one another. Weapons have evolved to the point where they have rendered war obsolete and with it much of the rationale and capacities for control of the state. Armed forces will not cease to exist, but they will matter less and less as a means of political decision (van Creveld 1991). They cannot decide matters between advanced states. And the disparity of forces between the Great Powers and major states in the Third World is so great that the latter cannot rearrange matters to their advantage by conventional armed force – that is, when the Great Powers perceive their vital interests to be at stake, as the Gulf War of 1991 proved.

This does not mean we shall live in a peaceful world. Lesser states will fight one another. Advanced states will be threatened by terrorism. Revolutionary movements will continue to arise on the impoverished periphery, new but local 'beggars' armies' like the Zapatistas in Chiapas. Revolutionary movements will articulate specific local antagonisms, but they will no longer seem to be detachments of a single struggle united by a common anti-capitalist and anti-imperialist ideology. But it does mean, in the advanced states at least, that governments are unlikely to have the occasion to call on the lives and property of their citizens for war. They will no longer be able to mobilize their societies and demand and create the solidarity and common identification with authority necessary to the effective pursuit of total war. War, the presence of a genuine enemy, reinforced national solidarity and made credible the claim to national cultural homogeneity.

Without war, without enemies, the state becomes less significant to the citizen. When peoples really faced enemies, invaders and conquerors, they needed their state and their fellow citizens. The liberal state, which claimed to live peacefully with its neighbours and to make limited demands on its own people, could claim great legitimacy if attacked, thereby rousing its people to a degree of commitment and common effort that authoritarian states could seldom match. These legitimations are gone, and with them whole classes of provision for 'national' needs justified by the possible contingency of war: 'national' industries, health and welfare to promote 'national efficiency', and social solidarity to unite rich and poor in a common struggle. Social democracy profited from industrialized conventional war: it could deliver organized labour to the all-out war effort at the price of economic and social reforms.

States in the advanced world no longer have war as a central support for their claims to 'sovereignty'. They are no longer conceivable as autonomous actors, free to pursue any external policy in the anarchical society of states. The society of states has passed from an anarchical condition to a quasi-civil one. The vast majority of states are bound together in numerous ways in what amounts to an international political society, and in the case of the major advanced states of the G7 and OECD, a virtual standing association of states with its own rules and decision procedures. This does not mean that national states are irrelevant, but it does mean that their claim to a monopoly of the means of legitimate violence within a given territory is no longer so definitive of their existence.

Just as nuclear weapons have transformed the conditions of war, weakening in the process the central rationale for the state, so too the new communications and information technologies have loosened the state's exclusiveness of control of its territory, reducing its capacities for cultural control and homogenization. It is a commonplace that digitized communications – satellites, fax machines, computer networks – have rendered the state licensing and control of information media all but impossible, undermining not merely ideological dictatorships but also all attempts to preserve cultural homogeneity by state force.

Modern communications form the basis for an international civil society, people who share interests and associations across borders. The international media also make possible a set of cosmopolitan cultures, both elite and popular, scientific and artistic, that are linked through the medium of English as a universal rather than a national language. Such cultures, from children watching 'Tom and Jerry' on TV to physicists gossiping on e-mail, are inevitably international. Cultural homogeneity becomes increasingly problematic: 'national' cultures are merely members of a set of cultures in which people participate for different purposes. Cosmopolitan and national cultures interact. Complete cultural homogeneity and exclusiveness are less and less possible. 'National' cultures that aim to be dominant over their member individuals are increasingly projects of resistance to and retreat from the world. Inward-looking nationalism and cultural fundamentalism are, to put it bluntly, the politics of losers. It is virtually impossible to continue to operate in the various world markets and ignore at the same time the internationalized cultures that go along with them. Such inward-looking nationalisms do exist and will continue to develop but, to the degree that their political projects are successful, they have the effect of marginalizing their societies. Although they are responses to economic backwardness, such nationalisms act to reinforce it. The same is true of social groups within advanced states that claim an all-pervasive identity, be that ethnic, religious or whatever: they condemn their members to social marginality.

The existence of different languages and religions, as Kant (1991) argued, virtually guarantees cultural diversity. Distinct local cultural traditions will continue to coexist with cosmopolitan cultural practices. What is threatened, however, is the idea of an exclusive and virtually self-sufficient 'national' culture, of which individuals are simply exemplars, sharing a common language, beliefs and activities. States strenuously attempted to create such cultures through common systems of national education, military service, etc. (Anderson 1991). That such projects are no longer possible for advanced states means that they have to seek bases of citizen loyalty outside primitive cultural homogeneity. In the major cities of most advanced states dozens of languages and almost every conceivable religion are in common usage. As we shall see, the state will probably find a new rationale in managing this very diversity, acting as the public power that enables such parallel communities to coexist and to resolve conflicts. Space and culture have no definite relation. In the great cities of the advanced countries at least, the cultures of the world are more or less randomly mixed. The state in the era of 'nation building' tried to turn its people into artefacts of itself, representative specimens of the 'national' culture. In the interest of individual liberty and the values of cosmopolitanism and cultural diversity, we should be grateful that states can make fewer and less credible claims on our imaginations and beliefs.

The state may have less control over ideas, but it remains a controller of its borders and the movement of people across them. As we have seen, apart from a 'club class' of internationally mobile, highly skilled professionals, and the desperate poor migrants and refugees who will suffer almost any hardship to leave intolerable conditions, the bulk of the world's populations now cannot easily move. Workers in advanced countries have no 'frontier' societies like Australia or Argentina to migrate to as they did in huge numbers in the nineteenth century and in lesser numbers into the 1970s. Increasingly the poor of Eastern Europe and the Third World are unwelcome in advanced countries except as guest workers or illegal migrants working for poverty wages. Western societies are shedding labour and local unskilled labour finds it harder and harder to get jobs, hence the pressure to exclude poor migrants. In the absence of labour mobility states will retain powers over their peoples: they define who is and is not a citizen, who may and may not receive welfare. In this respect, despite the rhetoric of globalization, the bulk of the world's population live in closed worlds, trapped by the lottery of their birth. For the average worker or farmer with a family, one's nation state is a community of fate. Wealth and income are not global, but are nationally and regionally distributed between poorer and richer states and localities. For the vast majority of people nation states are not just municipalities or local authorities, providing services that one chooses according to their relative quality and cost.

Nationally rooted labour has to seek local strategies and local benefits if it is to improve its lot. The question is whether business is similarly constrained, or whether it can simply choose new and more optimal locations. Internationally open cultures and rooted populations present an explosive contradiction. The impoverished can watch 'Dallas'. They know another world is possible, whether they are watching it in a slum apartment in an advanced country or a shanty town in a Third World country. The ideology of socialist revolution may have few takers but one should not imagine that the world's poor will remain cowed or passively accept their poverty. Their responses, whether of street crime or guerrilla struggles like Chiapas, will be far harder to cope with than old-style communist-directed revolts. Such responses will be local, and less aggregated in ideological terms with other conflicts. Hence such struggles will be left in the main to local states and local elites to contain. The advanced world currently does not think its frontier begins in the jungles of Yucatán in the way it once thought it did in the jungles of Vietnam or Bolivia.

As the advanced countries seek to police the movement of the world's poor and exclude them, the capriciousness of the notions of citizenship and of political community will become ever more evident. Advanced states will not be able effectively to use as a principle of exclusion the claim to cultural homogeneity – for they are ethnically and culturally pluralistic. Exclusion will be a mere fact, with no other logic or legitimacy than that states are fearful of the consequences of large-scale migration. A world of wealth and poverty, with appalling and widening differences in living standards between the richest and the poorest nations, is unlikely to be secure or stable. Industrial workers in the advanced countries fear the cheap labour of well-educated and skilled workers in the upper tier of developing countries like Taiwan or Malaysia. The poor of the Third World see themselves as abandoned by a rich world that trades more and more with itself and with a few favoured NICs. Both groups are stuck within the borders of states, forced to regard their countries as communities of fate and to seek solutions within the limits of their enforced residence.

However, as we have argued above, mere nationalism as such will provide no solution to these problems. The assertion of ethnic cultural or religious homogeneity may serve as a cultural compensation for poverty, as an opium of the economically backward, but it will not cure it. The appeal of fundamentalist Islam or other forms of cultural nationalism is to the poor and excluded. Such localizing ideologies will continue to be politically successful in areas where significant numbers of people see they have benefited not at all from the world free-trade order. But such ideologies will not alter the fact of poverty.[4]

Third World national revolutions as projects of economic and social modernization have proved failures. They required autarchic withdrawal from world markets, the socialization of agriculture, and forced-march industrialization. Where such revolutions were most complete, as in Albania or North Korea, they led to societies that reproduced the worst features of the Soviet system. Unfortunately for the world's poor they could not exit the free-trade system and transform their societies by their own efforts within their own borders. The problem is that without a transformation in the international economic order, without new strategies and priorities in the advanced countries towards the Third World, and without large-scale foreign capital investment, poor countries are unlikely to benefit much from turning away from autarchy either. The point is that in the 1960s the national state solution still seemed viable for the Third World, using the state power available after independence and the legacy of solidarity from the anti-colonial struggle to build a new society. Such Third World revolutionary strategies are no more viable now than are conventional, social democratic, national Keynesian strategies in the advanced countries.

Governance and the world economy

There can be no doubt that the era in which politics could be conceived almost exclusively in terms of processes within nation states and their external billiard-ball interactions is passing. Politics is becoming more polycentric, with states as merely one level in a complex system of overlapping and often competing agencies of governance. It is probable that the complexity of these superimposed authorities, both territorial and functional, will soon come to rival that of the Middle Ages. But this complexity and multiplicity of levels and types of governance implies a world quite different from that of the rhetoric of 'globalization', and one in which there is a distinct, significant and continuing place for the nation state.

We should again make it clear at this point that the issue of control of economic activity in a more integrated internationalized economy is one of *governance* and not just of the continuing roles of *governments*. Sovereign nation states claimed as their distinctive feature the right to determine how any activity within their territory was governed, either to perform that function themselves or to set the limits of other agencies. That is, they claimed a monopoly of the function of governance. Hence the tendency in common usage to identify the term 'government' with those institutions of state that control and regulate the life of a territorial community. 'Governance' – that is, the control of an activity by some means such that a range of desired outcomes is attained – is, however, not just the province of the state. Rather it is a function that can be performed by a wide variety of public and private, state and non-state, national and international institutions and practices.[5] The analogy with the Middle Ages simply helps us to grasp this by thinking back to a period before the attempt at the monopolization of governance functions by sovereign nation states. That is its only and limited purpose.

The analogy with the Middle Ages is at best metaphoric and in some ways is far from apt. We are *not* returning to a world *like* the Middle Ages and before the development of national 'sovereignty'. This is not just because national states and the 'sovereign' control of peoples persist. The scope and role of forms of governance are radically different today, and this has distinct implications for the architecture of government. In the Middle Ages the coexistence of parallel, competing and overlapping authorities was possible, if conflictual, because economies and societies were less integrated. The degree of division of labour and economic interdependence was relatively low, whereas today communities depend for their very existence on the meshing and coordination of distinct and often remote activities. Markets alone cannot provide such interconnection and coordination, or rather they can only do so if they are appropriately governed and if the rights and expectations of distant participants are secured and sustained (Durkheim 1893).

Hence governing powers cannot simply proliferate and compete. The different levels and functions of governance need to be tied together in a division of control that sustains the division of labour. If this does not happen then the unscrupulous can exploit and the unlucky can fall into the 'gaps' between different agencies and dimensions of governance. The governing powers (international, national and regional) need to be 'sutured' together into a relatively well-integrated system. If this does not happen then these gaps will lead to the corrosion of governance at every level. The issue at stake is *whether* such a coherent system will develop, and it takes priority over the question of whether international governance can be democratic (as forcefully argued by Held 1991, for example). The answer to the former question remains moot. But simplistic versions of the globalization thesis do not help to resolve it because they induce fatalism about the capacity of the key agencies in promoting coherent national strategies.

The nation state is central to this process of 'suturing': the policies and practices of states in distributing power upwards to the international level and downwards to sub-national agencies are the sutures that will hold the system of governance together. Without such explicit policies to close gaps in governance and elaborate a division of labour in regulation, vital capacities for control will be lost. Authority may now be plural within and between states rather than nationally centralized, but to be effective it must be structured by an element of design into a relatively coherent architecture of institutions. This the more simplistic 'globalization' theorists deny, either because they believe the world economy is ungovernable, given volatile markets and divergent interests, and therefore that no element of design is possible, or because they see the market as a mechanism of coordination in and of itself that makes any attempt at an institutional architecture to govern it unnecessary. The market is a substitute for govern*ment* because it is held to be a satisfactory mode of govern*ance*: it produces optimal outcomes when its workings are least impeded by extraneous institutional regulation.

Extreme 'globalization' theorists like Ohmae (1990) contend that only two forces matter in the world economy, global market forces and transnational companies, and that neither of these is or can be subject to effective public governance. The global system is governed by the logic of market competition, and public policy will be at best secondary, since no governmental agencies (national or otherwise) can match the scale of world market forces. To repeat, this view regards national governments as the municipalities of the global system: their economies are no longer 'national' in any significant sense and they can only be effective as governments if they accept their reduced role of providing locally the public services that the global economy requires of them. The question, however, is whether such a global economy exists or is coming into being. As we have seen, there is a vast difference between a strictly *global* economy and a highly *internationalized* economy in which most companies trade from their bases in distinct national economies. In the former national policies are futile, since economic outcomes are determined wholly by world market forces and by the internal decisions of transnational companies. In the latter national policies remain viable, indeed they are essential in order to preserve the distinct styles and strengths of the national economic base and the companies that trade from it. A world economy with a high and growing degree of international trade and investment is not necessarily a globalized economy in the former sense. In it nation states, and forms of international regulation created and sustained by nation states, still have a fundamental role in providing governance of the economy.

The issue, therefore, turns on what type of international economy exists at present or is coming into being: one that is essentially supranational, or one in which, despite high levels of international trade and investment, nationally located processes and economic actions still remain central. The evidence we have considered so far on the key aspects of this question – the character of the world financial markets, the pattern of world trade and FDI, the number and role of MNCs, and the prospects for growth in the developing world – all confirm that there is no strong tendency toward a globalized economy and that the major advanced nations continue to be dominant. If that is so we should ditch the over-fashionable concept of 'globalization' and look for less politically debilitating models. The issue here is not merely one of assessing evidence, but one of providing political concepts that restate the possibilities for economic governance and the role of the modern state in such governance.

Earlier in the book we saw that the ongoing battles between the public policy of the advanced nations and the major financial markets are by no means settled, but that there is no reason to believe market forces will invariably and inevitably prevail over regulatory systems, despite setbacks like the unravelling of the EMS. The reason is that most players in the international economy have an interest in financial stability, including the major companies, for whom the reduction in uncertainty is of obvious advantage in their planning of investment, and in their production and marketing strategies. The idea, common among extreme globalization theorists, that major companies will benefit from an unregulated international environment remains a strange one. Calculable trade rules, settled and internationally common property rights, and exchange rate stability constitute a level of elementary security that companies need to plan ahead, and therefore a condition of continued investment and growth. Companies cannot create such conditions for themselves, even if they are transnational. Stability in the international economy can only be had if states combine to regulate it and to agree on common objectives and standards of governance. Companies may want free trade and common regimes of trade standards, but they can only have them if states work together to achieve common international regulation.[6]

Equally, the notion that companies should wish to be transnational in the sense of extra-territorial is also a strange one. The national economic bases from which most companies operate actually contribute to their economic efficiency and not just in the sense of providing low-cost infrastructure. Most firms are embedded in a distinct national culture of business that provides them with intangible but very real advantages. Managers and core staff have common understandings that go beyond formal training or company policies. Genuinely transnational companies, with no primary location and a multinational workforce, would have to try to create *within* the firm the cultural advantages and forms of identification that other firms get almost free from national institutions. They would have to get core workers to put the company first as a source of identification and build a cohesive non-national managerial elite that can communicate implicitly one with another. This transnationality has traditionally only been achieved by non-economic organizations with a strong ideological mission as an alternative focus of loyalty to countries and states, such as the Society of Jesus. This would be difficult for companies to match. After all, the Jesuits are culturally distinct even if multinational – the products of a distinctive Latin Catholic environment and education. It is difficult to make the firm the exclusive *cultural* focus of an individual's life, and for individuals to make an ongoing commitment to one company, entirely removed from national connections. The Japanese managers and core workers who see the firm as a primary and ongoing social community do this in a *national* context where this makes sense.

Companies benefit not just from national business cultures, but from nation states and national communities as social organizations. This is emphasized by the literature on national systems of innovation (Ludval 1992; Nelson 1993; Porter 1990) and on national business systems (Whitley 1992a; 1992b). These national business systems are quite distinct from the forms of homogeneity preached by cultural nationalists, but they remain tenaciously distinctive in a way that many other forms of national culture do not. Companies benefit from being enmeshed in networks of relations with central and local governments, with trade associations, with organized labour, with specifically national financial institutions oriented toward local companies, and with national systems of skill formation and labour motivation. These networks provide information, they are a means to cooperation and coordination between firms to secure common objectives, and they help to make the business environment less uncertain and more stable. A national economic system provides forms of reassurance to firms against the shocks and the risks of the international economy. As we have argued, such national business-oriented systems have been most evident in the developed world in Germany and Japan, both of which have had strongly solidaristic relationships between industry, labour and the state, and in the developing world in such countries as South Korea and Taiwan.

But national advantages are not confined to those societies whose institutions promote solidarity in order to balance cooperation and competition between firms and between the major social interests. The USA has a national business culture that emphasizes competition and the autonomy of the individual corporation. But, *contra* fashionable arguments like those of Reich (1992), US firms have very real benefits in remaining distinctly American that stem from the power and functions of the national state (Kapstein 1991; Tyson 1991): for example, that the dollar remains the medium of international trade, that regulatory and standard-setting bodies like the FAA and FDA are world leaders and work closely with US industry, that the US courts are a major means of defence of commercial and property rights throughout the world, that the federal government is a massive subsidizer of R&D and also a strong protector of the interests of US firms abroad.

The extreme globalization theorists paint a picture of a world set free for business to serve consumers. States and military power cease to matter in the face of global markets. In this view economics and politics are pulling apart, and the latter is declining at the expense of the former. As markets dominate and the results of markets are legitimated by free competition and seen to be beyond national control, so states come to have less capacity to control economic outcomes or to alter them by force. Attempts to use military force for economic objectives against the interests of world markets would be subject to devastating, if unplanned, economic sanction: plunging exchange rates, turbulent stock exchanges, declining trade, etc. War would cease to have any connection with economic rationality: most societies would have become inescapably 'industrial' rather than 'militant'. War would become the recourse of failed and economically backward societies and political forces, driven by economically irrational goals like ethnic homogeneity or religion. This world free for trade is the dream of classical economic liberalism since its inception.

Markets and companies cannot exist without a public power to protect them, whether it is at the world level with the major states confronting authoritarian regional powers seeking to annex wealth by force, as with Saddam Hussein's seizure of Kuwait, or at the local level of policing against pirates and gangsters. The advanced states do at present trade predominantly one with another and, indeed, are unlikely to fight one another. But the world's free-trading order does require military force to back it, and this only the advanced countries, and in particular the USA, can provide (Hirst 1994b).

The advantages provided by public power to companies and markets are not confined to the national level. Indeed, for many vital services to business and forms of cooperation between firms, national-level institutions are too remote for adequate local knowledge and effective governance. We have argued earlier that regional governments are providers of vital collective services to industry throughout the advanced industrial world. In particular, regional governments are the public articulation of industrial districts composed of small and medium firms, and are a major reason why such firms can be internationally competitive and enjoy advantages comparable to the economies of scale of larger firms. Regional economic governance, thriving industrial districts, and an effective partnership and division of labour between national states and regional governments are central components of the success of national economies in world markets.[7]

If the foregoing arguments are true then the majority of companies, large and small, that are active in international markets have a strong interest in the continued public governance, national and international, of the world economy. Internationally they seek a measure of security and stability in financial markets, a secure framework of free trade, and the protection of commercial rights. Nationally they seek to profit from the distinct advantages conferred by the cultural and institutional frameworks of the successful industrial states. If companies have such interests then it is highly unlikely that an ungoverned global economy composed of unregulated markets will come into existence. Globalization theorists tend to rely either on the providentialist assumptions derived from a simplistic reading of neo-classical economics, that as markets approach perfection and freedom from external intervention they become more efficient as allocative mechanisms; or on the gloomy suppositions of the Marxist left, that international capital is an unequivocally malevolent force and one indifferent to national or local concerns. In the former case, the public power is a virtual irrelevance: its actions (beyond essential tasks like the protection of property) can do little but harm. In the latter case political authority submits to the will of capital and can do nothing to counter it within the existing world system.

In this and previous chapters we have argued that there are good economic grounds for believing that the international economy is by no means ungovernable. To recap from chapter 6, therefore, governance is possible at five levels from the international economy to the industrial district:

1   through agreement between the major advanced states, and particularly the G3;
2   through a substantial number of states creating international regulatory agencies for some specific dimension of economic activity, like the WTO;
3   through the control of large economic areas by trade blocs such as the EU or NAFTA;
4   through national-level policies that balance cooperation and competition between firms and the major social interests;
5   through regional-level policies of providing collective services to industrial districts.

Such institutional arrangements and strategies can assure some minimal level of international economic governance, at least to the benefit of the major advanced industrial nations. Such governance cannot alter the extreme inequalities between those nations and the rest, in terms of trade and investment, income and wealth. Unfortunately, that is not really the problem raised by the concept of globalization. The issue is not whether the world's economy is governable toward ambitious goals like promoting social justice, equality between countries and greater democratic control for the bulk of the world's people, but whether it is governable *at all*.

The new sovereignty

If such mechanisms of international governance and re-regulation are to be initiated then the role of nation states is pivotal. Nation states should be seen no longer as 'governing' powers, able to impose outcomes on all dimensions of policy within a given territory by their own authority, but as loci from which forms of governance can be proposed, legitimated and monitored. Nation states are now simply one class of powers and political agencies in a complex system of power from world to local levels, but they have a centrality because of their relationship to territory and population.

Populations remain territorial and subject to the citizenship of a national state. States remain 'sovereign', not in the sense that they are all-powerful or omnicompetent within their territories, but because they police the borders of a territory and, to the degree that they are credibly democratic, they are representative of the citizens within those borders. Regulatory regimes, international agencies, common policies sanctioned by treaty, all come into existence because major nation states have agreed to create them and to confer legitimacy on them by pooling sovereignty. Sovereignty is alienable, states cede power to supra-state agencies, but it is not a fixed quantum. Sovereignty is alienable and divisible, but states acquire new roles even as they cede power: in particular, they come to have the function of legitimating and supporting the authorities they have created by such grants of sovereignty. If 'sovereignty' is of decisive significance now as a distinguishing feature of the nation state, it is because the state has the role of a source of legitimacy in transferring power or sanctioning new powers both 'above' it and 'below' it: above, through agreements between states to establish and abide by forms of international governance; below, through the state's constitutional ordering within its own territory of the relationship of power and authority between central, regional and local governments and also the publicly recognized private governments in civil society. Nation states are still of central significance because they are the key practitioners of the art of government as the process of distributing power, ordering other governments by giving them shape and legitimacy. Nation states can do this in a way no other agencies can: they are pivots between international agencies and sub-national activities, because they provide legitimacy as the exclusive voice of a territorially bounded population. They can practise the art of government as a process of distributing power only if they can credibly present their decisions as having the legitimacy of popular support.

In a system of governance in which international agencies and regulatory bodies are already significant and are growing in scope, nation states are crucial agencies of representation. Such a system of governance amounts to a global polity and in it the major nation states are the global 'electors'.[8] States ensure that, in a very mediated degree, international bodies are answerable to the world's key publics, and that decisions backed by the major states can be enforced by international agencies because they will be reinforced by domestic laws and local state power.

Such representation is very indirect, but it is the closest to democracy and accountability that international governance is likely to get. The key publics in advanced democracies have some influence on their states and these states can affect international policies. Such influence is the more likely if the populations of several major states are informed and roused on an issue by the world 'civil society' of transnational non-governmental organizations (NGOs). Such NGOs, like Greenpeace or the Red Cross, are more credible candidates to be genuine transnational actors than are companies. It is easier to create a cosmopolitan agency for common world causes like the environment or human rights than it is to build a rootless business whose staff are asked to identify with its mundane activities above all else in the world.

Moreover, the category of non-governmental organizations is a misnomer. They are not governments, but many of them play crucial roles of governance, especially in the interstices between states and international regulatory regimes. Thus Greenpeace helps effectively to police international agreements on whaling. Equally, where nation states are indeed as weak and ineffective as the 'globalization' theorists suppose *all* states to be, as in parts of Africa, NGOs like Oxfam provide some of the elementary functions of government, such as education as well as famine relief.

An internationally governed economic system, in which certain key policy dimensions are controlled by world agencies, trade blocs, and major treaties between nation states ensuring common policies, will thus continue to give the nation state a role. This role stresses the specific feature of nation states that other agencies lack: their ability to make bargains stick, upwards because they are representative of territories, and downwards because they are constitutionally legitimate powers. Paradoxically then, the degree to which the world economy has internationalized (but not globalized) reinstates the need for the nation state, not in its traditional guise as the sole sovereign power, but as a crucial relay between the international levels of governance and the articulate publics of the developed world.

Nation states and the rule of law

So far we have discussed the persistence of the nation state primarily in terms of its role within a system of international governance. There is, however, another reason to argue that the 'nation' state will persist as an important form of political organization, a reason closely connected with one of the central traditional claims to 'sovereignty': that is, to be the primary source of binding rules – law – within a given territory. This role of the state as monopoly law-maker was closely connected with the development of a monopoly of the means of violence and with the development of a coherent system of administration providing the principal means of governance within a territory. Today, however, this role of upholding the rule of law is relatively independent of those other elements in the historical process of the formation of the modern state.

To sum up the argument in advance: nation states as sources of the rule of law are essential prerequisites for regulation through international law and they are, as overarching public powers, essential to the survival of pluralistic 'national' societies with diversified forms of administration and community standards. States may be the key source of the rule of law without being 'sovereign' in the traditional sense, that is, standing against all external entities as the sole means of government in a territory, or standing above sub-national governments and associations as the body from which they derive their powers by recognition and concession. Omnicompetence, exclusivity and omnipotence of the state are not necessary to the rule of law: indeed, historically these have been the attributes of states deriving from the portmanteau theory of sovereignty that have served to undermine it.

States have been Janus faced: on the one side the centres of substantive decision-making and administrative powers, and on the other the sources of rules limiting their own actions and those of their citizens. These two aspects may be pulling apart, and in large measure for the good. The power of nation states as administrative and policy-making agencies has declined. We have seen that the decline in the salience of war and the restriction of the scope of national economic management have lessened the claim that states as governing agencies can make upon their societies. This does not mean that the law-making and constitutional ordering functions of states will decline in the same measure. One aspect of the state is substantive and outcome oriented, a matter of political decision and the implementation of such decisions through administration; the other aspect is procedural and concerns the state's role as regulator of social action in the widest sense, of rules as guides to action and of constitutional ordering as adjudicating between the competing claims of corporate entities and citizens.

The state as a source of constitutional ordering, limiting its own and others' powers, and guiding action through rights and rules, is central to the rule of law (Hirst 1994b). Commercial societies require that minimum of certainty and constancy in the action of administrators and economic actors that the rule of law implies. Western societies have been economically successful and relatively civilized in their treatment of their members when they have provided the security and the certainty of the rule of law – limiting the harms that citizens, companies and governments could do. Politics, ideology and state policy have frequently undermined the rule of law, governments abandoning the civilized limits of state action in the pursuit of overarching political goals.

If we are moving into a more complex and pluralistic social and political system then the rule of law will become more important rather than less. Even more so than in the sphere of administrative regulation, 'gaps' between jurisdictions are fatal to the certainty and security necessary for actors in a commercial society, for they allow the unscrupulous to evade their own obligations and to violate others' rights. For example, tax havens, flags of convenience, dumping grounds for pollution, etc. all allow advanced world economic actors to avoid First World obligations. A world composed of diverse political forces, governing agencies, and organizations at both international and national levels will need an interlocking network of public powers that regulate and guide action in a relatively consistent way, providing minimum standards of conduct and reliefs from harms. In this sense we are considering constitutional ordering in its aspect as a *pouvoir neutre*, not as part of issue-oriented politics or administrative regulation. Our model for such a power remains the *Rechtsstaat*, and national states are its primary embodiment in so far as they correspond to that conception of authority as a source of law that is itself lawful and limited in its action by rules.

Within states the role of such an independent public power that arbitrates between other powers, that is neutral between plural and competing social communities with different standards, and that provides highly individuated citizens with a common procedural basis by which to regulate their interactions, will become more important rather than less. A pluralistic system of authority and pluralistic communities require a public power as the medium through which they may contain their conflicts. As J.N. Figgis (1913) argued at the beginning of the century, the decline of the excessive claims of state 'sovereignty' does *not* mean the end of a law-making public power. The state may no longer be 'sovereign' in this old sense – it may share authority with sub-national governments whose specific autonomous powers are guaranteed, it may no longer view associations and corporate bodies as legal fictions that have their limited powers granted by its own revocable fiat – but it will define the scope of legitimate authority and legitimate action in its roles as constitutional arbitrator and law-maker.

In an individualistic and pluralistic society, where there are few common standards, where strong binding collectivities have declined and been replaced by communities of choice, and where informal social sanctions have weakened, the rule of law is more rather than less necessary. This does not mean that states will be able to cope fully with the multiple problems and conflicts that arise from the growing pluralism of modern societies: rather we are claiming that without a public power that mediates between these plural groups through the rule of law, such conflicts will become intolerable (Hirst 1993, ch. 3). In a sense the decline of war as a source of national cohesion, and the lessening role of the state as an economic manager, reduce the power and claims that states can exert over society as administrative agencies and foci of political identification. They have less capacity to impose external cohesion on groups. The other consequence of this is that they are becoming less Janus faced, less encumbered with the need to balance their roles as primary administrator and neutral public power in a way that makes it easier for them credibly to give primacy to the latter role. A cooling of national politics gives states the space to expand their roles as an internal *pouvoir neutre* and an arbiter between conflicting interests, something that the excessive and overcharged claims to 'sovereignty' as omnicompetence made problematic.

Externally, the role of states as sources of the rule of law will also become more central. As international economic, environmental and social governance expands, so the role of international law will increase. International agencies, international regimes based on treaties and inter-state agreements, international 'civil' agencies performing world public functions in the defence of human rights and environmental standards, all imply an extension of the scope of international law. However, international law cannot function without national states, not merely as its material supports and the agents to whom it is addressed, but as *Rechtsstaaten,* agencies that create and abide by law. International law without a significant population of states that are sources of the rule of law is a contradictory enterprise. It is like states imposing laws on citizens who do not internalize rules or govern their actions by such rules. An international society as an association of states cannot rely on supranational bodies to make and enforce laws but requires states that accept constitutional limitations above and below them. In this sense the move from an anarchical society of states to a world in which states are part of a common association requires that the member states of that association accept international legal obligations and also govern internally according to the requirements of the rule of law. In this sense the state as the source and the respecter of binding rules remains central to an internationalized economy and society.

9

Conclusion

In the preceding chapters we have presented an argument against the idea that the international economy has become or is becoming 'globalized' as defined by us in chapter 1. 'Globalization' has become a fashionable concept both in the social sciences and among management thinkers. It is widely asserted that a truly global economy has emerged or is emerging in which distinct 'national' economies and, therefore, domestic strategies of national economic management are increasingly irrelevant. The world economy has internationalized in its basic dynamics, is dominated by uncontrollable global market forces, and has as its principal actors and major agents of change truly transnational corporations (TNCs), which owe allegiance to no nation state and locate wherever in the globe market advantage dictates.

In this book we questioned the validity and accuracy of many of the strong claims made about 'globalization'. We have pointed out the following problems for the globalization thesis: first, that few exponents of globalization develop a coherent concept of the world economy in which supra-national forces and agents are decisive; second, that pointing to evidence of the enhanced internationalization of economic relationships since the 1970s is not in itself proof of the emergence of a distinctly 'global' economic structure; third, that the international economy has been subject to major structural changes in the last century and that there have been earlier periods of internationalization of trade, capital flows and the monetary system, especially 1870–1914; fourth, that truly global TNCs are relatively few and that most successful multinational corporations continue to operate from distinct national bases; and lastly, that the prospects for regulation by international cooperation, the formation of trading blocs, and the development of new national strategies that take account of internationalization are by no means exhausted. Indeed, we have argued that entities like the European Union and the collaboration of the G3 indicate emerging potentialities for the governance of the world economy. Thus we remain sceptical about the more extreme claims for economic globalization, whilst at the same time accepting that the international economy has changed radically in structure and forms of governance from those that prevailed in the long boom from the early 1950s to the 1973 oil crisis.

In the course of the analysis of the previous chapters we have identified five major characteristics of the emerging international economy that are worth reiterating as part of this conclusion.

First, within the contemporary international economy the important relationships remain those between the more developed economies, particularly the members of the OECD. Indeed, these economies have increased in their relative importance over recent years in terms of their share of world trade and investment. In the early 1990s about 80 per cent of world trade was conducted between the OECD economies, and this rises to 85 per cent if the former Eastern European and Soviet economies are included. The Group of Five (G5) main economies accounted for approximately 70 per cent of foreign direct investment. Thus for all practical intents and purposes it is the advanced industrial economies that constitute the membership of the 'global' economy, if that entity can be said to exist. The less developed countries (LDCs), and even the NICs, still constitute a very small part of the international economy, however regrettable or disappointing that may be. The primary producers are more or less totally dependent upon the more developed countries (MDCs) for markets and investment, which is a position that has not significantly changed for many decades.

Second, there is little doubt that there has been a progressive internationalization of money and capital markets since the 1970s, and this is a marked change in the post-war period. Many have seized upon this as a sign of the radical change towards a globalizing economy in the post-1970s period. It has led to the strong argument that national economies are no longer governable because they have become increasingly penetrated by 'international financial capital'. This inability to control capital flows undermined any remaining credibility of the policies of national macroeconomic management.

But the implications of this internationalization of financial markets are not unambiguous. We have shown that the international financial penetration of the UK and other economies (in terms of openness to capital flows) was *greater* between 1900 and 1914 than it was in the late 1980s, and similar results emerge for foreign trade as a percentage of GDP. Thus it is important to remember that the international economy was hardly less integrated before 1914 than it is today. Financial and other major markets were closely integrated once the system of international submarine telegraph cables was in place and in a way not fundamentally different from the satellite-linked and computer-controlled markets of today. Commentators sometimes forget that today's open world economy is not unique.

Moreover, we must be careful to elaborate the reasons for the admittedly phenomenal recent growth of international financial flows and liquidity. Here we need to emphasize (a) the floating of exchange rates, (b) the oil price hike and consequent Third World debt problem, (c) the unexpected emergence of vast and mobile OPEC funds, (d) the international recession and the growth in government debt through the 1970s, (e) the emergent structural imbalances in payments for a number of large economies, and finally (f) the liberalization and deregulation of financial markets by national governments, and the abandonment of capital control. All these features went to increase the extent of international capital flows. If we were to single out one central feature it would surely be the floating of exchange rates. Many of the other features followed as a consequence of this (e.g. the undermining of capital controls and the integration of trading on currency and equity markets, which *is* a new feature of the present period).

This demonstrates how many of these changes may be temporary. They are not irreversible. Volatility on the international currency markets could diminish. The major international currencies are to some degree 'managed' currencies, though there remains a lack of political will on the part of the main players to extend existing forms of management. Furthermore, after an initial enthusiastic embrace of market liberalization and deregulation the authorities are recognizing that there are undesirable consequences of this and the trend now is for re-regulation. In addition, there are signs that the structural imbalances on the payments accounts of the main players, and of the USA in particular, are at last beginning to ease – and similarly with the rate of growth of government fiscal imbalances. Overall the fiscal stance of the important economies has moved into a position of 'structural improvement' since the late 1970s and early 1980s. All these trends could help to 'cool the casino' more or less automatically, without further major structural changes in international governance.

Third, there has been an increasing volume of trade in semi-manufactured and manufactured goods between the industrialized economies. Most markets for major industrial products are now international and major economies both import and export significant volumes of such goods, whereas before the 1960s home sourcing was dominant and export markets were more specialized. This has had an inevitable impact on the ability of individual economies to exercise national macro-management strategies. But it is important to recognize that the European Union as a whole and the other large bloc economies still export a surprisingly low proportion of their overall GDP.

Fourth, one of the main concomitants of the growth in interdependent trade relations, limited though these may still be, is the progressive development of internationalized companies. This also involves foreign direct investment. The potential role of the TNCs in undermining a national government's conduct of an independent economic policy has already been raised. But the extent of these developments is questionable. Most international companies still only operate in a small number of countries, or at most regionally. In other words there are few true TNCs: the MNC form continues to dominate, and the few exceptions to this do not yet make the rule. In addition, most MNCs adapt passively to governmental policy rather than continually trying to undermine it. The real question to ask of MNCs is not why they are always threatening to up and leave a country if things seem to go badly for them there, but why the vast majority of them fail to leave and continue to stay put in their home base and major centres of investment. MNCs are very reluctant to uproot themselves because they get entrenched in specific national markets, and with local suppliers and dealers. This makes it both difficult and expensive to leave given national markets unless there are fundamental structural disincentives, rather than conjunctural difficulties or specific policy constraints imposed by national governments.

Nor is direct foreign investment as important as is often believed. In relation to trade growth since the Second World War, for instance, the aggregate growth of direct investment has, until very recently, been small. In general the most successful industrial nations (e.g. Germany and Japan) have shown a great reluctance to invest and develop core manufacturing activity abroad; they have kept the bulk of their value-adding capacity at home (though this may be changing as these countries are forced to react to the seemingly relentless appreciation of their currencies). In both cases this is for a variety of reasons, not all of which can be summed up in market efficiency or balance sheet terms. German and Japanese financial capital remains 'nationalistic', committed to its domestic manufacturing sector in a way Anglo-American capital is not. German and Japanese firms have a strong commitment to highly skilled and motivated labour forces, and a national 'deal' between labour and capital to sustain prosperity is a core part of their post-1945 politico-economic settlements. In both countries there would be a massive political price to pay were a major part of manufacturing to be shipped abroad and the prosperity of recent decades to falter.

Fifth, perhaps the most significant post-1970s development, and the most enduring, is the formation of supra-national trading and economic blocs. The major problem that the development of a more regionalized international economy presents is the protectionist sentiments that it may engender. If such sentiments were to strongly emerge they could undermine some of the other trends towards internationalization identified in the book, like the increase in interdependent world trade flows in particular, but also the further integration of financial markets. This issue needs a little closer examination. The general question is the form of the global economy as the liberal multilateralism of the post-war period is forced onto the defensive. Clearly this is the dominant trend of the present period, and it allows us to sum up on an important question examined in this book. Will 'globalization' replace the existing emphasis on liberal multilateralism (or minilateralism – see below) and further internationalization of economic activity? Our response is to suggest not. A more likely outcome is the further development of a newly regionalized international economy, possibly dominated by a trilateralism of the US/NAFTA, the (expanding) EU, and Japan (with or without possible Pacific Rim allies). This itself will also involve an increase in bilateral negotiation between these major players and other lesser parties – what was termed in chapter 6 'minilateralism'. If one calls this outcome 'globalization' so be it, but it does not conform to the ideal type elaborated in chapter 1.

The above discussion indicates that, whilst classical *national* economic management now has limited scope and multilateral mechanisms of governance of the international economy in the 1945–73 period are now largely obsolete, there are emerging issues for possibilities of governance that require theoretical specification and analysis. As we have argued in earlier chapters, the economies of nation states are less subject to the actions of 'government', that is, to the territorially bounded authority of agencies with the capacity to make specific and effective policy dispositions. It does not follow, however, that economic relations at both international and national levels are beyond 'governance', that is, means of regulation and control. The agencies of governance are less likely to be nation states or their officials. The issue of governance without or beyond government is now central, and in particular the possible agencies of and mechanisms for the control, stabilization and redistribution of key economic functions. Chief amongst these factors are exchange rate stability and flows of FDI. It has proved difficult to manage exchange rates without strong capital controls. But a return to any Bretton Woods style capital controls looks increasingly unfeasible, though the alternative of completely floating rates is equally unlikely to prove acceptable to the international political community. Thus further attempts to institute some 'intermediate' position of regulation around target zones and taxes on purely speculative activity seems more than likely. International coordination, governance by cooperation between the major trade blocs, and national-level mobilization in favour of such international objectives offer possibilities for creating a newly ordered and prosperous world economy. One of the reasons such possibilities are not seized upon is the prevailing pessimism about the feasibility of regulatory action in the face of global markets, and in this respect the most enthusiastic proponents of 'globalization' encourage passivity.

Some of the emerging agencies of economic governance, like the EU, remain poised between the old era of national economic management and the new. The creation of the single market is forging an integrated regional economy, but without appropriate institutional structures or policy mechanisms to regulate it. The EU will not become a unitary super-state; equally it cannot function effectively if it remains a loose federation of states with no settled distribution of regulatory powers between trade bloc, national and regional levels. If this mismatch continues, the prospect is for greater 'disintegration' as economic forces and problems slip through gaps in the different levels of governance. If a coherent policy does emerge it will be to create an 'economic Europe' governed at the highest level by functionally specific confederal public powers. These will be different from a traditional state; they will have limited and defined functions and they will lack the authority to impose their will on subsidiary political bodies. The main capacity that will define and sustain these public powers is that they, and only they, can effectively shape and coordinate policy *outwards* with respect to and in cooperation with the other major trading blocs like NAFTA and Japan. Thus the EU will be most successful if it acts to promote *international* economic governance rather than introduces inward-looking and territorially bounded policy measures. If Europe requires a new idea of the role of agencies of economic governance, then this is also true of strictly international forms of cooperation and coordination.

As this book was being finalized, two important events for the international economy were taking place. The first of these was the Barings crisis when the oldest and most distinguished of Britain's merchant banks went into insolvency as its Singapore trading in futures contracts opened it to potentially incalculable losses. This crisis involved the issue of 'derivatives' discussed in chapter 6. The other event involved a potentially much more disruptive development for the international economy, the exchange rate turmoil sparked off by the rapid depreciation of the Mexican peso, first of all involving just the 'emerging markets' in a number of the new financial centres in Latin America and East Asia, but then spilling over into the well-established markets where the US dollar and sterling experienced sustained depreciationary pressure against the Japanese yen and particularly the German Deutschmark.

What are we to make of these twin developments in terms of the features and arguments advanced in the previous chapters about the international economy still being relatively un-integrated? On the surface, at least, these two events would seem to indicate the very close integration of the financial system, where events at one location in the international financial system quickly spill over into other centres.

Our argument is not that financial centres are un-integrated – they are clearly integrated. The point is rather the extent of such integration and the nature of the links in operation. The US could not put together a coherent package to save the peso, even though it is supposed to be integrating with Mexico's real economy through the NAFTA process. The crisis in Mexico indicates the still precarious nature of the growth potential and stability of the newly revitalized economies in Latin America and beyond. The wider exchange rate turmoil indicates the need to regulate further the international financial system, not to abandon it to the forces of speculation and market advantage. What this highlights is the ongoing battle between the public authorities at various levels and short-term market dictated outcomes. It again raises the issue of the possible terms and mechanisms of macro-governance at national and international levels so as to contain the undesirable effects of market operations. Similar points can be made about the Barings crisis, but at more of a micro-level. Regulation to more effectively monitor the internal liquidity and potential insolvency position of international banks is posed by this event. It is a question not just of recalcitrant or omnipotent dealers but of the systemic nature of markets and financial flows. Any attempt to hedge against the uncertainties endemic in the present arrangements of international financial markets – to get around those risks – remains a highly dangerous bet. Under these circumstances very legitimate public concerns and interests are at stake which warrant not less but more regulation and better governance.

Appendix

Data Set Construction

The first data set used in chapter 4 is derived from information found in two published sources: the *Macmillan Directory of Multinational Corporations* and the *UNCTAD/Moody's Directory of Multinational Service Companies*. The second data set is derived from the *Worldscope Global* disk of company financial information available on CD-ROM. Each of the two newly formed data sets derived from these sources now exists in an Excel spreadsheet format, from which the analysis in chapter 4 was generated.

The first of the data bases contains information on 533 of the largest MNCs for the late 1980s, mostly for the 'year' 1987. Three hundred and fifty of these companies are what are termed here 'manufacturing' companies, but include some primary producers, while the other 183 are service sector companies. There is some slight imprecision in the 'year' for which these data are recorded. This is because the companies included in the original sources did not provide information in their accounts for a uniform period: financial years differ and some report on a calendar year basis. As far as possible the financial year 1987–8 was the one designated, but to keep the coverage comprehensive there was some variation around this. Thus the analysis completed for this period should be taken as indicative of the position in the late 1980s.[1] The full data set is coded according to the main activity four-digit international standard industrial classification (ISIC) number of the company, and information is available on the geographical distribution of assets, profits, sales and affiliates for companies. Not all companies report information on all of these, so coverage is patchy.

The data apply to those companies with a 'home base' in one of the following five countries: Canada, Germany, Japan, the UK and the USA. These were the countries with a reasonable number of companies reporting in the original information sources. This is not a sample population in the true sense, since all the companies from the five countries found in the published sources that provided the relevant data are included in the population sets. Table A.1 shows a breakdown of these companies.

The second data set pertains to the year 1992–3, though with similar caveats as indicated above. It takes data from what was available in the first quarter of 1994 on the *Worldscope Global* data disk (the *Worldscope Global* disk is updated quarterly). These data only show the geographical distribution of company sales and assets. Again, they are coded on a four-digit ISIC basis. However, there are many more companies in the data set, which in this instance is organized in terms of six 'home countries': France, Germany, Japan, the Netherlands, the UK and the USA. Again, these countries were the ones with the most extensive coverage for their companies reported on the original data disk. Table A.2 gives the breakdown of companies.

Table A.1   Breakdown of companies for 1987 analysis

Country of origin	Number	%
Canada	20	3.8
Germany	35	6.6
Japan	90	16.9
UK	82	15.4
USA	306	57.4
Total	533	100

Source: Data set, see text

Table A.2   Breakdown of companies for 1992–3 analysis

Country of origin	Total companies on disk	Companies with some geographical breakdown	%
France	572	324	57
Germany	483	298	62
Japan	1,606	1,098	68
Netherlands	166	103	62
UK	1,714	1,388	81
USA	3,300	2,332	71
Total	7,841	5,543	71

Source: *Worldscope Global* data disk

In all there are data for nearly 11,000 companies on the *Worldscope* disk, so those with home base in our six countries comprised approximately 70 per cent of the total; and of these companies, those that give some geographical breakdown of their activity amounted to 71 per cent, as shown in table A.2. The companies as sorted in table A.2 were the ones used for the basic analysis reported in the main text, but with one additional adjustment to restrict them to those that showed a geographical breakdown of their activity beyond their own domestic territory. Table A.3 gives the breakdown of these companies.

It is worth sounding a note of caution about the quality of the data on both these data sets. Reporting of information can differ significantly within countries, but perhaps more importantly between countries. In general, the information from the US, the UK, Canada and the Netherlands is more extensive and more uniform than that from the other countries covered. In particular Japanese and German companies report very little geographically specified information. This is largely because of different accounting conventions between countries. The US, the UK and Canada are required by law and convention to disclose more information in their accounts, and this translates through into more geographically specified data.

Finally, table A.4 shows the geographical breakdown of company activity as adopted in this study.

Table A.3 Number and origin of companies used for main 1992–3 MNC sales and asset analysis

Country of origin	Sales	Assets
France	208	22
Germany	257	–
Japan	389	719
Netherlands	103	7
UK	896	419
USA	815	810
Total	2,668	1,977

Source: Data set, see text

Table A.4   Country location definitions

Europe	South East Asia	Pacific	Middle East	Latin America	Caribbean
Included					
EEC member	S. Korea	Thailand	Israel	Brazil	Netherlands
states	Singapore	Australia	UAE	Argentina	Antilles
Eastern	Malaysia	New Zealand		Mexico	CARICOM
Europe	India	Fiji		Puerto Rico	member
	Hong Kong				states
	Philippines				
Excluded					
Turkey				Belize	Bermuda
				Guyana	

Notes

Chapter 1 Introduction: Globalization – a Necessary Myth?

1 This distinction between MNCs and TNCs is not usual. There is a tendency to use them interchangeably, increasingly with the use of TNC as a generally accepted term for both types. Where we use the term TNC it should be clear that we are referring to a *true* TNC in the context of discussing the strong globalizers' view.

2 Obviously, conjunctural changes *could* result in a change of international economic system: the question is whether they have. Our point here is to caution against citing phenomena generated by such changes as if they were part of and evidence for a process of structural transformation driven by deep-seated causes, called 'globalization'.

Chapter 2 Globalization and the History of the International Economy

1 By the term 'autonomy' we mean the ability of the authorities in a national economy to determine their own economic policy and implement that policy. This is obviously a matter of degree. Autonomy is closely linked to 'openness', 'interdependence' and 'integration', three other categories used in this and subsequent chapters. Openness implies the degree to which national economies are subject to the actions of economic agents located outside their borders and the extent to which their own economic agents are oriented towards external economic activity. This is in turn linked to the degree of interdependence of the economic system in which these agents operate. Thus interdependence expresses the systemic links between all economic activity within a system or regime. Integration is the process by which interdependence is established.

2   France devalued twice, in 1957 and 1958, Germany in 1961, Britain in 1967 and Germany and France again in 1969, all against the US dollar: hence the designation of this period as a dollar standard.

3   This refers to the exchange rate element of the BWS only. The total BWS comprised not just its exchange rate part but also the activity of the IMF and the IBRD (World Bank). In so far as these two institutions still exist and function much as planned at the BW Conference, these elements of the BWS still operate.

4   Take possibly the simplest case of short-term interest rate differentials. These rates will vary with local regulations, with the riskiness and precise duration of the loans, as local structural conditions vary the possibilities of generating monopoly rents, and so on. Thus differences between rates in financial centres could be due to these local conditions rather than to the integration or separation of markets as such.

5   This scepticism is registered in the careful analyses contained in Banuri and Schor (1992).

6   Before 1870 the British suspended convertibility in 1847, 1857 and 1866, but each time restored it quickly at the previous parity. It should be noted, however, that there were a large number of suspensions of, withdrawals from and readmissions to the system amongst the peripheral economies.

7   This is a somewhat controversial position: the general sentiment is that the US Federal Reserve was unique amongst central banks in being able to unilaterally stabilize its own price level – inclusive of tradable goods.

Chapter 3   Trade, Foreign Direct Investment and International Inequality

1   The UN has adopted the term 'transnational corporations' (TNCs) to designate what are here termed MNCs. The distinction we adopt pertains to the discussion in chapter 1, and we use MNC here and in the following chapter, other than where an organization so obviously corresponds to our definition of a TNC. The reason for this usage will become clear as a result of the analysis of the following chapter.

2   In fact, the empirical results emerging from NTT models have only been modest, particularly in the case of positive effects of strategic trade policy (CERP 1994).

3   As indicated earlier, from 1995 the GATT mechanism is to be replaced by a World Trade Organization (WTO). We discuss this change further in chapter 6, but the point being made here remains.

4   Similar remarks could be made about the position developing *within* just the EU in the 'post-1994' period (see Colombo and Mariotti 1994, particularly pp. 153–5).

5   In 1994, China became the single most important country of destination for FDI. See also the analysis of chapter 5.

6   In terms of measures that try to present comparable distributional evidence on a consistent and deflated basis, the distribution of world income remains about the same between the two periods shown.

7   UNCTAD has called for a new international 'speculation tax' on short-term
    financial flows to finance a modest redistribution to the poorer nations. This
    tax proposal was endorsed by the March 1995 Copenhagen UNESCO-spon-
    sored World Summit for Social Development. In chapter 6 we review this
    proposal further.

Chapter 4   Multinational Corporations and the Globalization Thesis

1   This 'other' category also captures some ambiguity in classifying how com-
    panies register the geographical distribution of their sales. The 'other' cat-
    egory is sometimes used as a catch-all category to allocate sales when limited
    geographical areas are used. In as much as this occurs, it underestimates some
    of the designated area distribution shown in the figures (though the relative
    importance of the 'other' category is small in most of the figures). In addition,
    sales are sometimes allocated geographically on a 'production zone' basis
    rather than on a 'sales zone' basis, although the difference between these is
    not always apparent.
2   Note that no primary sector asset information was reported for France or the
    Netherlands.
3   Thus the 'home region' for German companies in both years comprises
    Germany itself, the rest of Europe, the Middle East and Africa (although
    these latter two areas account for very little overall sales); 'home region' for
    Japanese companies comprises Japan and South East Asia; for the UK it
    comprises the UK itself, the rest of Europe, the Middle East and Africa
    (again, where the latter two areas are not very important); and for US
    companies it includes the US and Canada. These aggregations are dictated by
    the way it was possible to code the 1987 data.
4   The argument is not that there are *no* TNCs. There clearly are some firms,
    usually very large ones and probably a very small number, that have adopted
    a more TNC style of operation. Our analysis pertains to the *aggregate* of
    international companies, though these are 'large' in the usual sense of that
    definition.

Chapter 5   Economic Backwardness and Future Prosperity: the Developing Economies and Globalization

1   On East Asian industrialization and especially the role of the state and public
    policy, see Applebaum and Henderson (1992), Amsden (1989), Deyo (1987),
    Haggard (1990), Henderson (1989) and Wade (1990). For a comparison of
    East Asian and Latin American industrialization, see Gereffi and Wyman
    (1990).

Chapter 6   Economic Governance Issues in General

1   Another example would be that the domestic structure and organization of
    Japanese retailing can preclude the implementation of internationally agreed

norms for 'market access', and there is little that Japanese governments can do about this.

2   Clearly, this relationship between the USA and Japan would seem to break the high correlation between national savings and investment ratios discussed in chapter 2. However, while it does this for these two countries, there is no indication that things have dramatically changed in other countries, and Europe as a whole has not followed the trend. Also, this pertains to overall financial flows, not necessarily just to private real resource flows. Finally, of course, there is no necessary reason why this situation should continue indefinitely. The old relationships could be re-established.

3   Here our conclusion very much resembles that of Gilpin (1987).

4   The IOSCO promotes harmonization and cooperation between different national regulatory environments. Among the major issues discussed at its recent meetings are capital adequacy standards, supervision of financial conglomerates, international auditing standards, coordination between cash and derivatives markets, money laundering, means of combating insider dealing, transparency in secondary market transactions, and emerging securities markets. It has set up a number of technical committees to investigate these areas, with the aim of agreeing regulatory principles for them.

5   This chapter was completed before the Barings crisis of March 1995, but the remarks here prefigure that crisis and in part help to explain it. The fuller implications of the Barings crisis are discussed in the concluding chapter to this book.

6   This was confirmed by the Barings crisis of March 1995 where, although the Singapore authorities took an obvious and active interest in the outcome of the crisis, it was within the City of London and its supervisory network that the final deals were done and the regulatory issues investigated.

7   The Final Act was signed in Marrakesh, Morocco, on 15 April 1994.

8   At the international level UNCTAD conducts this kind of analysis from the Geneva headquarters of its Division on Transnational Corporations and Investment. UNCTAD and the DTCI also have extensive expertise on issues such as transfer pricing.

9   Clearly, the case of the UK alcohol market has shown that some people will travel to continental Europe to obtain their purchases at a lower tax rate. While this is an important example it should not be exaggerated: there is extensive compliance with the existing situation by most consumers.

Chapter 8   Globalization, Governance and the Nation State

1   This discussion of nationalism draws on two quite contrary approaches, that of Benedict Anderson (1991) which stresses the character of cultural homogeneity as a political project, and that of Eric Hobsbawm (1992) whose scepticism about nationalist politics and whose practice of confronting the rhetoric of nationalists with the political and cultural complexities they seek to homogenize is a healthy corrective. Weber (1979) is an excellent study of the creation of cultural homogeneity in France.

2   This is in many ways the entry of states into a 'civil order' and no longer an anarchy: it moves international relations on beyond the 'deterred state' and closer to the nuclear stand-off advocated by Schell (1984).

3   Proliferation is unlikely to undermine this proposition. The mutual pos-
    session of nuclear weapons by antagonistic regional powers (like India and
    Pakistan) will result in a state of deterrence and also a curb on conventional
    military adventures. Major nuclear powers will strive to disarm pariah states
    like Iraq or North Korea, probably with some degree of success. The real
    dangers stem from the breakup of unstable regimes with nuclear weapons
    and nuclear terrorism. The former will probably be subject to political and
    military sanction by the Great Powers, and the latter, while a real threat,
    cannot be contained either by deterrence or by conventional war, but is an
    intelligence and police matter.
4   It has become fashionable to erect political Islam, and other anti-Western
    movements, into a major threat: see for example Huntingdon (1993). He
    argues that after the ending of the conflict of ideologies we are moving into a
    new era of the 'clash of civilizations'. Four points can be made against this
    claim: (1) that it is not evident that there are homogeneous 'civilizations'
    opposed one to another in essence, rather there are relatively brittle politico-
    religious ideologies that are highly particular constructions of Islam or,
    among fundamentalist conservatives in the West, Christianity; (2) that radical
    political Islam lacks a coherent and practical strategy for economic and social
    life; (3) that in the case of Islam such politics are those of protest rather than
    being general and allegedly hegemonic alternatives to capitalism, as socialism
    claimed to be in the East and West; (4) that Islamic fundamentalist regimes
    are radically different in character and often extremely hostile one to
    another. On political Islam see Zubaida (1993).
5   For an interesting series of discussions of the difference between governance
    and government and of the possible forms of non-state regulation in inter-
    national arenas see Rosenau and Czempiel (1992); see also the World Bank's
    attempt to define the roles of states in respect to good governance in its 1994
    report *Governance*.
6   It is probably the case that Keynes's main legacy to the modern world is not
    his account of the management of national economies in *The General Theory*
    but his long-term emphasis on the corrosive effects of uncertainty on invest-
    ment, output and trade and the value of a calculable international monetary
    framework in stabilizing expectations. Skidelsky's biography (1992) is excep-
    tionally valuable and suggestive in demonstrating the importance of Keynes's
    ideas today, for it shows him (especially in the 1920s) wrestling with the
    problem of national policy in a highly internationalized and volatile world
    economy.
7   See Ohmae (1993) for the argument that region states can become salient in
    an era where nation states are declining. Region states or networks of city
    states are another thing entirely from the organized industrial district or
    subsidiary regional governments, and, although a fashionable idea (building
    on the success of Singapore or Hong Kong), are unlikely to become a wide-
    spread *alternative* to nation states. They rely both on strong international
    economic governance and on the collective security provided by major
    states. They are too small to survive alone in the face of less economically suc-
    cessful but militarily strong political powers. They cannot bear the full
    costs of security or economic regulation alone without losing competitive

advantage, and larger political entities will not allow them a free ride if they become differentially successful and put competitive pressure on their own economies.

8   The reference here is to those princes of the Holy Roman Empire who enjoyed the right to elect the Emperor. The Empire was not a 'sovereign' state but a political entity made up of associated institutions with varying powers of governance: its policies were determined by the Emperor, the Electors and the Imperial Diet. It could hardly be a model for the modern world, but given our need to understand emerging political relationships it has some limited value as an analogy. For debates on the constitutional states of the Empire at the period of the formation of the modern state see Franklin (1991).

Appendix   Data Set Construction

1   The *Macmillan Directory,* on which part of this data set was based, has recently been updated with an edition that reports data for 1992.

Further Reading

The literature on globalization is vast and, apart from extreme views, many authors argue that a fundamental shift has taken place in the international economy: see Chase-Dunn (1989), Dicken (1992), Dunning (1993), Julius (1990), Kennedy (1993). For judicious overviews of the world economic system see Gilpin (1987) and Wallace (1990). Lang and Hines (1993) see a global free-market economy as the dominant trend but argue that its consequences will be disastrous and that production needs to be relocalized to the benefit of advanced and developing countries alike. We have discussed and criticized some of these arguments and tendencies (Hirst and Thompson 1992).

For sociological views of globalization, see Featherstone (1990), Robertson (1992) and Sklair (1991).

For views of the political system, see Camilleri and Falk (1992) for a careful review of recent developments on national sovereignty, and Horsman and Marshall (1994) for an argument that world economic and social changes are rapidly reducing the power of the nation state. Rosenau (1990) is a valuable review of the changing faces and issues in world politics, as is McGrew and Lewis (1992). Rosenau and Czempiel (1992) is the most suggestive source on forms of governance beyond the nation state. Ostrom (1990) is a powerful argument about conditions in which it is possible to regulate the use of common resources, and shows the formidable difficulties experienced by regimens in governing the 'global commons'. Held (1991; 1993a; 1993b; 1994) raises the legitimate if deeply problematic issue of democratic government in an internationalizing world.

References

Akyuz, Y. and Cornford, A. (1995) 'Controlling Capital Movements: Some Proposals for Reform' in Michie, J. and Grieve-Smith, J. (eds) *Managing the Global Economy*. Oxford: Oxford University Press.

Albert, M (1993) *Capitalism Against Capitalism*. London: Whurr.

Amsden, A.H. (1989) *Asia's Next Giant: South Korea and Late Industrialization*. New York: Oxford University Press.

Anderson, B. (1991) *Imagined Communities*. London: Verso.

Applebaum, R.P. and Henderson, J. (1992) *States and Development in the Asian Pacific Rim*. Newbury Park, CA: Sage.

Archibugi, Daniele and Michie, Jonathan (1995) 'The Globalisation of Technology: A New Taxonomy' *Cambridge Journal of Economics*, vol. 19, pp. 121–140.

Archibugi, Daniele and Pianta, Mario (1992) *The Technological Specialization of Advanced Countries*. Dordrecht: Kluwer.

Artis, M. and Ostry, S. (1986) 'International Policy Coordination' *Chatham House Papers*, no. 30. London: Royal Institute for International Affairs.

Atkinson, D. and Kelly, R. (1994) *The Wrecker's Lamp: Do Currency Markets Leave Us on the Rocks?* London: IPPR.

Bailey, D., Harte, G. and Sugden, R. (1994) *Making Transnationals Accountable*. London: Routledge.

Banuri, T. and Schor, J.B. (eds) (1992) *Financial Openness and National Autonomy*. Oxford: Clarendon Press.

Barrington Moore, J.M. (1967) *The Social Origins of Dictatorship and Democracy*. London: Allen Lane.

Bartlett, C.A. and Ghoshal, S. (1989) *Managing Across Borders – The Transnational Solution*. Boston: Harvard Business School Press.

Bayoumi, T.A. (1990) 'Saving–Investment Correlations: Immobile Capital, Government Policy or Endogenous Behaviour?' *IMF Staff Papers*, vol. 37, no. 2, June, pp. 360–87.

Bayoumi, T.A. and Rose, A.K. (1993) 'Domestic Savings and Intra-national Capital Flows' *European Economic Review*, vol. 37, pp. 1197–202.

Bergsten, C. Fred (1994) 'Managing the World Economy of the Future' in Kenen, P.B. (ed.) *Managing the World Economy: Fifty Years after Bretton Woods*. Washington, DC: Institute for International Economics.

Bergsten, C. Fred and Graham, Edward M. (1992) 'Needed: New International Rules for Foreign Direct Investment' *The International Trade Journal*, vol. VII, no. 1, Fall, pp. 15–44.

Bodin, J. (1576) *On Sovereignty*, ed. Franklin, J.H. Cambridge: Cambridge University Press.

Bonturi, Marcos and Fukasaku, Kiichiro (1993) 'Globalisation and Intra-Firm Trade: An Empirical Note' *OECD Economic Studies*, no. 20, Spring, pp. 145–59.

Bosworth, B.P. (1993) *Saving and Investment in a Global Economy*. Washington, DC: Brookings Institution.

Brodie, B. (1946) *The Absolute Weapon*. New York: Harcourt Brace.

Brodie, B. (1965) *Strategy in the Missile Age*. Princeton: Princeton University Press.

Bull, H. (1977) *The Anarchical Society: A Study of Order in World Politics*. London: Macmillan.

Camilleri, J.A. and Falk, J. (1992) *The End of Sovereignty*. Aldershot: Edward Elgar.

Cantwell, J. (1992) 'The Internationalisation of Technological Activity and its Implications for Competitiveness' in Granstand, O., Hakanson, L. and Sjolander, S. (eds) *Technology Management and International Business*. Chichester: Wiley.

Casson, M., Pearce, R.D. and Singh, S. (1992) 'Global Integration through the Decentralisation of R&D' in Casson, M. (ed.) *International Business and Global Integration*. Basingstoke: Macmillan.

Castles, S. and Miller, M.J. (1993) *The Age of Mass Migration*. Basingstoke: Macmillan.

CERP (1994) *New Trade Theories: A Look at the Empirical Evidence*. London: Centre for Economic Policy Research.

Chase, B.F. (1993) 'Tropical Forests and Trade Policy: The Legality of Unilateral Attempts to Promote Sustainable Development under the GATT' *Third World Quarterly*, vol. 14, no. 4, pp. 749–74.

Chase-Dunn, C. (1989) *Global Formation: Structures of the World Economy*. Oxford: Basil Blackwell.

Colombo, M.G. and Mariotti, S. (1994) 'Europe and Cross-Border M&As' in Commission of the European Communities. *The European Community and the Globalization of Technology and the Economy*. Forecasting and Assessment in Science and Technology Report, EUR 15150, Brussels.

Commission of the European Communities (1990) 'One Market, One Money' *European Economy*, no. 44, October. Brussels.

Commission of the European Communities (1994) *The European Community and the Globalization of Technology and the Economy*. Forecasting and Assessment in Science and Technology Report, EUR 15150, Brussels.

Corley, T.A.B. (1994) 'Britain's Overseas Investments in 1914 Revisited' *Business History*, vol. 36, no. 1, January, pp. 71–88.

Cosh, A.D., Hughes, A. and Singh, A. (1992) 'Openness, Financial Innovation, Changing Patterns of Ownership, and the Structure of Financial Markets' in Banuri, T. and Schor, J.B. (eds) *Financial Openness and National Autonomy*. Oxford: Clarendon Press.

Deyo, F.C. (ed.) (1987) *The Political Economy of the New Asian Industrialization*. Ithaca, NY: Cornell University Press.

Dicken, P. (1992) *Global Shift: The Internationalization of Economic Activity* (2nd edn). London: Chapman and Hall.

Doyle, M.W. (1983) 'Kant, Liberal Legacies and Foreign Affairs' *Philosophy and Public Affairs*, vol. 12, part 1 pp. 205–35, part 2 pp. 325–53.

Dunning, J.H. (1993) *Multinational Enterprises and the Global Economy* Wokingham: Addison-Wesley.

Durkheim, E. (1893) *The Division of Labour in Society*. New York: Free Press, 1964.

Economist (1994) 'The Global Economy' *The Economist*, 1 October, pp. 3–46.

Eichengreen, B. (1990) *Elusive Stability*. Cambridge: Cambridge University Press.

Eichengreen, B. (1994) *International Monetary Arrangements for the 21st Century*. Washington, DC: Brookings Institution.

Eichengreen, B., Tobin, J. and Wyplosz, C. (1995) 'Two Cases for Sand in the Wheels of International Finance' *The Economic Journal*, vol. 105, January, pp. 162–72.

Featherstone, M. (ed.) (1990) *Global Culture: Nationalism, Globalisation and Modernity*. London: Sage.

Feldstein, M. (1983) 'Domestic Savings and International Capital Movements in the Long Run and the Short Run' *European Economic Review*, vol. 21, pp. 129–51.

Feldstein, M. and Horioka, C. (1980) 'Domestic Saving and International Capital Flows' *Economic Journal*, vol. 90, pp. 314–29.

Figgis, J.N. (1913) *Churches in the Modern State*. London: Longmans Green.

Frankel, J.A. (1992) 'Measuring International Capital Mobility: A Review' *American Economic Review*, vol. 82, no. 2, pp. 197–202.

Frankel, J.A., Dooley, M. and Mathieson, D. (1986) 'International Capital Mobility in Developing Countries *vs* Industrial Countries: What Do Saving–Investment Correlations Tell Us?' *NEBR Working Paper Series,* no. 2043, October, Cambridge, MA.

Franklin, J.H. (1991) 'Sovereignty and the Mixed Constitution' in Burns, J.H. (ed.) *The Cambridge History of Political Thought* 1450–1700. Cambridge: Cambridge University Press, pp. 309–28.

Galbraith, J.K. (1993) *The Culture of Contentment*. London: Penguin.

Gales, B.P.A. and Sluyterman, K.E. (1993) 'Outward Bound: The Rise of Dutch Multinationals' in Jones, G. and Schröter, H.G. (eds) *The Rise of Multinationals in Continental Europe*. Aldershot: Edward Elgar.

Garber, P. and Taylor, M.P. (1995) 'Sand in the Wheels of Foreign Exchange Markets: A Sceptical Note' *The Economic Journal*, vol. 105, January, pp. 173–80.

GATT Secretariat (1993) 'The Draft Act of the Uruguay Round Press Summary' *The World Economy*, vol. 16, no. 2, March, pp. 237–59.

Gereffi, G.S. and Wyman, D.L. (eds) (1990) *Manufacturing Miracles: Paths of*

Industrialization in Latin America and East Asia. Princeton, NJ: Princeton University Press.

Gershenkron, A. (1966) *Economic Backwardness in Historical Perspective.* Cambridge, MA: Belkamp.

Ghosh, A.R. (1995) 'International Capital Mobility amongst the Major Industrialised Countries: Too Little or Too Much?' *The Economic Journal*, vol. 105, January, pp. 107–28.

Gierke, O.Y. (1900) *Political Theories of the Middle Ages*, ed. Maitland, F.W. Cambridge: Cambridge University Press, 1988.

Gilpin, R. (1987) *The Political Economy of International Relations.* Princeton: Princeton University Press.

Goldsmith, J. (1994) *The Trap.* London: Macmillan.

Grahl, J. and Thompson, G.F. (1995) 'The Prospects for European Economic Integration: Macroeconomics, Development Models and Growth' in Arestis, P. and Chick, V. (eds) *Finance, Development and Structural Change: Post-Keynesian Perspectives.* Cheltenham: Edward Elgar.

Grassman, S. (1980) 'Long Term Trends in Openness of National Economies' *Oxford Economic Papers*, vol. 32, no. 1, pp. 123–33.

Haggard, S. (1990) *Pathways from the Periphery: The Politics of Growth in Newly Industrializing Countries.* Ithaca, NY: Cornell University Press.

Harden I. (1995) 'The Constitution of the European Union' *Public Law*, Winter, pp. 609–24.

Harris, L. (1995) 'International Financial Markets and National Transmission Mechanisms' in Michie, J. and Grieve-Smith, J. (eds) *Managing the Global Economy.* Oxford: Oxford University Press.

Held, D. (1991) 'Democracy, the nation-state and the Global System' *Economy and Society*, vol. 20, no. 2, May, pp. 138–72.

Held, D. (1993a) 'Democracy: From City-States to a Cosmopolitan Order' in Held, D. (ed.) *Prospects for Democracy.* Cambridge: Polity, pp. 13–52.

Held, D. (1993b) *Democracy and the New International Order.* London: IPPR.

Held, D. (1994) 'Democracy and the New International Order' in Archibugi, D. and Held, D. (eds) *Cosmopolitan Democracy.* Cambridge: Polity.

Helleiner, E. (1994) *States and the Reemergence of Global Finance: From Bretton Woods to the 1990s.* Ithaca, NY: Cornell University Press.

Henderson, J. (1989) *The Globalization of High Technology Production: Society, Space and Semiconductors in the Restructuring of the Modern World.* London: Routledge.

Herring, R.J. and Litan, R.E. (1995) *Financial Regulation in the Global Economy.* Washington, DC: Brookings Institution.

Hewitt, P (1990) *Green Taxes.* London: IPPR.

Hindess, B. (1991) 'Imaginary Presuppositions of Democracy' *Economy and Society*, vol. 20, no. 2, May, pp. 173–95.

Hindess, B. (1992) 'Power and Rationality: The Western Concept of Political Community' *Alternatives*, vol. 17, no. 2, Spring, pp. 149–63.

Hinsley, H. (1986) *Sovereignty* (2nd edn). Cambridge: Cambridge University Press.

Hirst, P.Q. (1993) *Associative Democracy.* Cambridge: Polity.

Hirst, P.Q. (1994a) 'Why the National Still Matters' *Renewal*, vol. 2, no. 4, October, pp. 12–20.

Hirst, P.Q. (1994b) 'Security Challenges in Post-Communist Europe' in Freedman, L. (ed.) *Military Intervention in European Conflicts*. Oxford: *Political Quarterly*, Basil Blackwell.

Hirst, P.Q. (1995) 'The European Union at the Crossroads – Integration or Decline?' in Bellamy, R., Bufacchi, V. and Castiglione, D. *Democracy and Constitutional Culture in Europe*. London: Lothian Foundation.

Hirst, P.Q. and Thompson, G.F. (1992) 'The Problem of "Globalisation": International Economic Relations, National Economic Management and the Formation of Trading Blocs' *Economy and Society*, vol. 21, no. 4, November, pp. 357–96.

Hirst, P.Q. and Thompson, G.F. (1994) 'Globalization, Foreign Direct Investment and International Economic Governance' *Organization*, vol. 1, no. 2, pp. 277–303.

Hirst, P. and Zeitlin, J. (1989) 'Flexible Specialization and the Failure of UK Manufacturing' *The Political Quarterly*, vol. 60, no. 2, April/June, pp. 164–78.

Hirst, P. and Zeitlin, J. (1993) 'An Incomes Policy for Sustained Recovery' *The Political Quarterly*, vol. 64, no. 1, January/March, pp. 60–83.

Hobsbawm, E. (1992) *Nations and Nationalism since 1780*. Cambridge: Cambridge University Press.

Holtham, G. (1989) 'Foreign Exchange Markets and Target Zones' *Oxford Review of Economic Policy*, vol. 5, no. 3, Autumn.

Holtham, G. (1995) 'Managing the Exchange Rate System' in Michie, J. and Grieve-Smith, J. (eds) *Managing the Global Economy*. Oxford: Oxford University Press.

Horsman, M. and Marshall, A. (1994) *After the Nation State*. London: Harper Collins.

Howells, Jeremy and Wood, Michelle (1993) *The Globalisation of Production and Technology*. London: Belhaven.

Huntingdon, S. (1993) 'The Clash of Civilisations' *Foreign Affairs*, vol. 72, no. 3, Summer, pp. 22–49.

Hutton, W. (1995) *The State We're In*. London: Cape.

IMF (1993) 'Regional Trading Arrangements' *World Economic Outlook*, Annex III, May. Washington, DC: IMF.

Jackson, J.H. (1994) 'Managing the Trading System: The World Trade Organization and the Post-Uruguay GATT Agenda' in Kenen, P.B. (ed.) *Managing the World Economy*. Washington, DC: IIE.

Jones, G. (1994) 'The Making of Global Enterprise' *Business History*, vol. 36, no. 1, January, pp. 1–17.

Julius, D. (1990) *Global Companies and Public Policy*. London: RIIA, Pinter.

Julius, D. (1994) 'International Direct Investment: Strengthening the Policy Regime' in Kenen, P.B. (ed.) *Managing the World Economy*. Washington, DC: IIE.

Kant, I. (1991) *Perpetual Peace* in Reiss, H. (ed.) *Kant – Political Writings* (2nd edn.). Cambridge: Cambridge University Press.

Kapstein, E.B. (1991) 'We Are Us: The Myth of the Multi-National' *The National Interest*, Winter, pp. 55–62.

Kapstein, E.B. (1994) *Governing the Global Economy: International Finance and the State.* Cambridge, MA: Harvard University Press.

Kenen, P.B. (1995) 'Capital Controls, the EMS and EMU' *The Economic Journal,* vol. 105, January, pp. 181–92.

Kennedy, E. (1991) *The Bundesbank.* London: RIIA, Pinter.

Kennedy, P. (1993) *Preparing for the Twenty-First Century.* New York: Random House.

Kern, H. and Sabel, C. (1994) 'Verblaßte Tügenden. Zur Krise des deutschen Produktionsmodells' Umbruche gesellschaftlicher Arbeiter (Special Issue 9), *Soziale Welt.* Göttingen: Otto Schwartz, pp. 605–24.

Kirkpatrick, C. (1994) 'Regionalisation, Regionalism and East Asian Economic Cooperation' *The World Economy,* vol. 17, no. 2, March, pp. 191–202.

Kitson, M. and Michie, J. (1995) 'Trade and Growth: A Historical Perspective' in Michie, J. and Grieve-Smith, J. (eds) *Managing the Global Economy.* Oxford: Oxford University Press.

Kline, John M. (1993) 'International Regulation of Transnational Business: Providing the Missing Leg of Global Investment Standards' *Transnational Corporations,* vol. 2, no. 1, February, pp. 153–64.

Krugman, P. (1986) *Strategic Trade Policy and the New International Economics.* Cambridge, MA: MIT Press.

Krugman, P. (1987) 'Is Free Trade *Passé?*' *Journal of Economic Perspectives,* vol. 1, no. 2, pp. 131–44.

Krugman, P. (1994a) 'Competitiveness: A Dangerous Obsession' *Foreign Affairs,* vol. 74, no. 2, March/April, pp. 28–44.

Krugman, P. (1994b) 'Does Third World Growth Hurt First World Prosperity?' *Harvard Business Review,* July–August, pp. 113–121.

Krugman, P. (1994c) 'The Myth of Asia's Miracle', *Foreign Affairs,* November–December, pp. 63–75.

Lang, T. and Hines, C. (1993) *The New Protectionism.* London: Earthscan.

Lash, S. and Urry, J. (1987) *The End of Organised Capitalism.* Cambridge: Polity.

Lenin, V.I. (1899) *The Development of Capitalism in Russia* in *Collected Works,* vol. 3, 1967, Moscow: Progress Publishers.

Lewis, A. (1981) 'The Rate of Growth of World Trade, 1830–1973' in Grassman, S. and Lundberg, E. (eds) *The World Economic Order: Past and Prospects.* Basingstoke: Macmillan.

Limm, P. (1984) *The Thirty Years War.* London: Longman.

Livi-Bacci, M. (1993) 'South–North Migration: A Comparative Approach to North American and European Experiences' in *The Changing Course of Migration.* Paris: OECD.

Lloyd, P.J. (1992) 'Regionalisation and World Trade' *OECD Economic Studies* no. 18, Spring, pp. 7–43.

Lorenz, N. (1989) 'The Search for Flexibility: Sub-Contracting Networks in French and German Engineering' in Hirst, P.Q. and Zeitlin, J. (eds) *Reversing Industrial Decline.* Oxford: Berg.

Lorenz, N. (1992) 'Trust, Community and Cooperation: Towards a Theory of Industrial Districts' in Storper, M. and Scott, A.J. (eds) *Pathways to Industrialisation and Regional Development.* London: Routledge.

Ludvall, Bengt-Äke (ed.) (1992) *National Systems of Innovation.* London: Pinter.

McGrew, A.G. and Lewis, P.G. (1992) *Global Politics*. Cambridge: Polity.

McKelvey, Maureen (1991) 'How Do National Systems of Innovation Differ? A Critical Analysis of Porter, Freeman, Ludvall and Nelson' in Hodgson, Geoffrey and Screpanti, Ernesto (eds) *Rethinking Economics*. Cheltenham: Edward Elgar.

McKinnon, R. (1993) 'The Rules of the Game: International Money in Historical Perspective' *Journal of Economic Literature*, vol. XXXI, March, pp. 1–44.

Maddison, A. (1962) 'Growth and Fluctuation in the World Economy, 1870–1960' *Banca Nazionale del Lavoro Quarterly Review*, no. 61, June, pp. 127–95.

Maddison, A. (1987) 'Growth and Slow-Down in Advanced Capitalist Economies: Techniques of Quantitative Assessments' *Journal of Economic Literature*, vol. XXV, no. 2, June, pp. 649–98.

Mansell, Robin (1994) *The New Telecommunications: A Political Economy of Network Organizations*. London: Sage.

Morse, E.L. (1971) *Modernization and the Transformation of International Relations*. New York: Free Press.

Moran, T.H. (1992) 'The Impact of TRIMs on Trade and Development' *Transnational Corporations*, vol. 1, no. 1, February, pp. 55–65.

Moss Kanter, R. (1991) *When Giants Learn to Dance*. London: Simon Schuster.

Mulgan, G. (1994) *Politics in an Anti-Political Age*. Cambridge: Polity.

Nader, R. et al. (1994) *The Case against Free Trade: GATT, NAFTA, and the Globalization of Corporate Power*. San Francisco: Earth Island.

Nairn, T. (1993) 'All Bosnians Now?' *Dissent*, Fall, pp. 403–10.

Neal, L. (1985) 'Integration of International Capital Markets: Quantitative Evidence from the Eighteenth to Twentieth Centuries' *Journal of Economic History*, vol. XLV, no. 2, June, pp. 219–26.

Nelson, R. (ed.)(1993) *National Innovation Systems*. Oxford: Blackwell.

Nicholls, D. (1995) *The Pluralist State* (2nd edn). London: Macmillan.

Northrope, M. (1993) 'The Uruguay Round: A GATTastrophe' *Alternatives*, vol. 18, no. 2, pp. 171–200.

OECD (1993) 'World Securities Markets: Looking Ahead' *OECD Financial Markets Trends*, no. 55, June. Paris: OECD.

OECD (1994) 'Desynchronisation of OECD Business Cycles' *OECD Economic Outlook*, no. 55, June, Paris: OECD.

OECD (1992) *International Direct Investment: Policies and Trends in the 1980s*. Paris: OECD.

Ohmae, K. (1990) *The Borderless World*. London, New York: Collins.

Ohmae, K. (1993) 'The Rise of the Region State' *Foreign Affairs*, Spring, pp. 78–87.

Ohmae, K. (1995) 'Putting Global Logic First' *Harvard Business Review*, January/February, pp. 119–25.

Ostrom, E. (1990) *Governing the Commons*. Cambridge: Cambridge University Press.

Oye, K.A. (1994) 'Comment' in Kenen, P.B. (ed.) *Managing the World Economy*. Washington, DC: IIE.

Padoa-Schioppa, T. and Saccomanni, F. (1994) 'Managing a Market-Led Global Financial System' in Kenen, P.B. (ed.) *Managing the World Economy*. Washington, DC: IIE.

Panagariya, A. (1994) 'East Asia and the New Regionalism in World Trade' *The World Economy*, vol. 17, pp. 817–39.

Patel, P. and Pavitt, K. (1992) 'Large Firms in the Production of the World's Technology: An Important Case of Non-Globalisation' in Granstand, O., Hakanson, L. and Sjolander, S. (eds) *Technology Management and International Business*. Chichester: Wiley.

Piore, M. and Sabel, C. (1984) *The Second Industrial Divide*. New York: Basic Books.

Porter, M. (1990) *Competitive Advantage of Nations*. London: Macmillan.

Prestowitz, C.V. (1994) 'Playing to Win' *Foreign Affairs*, vol. 74, no. 4, July/August, pp. 186–9.

Putnam, Robert D. and Bayne, N. (1987) *Hanging Together: Cooperation and Conflict in the Seven-Power Summits*. Cambridge, MA: Harvard University Press.

Reich, R.B. (1990) 'Who Is Us?' *Harvard Business Review*, January–February, pp. 53–64.

Reich, R.B. (1992) *The Work of Nations*. New York: Vintage.

Robertson, R. (1992) *Globalisation: Social Theory's Global Culture*. London: Sage.

Rodrik, D. (1994) 'King Kong Meets Godzilla: The World Bank and The East Asian Miracle' *Centre for Economic Policy Research Discussion Paper*, no. 944, April. London: CERP.

Rosenau, J.N. (1990) *Turbulence in World Politics*. Hemel Hempstead: Harvester/Wheatsheaf.

Rosenau, J.N. and Czempiel, E.-O. (1992) *Governance without Government: Order and Change in World Politics*. Cambridge: Cambridge University Press.

Rubery, J. (1994) 'The British Production Regime: A Societal-Specific System?' *Economy and Society*, vol. 23, no. 3, August, pp. 355–73.

Sabel, C. (1989) 'Flexible Specialisation and the Re-Emergence of Regional Economies' in Hirst, P.Q. and Zeitlin, J. (eds) *Reversing Industrial Decline*. Oxford: Berg.

Sabel, C. (1991) 'Moebius-Strip Organisation and Open Labour Markets', in Bordieue, P. and Coleman, J.S. (eds) *Social Theory for a Changing Society*. Boulder, CO: Westview.

Scaperlanda, Anthony (1993) 'Multinational Enterprises and the Global Market' *Journal of Economic Issues,* vol. XXVII, no. 2, June, pp. 605–16.

Scharpf, F. (1991) *Crisis and Choice in European Social Democracy*. Ithaca, NY: Cornell University Press.

Schell, J. (1984) *The Abolition*. London: Picador.

Schröter, V. (1984) *Die deutsche Industrie auf dem Weltmarkt 1929 bis 1933*. Frankfurt.

Segal, A. (1993) *Atlas of International Migration*. London: Hans Zell.

Serow, W.J., Nairn, C.B., Sly, D.F. and Weller, R.M. (eds) (1990) *Handbook on International Migration*. New York: Greenwood.

Singh, A. (1993) 'Asian Economic Success and Latin American Failure in the 1980s' *International Review of Applied Economics*, vol. 7, no. 3, October, pp. 267–89.

Skidelsky, R. (1992) *John Maynard Keynes. Vol. 2: The Economist as Saviour*

1920–1939. London: Macmillan.

Sklair, L. (1991) *The Sociology of the Global System.* London: Harvester/Wheatsheaf.

Streeck, W. and Schmitter, P. (1991) 'From National Corporatism to Transnational Pluralism: Organised Interests in the Single European Market' in *Politics and Society*, vol. 19, no. 2, pp. 133–64.

Thompson, G.F. (1992) *The Economic Emergence of a New Europe?* Cheltenham: Edward Elgar.

Thompson, G.F. (1995a) 'The Market System' in Macintosh, M. et al. (eds) *Economics and Changing Economies.* London: International Thompson.

Thompson, G.F. (1995b) 'Comment on "The Crisis of Cost Recovery and the Waste of the Industrialised Nations"' *Competition and Change*, vol. 1, no. 1, October.

Tobin, J. (1978) 'A Proposal for International Monetary Reform' *Eastern Economic Journal*, vol. 4, pp. 153–9.

Tobin, J. (1994) 'Speculators' Tax' *New Economy*, pp. 104–9.

Tomlinson, J. (1988) 'Can Governments Run the Economy?' *Fabian Tract*, no. 542, London: Fabian Society.

Turner, P. (1991) 'Capital Flows in the 1980s: A Survey of Major Trends' *BIS Economic Papers*, no. 30, April. Geneva: Bank for International Settlements.

Tyson, L. (1991) 'They Are Not Us: Why American Ownership Still Matters' *The American Prospect*, Winter, pp. 37–49.

Tyson, L. (1993) *Who's Bashing Whom? Trade Conflict in High Technology* Washington, DC: Institute for International Economics.

UNCTAD (1993) *Trade and Development Report, 1993.* New York: United Nations.

United Nations (1993a) *World Investment Report 1993. Transnational Corporations and Integrated International Production.* New York: United Nations.

United Nations (1993d) *World Investment Directory 1992. Vol. III: Developed Countries.* Transnational Corporations and Management Division, Department of Economic and Social Development, New York: United Nations.

United Nations (1993b) *Small and Medium-Sized Transnational Corporations: Role, Impact and Policy Implications.* New York: United Nations.

United Nations (1993c) *Explaining and Forecasting Regional Flows of Foreign Direct Investment.* New York: United Nations.

Van Creveld, M. (1991) *On Future War.* London: Brassey's.

Wade, R. (1990) *Governing the Market: Economic Theory and the Role of Government in East Asian Industrialization.* Princeton, NJ: Princeton University Press.

Wallace, I. (1990) *The Global Economic System.* London: Unwin Hyman.

Weber, E. (1979) *Peasants into Frenchmen.* London: Chatto and Windus.

Weber, M. (1968) *Economy and Society.* Vol. 1. New York: Bedminster Press.

Whitley, Richard (1992a) *Business Systems in East Asia: Firms, Markets and Societies.* London: Sage.

Whitley, Richard (ed.)(1992b) *European Business Systems: Firms and Markets in their National Contexts.* London: Sage.

Wilkinson, F. (1983) 'Productive Systems' *Cambridge Journal of Economics*, vol. 7, no. 3/4, pp. 413–30.

Williams, K., Haslam, C., Williams, J. and Adcroft, A. (1992) 'Factories as Warehouses: Japanese Manufacturing Foreign Direct Investment in Britain and the United States' *University of East London Occasional Paper on Business, Economy and Society*, no. 6.

Williams, K., Haslam, C., Williams, J., Sukhdev, J., Johal, A., Adcroft, A. and Willis, R. (1995) 'The Crisis of Cost Recovery and the Waste of the Industrialised Nations' *Competition and Change*, vol. 1, no. 1, October.

World Bank (1993) *The East-Asian Miracle: Economic Growth and Public Policy*. Oxford: World Bank, Oxford University Press.

World Bank (1994) *Governance: The World Bank's Experience*. Washington, DC: World Bank.

Yarbrough, B.V. and Yarbrough, R.M. (1992) *Cooperation and Governance in International Trade*. Princeton: Princeton University Press.

Young, A. (1994a) 'The Tyranny of Numbers: Confronting the Statistical Realities of the East Asian Growth Experience' *NEBR Working Paper*, no. 4680, March.

Young, A. (1994b) 'Lessons from the East Asian NICs: A Contrarian View' *European Economic Review*, vol. 38, nos 3/4, April, pp. 964–73.

Zeitlin, J. (1992) 'Industrial Districts and Local Economic Regeneration' in Pyke, F. and Sengenberger, W. (eds) *Industrial Districts and Local Economic Regeneration*. Geneva: International Institute of Labour Studies, ILO.

Zeitlin, J. (1994) 'Why Are There No Industrial Districts in the United Kingdom?' in Baguasco, A. and Sabel, C. (eds) *Ce que petit peut faire*. Les petites et les moyennes entreprises en Europe, Poitiers: OCSEO.

Zevin, R. (1992) 'Are World Financial Markets More Open? If So, Why and With What Effects?' in Banuri, T and Schor, J.B. (eds) *Financial Openness and National Autonomy*. Oxford: Clarendon Press.

Zubaida, S.D. (1993) *Islam, the People and the State* (2nd edn). London: Tauris.

Index